The Elderly and the Future Economy

The Elderly and the Future Economy

Lawrence Olson
Christopher Caton
Martin Duffy
with contributions by
Michael Shannon
Robert Tannenwald
Data Resources, Inc.

LexingtonBooks
D.C. Heath and Company
Lexington, Massachusetts
Toronto

Funded by the Corporation for Older Americans, Inc., in support of the Technical Committee on the Economy of the 1981 White House Conference on Aging.

Library of Congress Cataloging in Publication Data

Main entry under title:
The Elderly and the future economy.

Includes index.
1. Aged—United States—Economic conditions. 2. Income distribution—United States. 3. Age and employment—United States. 4. Aged—Employment—United States. 5. Economic forecasting—United States. I. Olson, Lawrence.
HQ1064.U5E4 338.5′443′0973 81—47543
ISBN 0-669-04651-5 AACR2

Published simultaneously in Canada

Printed in the United States of America

International Standard Book Number: 0-669-04651-5

Library of Congress Catalog Card Number: 81-47543

Contents

List of Figures

List of Tables

Preface

The research presented here was financed by the Corporation for Older Americans, Inc., to supplement the work of the Technical Committee on the Economy of the 1981 White House Conference on Aging. The committee felt a need for an analysis of the likely future for the elderly and the economy, and of how that future might differ under various suggested policy options.

The project addressed areas of research that were chosen with the guidance of the committee, and we are grateful for the committee's input. All results and conclusions, however, are ours and should not be construed as representing the views of the committee, the Corporation for Older Americans, or the White House Conference on Aging.

The tight time schedule under which this project was done reflected the committee's need for timely input into its decisions and recommendations. In order to meet an ambitious project schedule, a concerted team effort was required.

Among the technical staff at Data Resources, Inc., (DRI), a number of people were helpful. Carol Rapaport made valuable contributions to all parts of the project. Christopher Probyn was involved in the design of the study. Ann Stoddard assisted in the macroeconomic analysis. M. Carey Leahey contributed ideas relating to effects of economic changes on the federal government and the reverse. L. Douglas Lee provided numerous suggestions about the macroeconomic aspects of the study. Michael Flanagan, who had built the original version of the Demographic-Economic Model of the Elderly as part of an earlier study, helped guide the simulations and extensions of that model in this project. Evan Barrington contributed numerous comments and suggestions relating to labor-force behavior of the elderly.

Three outside consultants were involved in the project. Anthony Pellechio of the University of Rochester helped organize and analyze the many articles in the literature summary. He also contributed to the labor supply and income-guarantee simulations. Richard Wertheimer of the Urban Institute provided information on the schools of thought about the elderly and repeatedly redirected our interest toward the issue of the elderly poor. Joseph Anderson of ICF Inc. improved our understanding of how demographic trends interact with labor markets for older and younger workers.

Two members of the staff of the Technical Committee on the Economy of the 1981 White House Conference on Aging were involved in all aspects of the research. Matthew Lind, staff director for the committee, provided energy and imagination. His direction inspired us to extraordinary efforts, contributing greatly to the quality of this volume. Frank Campbell provided a stream of ideas and suggestions. His calm but insistent influence helped shape the research and keep it on course.

The production of a report of this scope within a tight schedule required dedicated efforts from the DRI support staff. The manuscript was ably typed by Terry Gill, Marilyn Galvin, Carol Hillman, and Eve Ntapolis, all of whom worked hard and long under trying circumstances. Katherine Kush helped coordinate typing and chart preparation, as well as editing parts of the manuscript. Vaidas Matulaitis prepared many of the charts and tables. Tobie McNeill, Cindy Adams, and Steven Brown of the DRI copying department handled our requests for duplication speedily and with care.

Lawrence Olson
Study Director
Washington, D.C.

Christopher Caton
Martin Duffy
Lexington, Massachusetts

1 Introduction

Recent years have witnessed rapid increases in the number of elderly Americans and their share of the total U.S. population.[1] From 1970 through 1978, the number of people aged 65 and over increased about 20 percent, while the total population rose only 7 percent. Today, 1 in 9 persons is 65 or older, an increase from a ratio of 1 in 25 at the turn of this century.

This 1 in 9 represents some 25 million elderly Americans. By the year 2000, there will be about 32 million citizens aged 65 or older, or 1 American in 8. Growth in the numbers of elderly Americans will be even more rapid in the twenty-first century, as the elderly share is expected to increase to almost 1 in 5 by 2030. This profound increase will be given added force by even more-rapid increases in the very old population of persons aged 75 and over. The population share of the very old will nearly double in the next 50 years. By 2030, the very old are forecast to rise to about 45 percent of all elderly persons.

Increases in the proportion of the elderly population and a rising awareness of future increases are occurring as questions about the relationships between the elderly and the economy are gaining new prominence. The 1970s witnessed substantial improvements in income made available to the elderly, primarily through social security. The share of government budgets and gross national product (GNP) allocated to transfers rose steadily in the 1970s, and much of this increase was due to programs benefiting the elderly. While money income and transfers grew, rising inflation erased much of the apparent gain and created particularly acute problems for the elderly. More recently, declining real growth in the economy and a rising burden of government expenditures have led to increased taxpayer resistance to financing further growth in transfers. The overall labor force grew very rapidly in the past few years, but labor-force participation among elderly Americans has been declining. In labor markets, older workers, particularly elderly and near-elderly men, have continued to decrease their labor-force participation. Earlier and earlier retirements have led both to the elderly's greater dependence on social solutions and the general population's rising clamor for stability in economic affairs, particularly in regard to inflation.

As the 1980s begin, it is important to understand what is known about the outlook for the economy and the elderly. Furthermore, it makes sense to consider the future both in light of current trends and policies and under various new policies suggested for future improvements. The available literature, a summary of which is included as chapter 2, is not sufficient for this task. Written material is not lacking, but its quality is uneven. Also, most of the available studies focus on the past, even though the future outlook is for significant changes from historical experience in some of the economy's key problems. The forward-looking studies, moreover, usually examine only a few economic indicators, and different studies make different assumptions about the basic future path of the economy. Therefore, a new study is needed to analyze the future outlook in a comprehensive and consistent fashion, examining that outlook both with and without new policy initiatives. This book represents an attempt to meet that need.

Chapter 3 reports on Data Resources, Inc.'s (DRI's) baseline simulation of the macroeconomic outlook and the outlook for particular age and income groups in the population. Due in large part to reduced labor-force growth, the outlook is for continued but diminished economic growth and only slowly declining inflation. The real income of the elderly is projected to continue to improve, but less rapidly than in the recent past, and the relative gains of the poorest elderly are also projected to slow. Therefore, large numbers of the elderly are projected to have very low income even into the twenty-first century.

This relatively poor outlook for the economy and the elderly motivates the form of the options that are simulated, each addressing a key assumption of the baseline. Option 1 (chapter 4) addresses the baseline assumption that the labor-force-participation rates of the elderly and near elderly will continue to decline. In this option, the participation rates of elderly and near-elderly men and women are assumed to return gradually to levels experienced in 1970. These net new workers increase overall growth while also providing more income for the elderly and a "fiscal dividend" of increased government expenditures. Gains accrue mainly to the younger and more-vigorous elderly, however, so the oldest and poorest elderly gain relatively little.

Option 2 (chapter 5) addresses the baseline assumption that current transfer programs for the elderly will not be liberalized. In this option, a new transfer program financed by increased income taxes is implemented to guarantee a minimum income for the elderly. The program costs $18.6 billion (1980 dollars) in its first year, falling to $11 billion in 2005 (because economic growth reduces the number of elderly who needs these transfers). Macroeconomic effects are trivial, but income taxes increase by about $70 (1980 dollars) per person in 1981 and by smaller amounts in later years.

Option 3 (chapter 6) addresses the baseline assumption that the saving rate will continue to be low. New saving amounting to about 2 percent of disposable income is assumed, with all the new saving being done by those under age 65. The reductions in consumption necessary for this new saving first depress the economy, but increased investment eventually leads to an improved economy. The elderly are projected to share in these initial reductions and subsequent improvements, but the lowest-income elderly gain relatively little from the eventual improvements. The new saving creates a stock of added household wealth that can help finance retirement expenses.

Option 4 (chapter 7) addresses the baseline assumption that only small corporate-tax cuts will occur over the next quarter-century. Larger cuts in corporate taxes are assumed in this option. After about one to two years, these cuts lead to increased economic growth and reduced inflation. The elderly are helped by this option but by less than are younger groups. In the absence of new transfer initiatives, however, the poorest elderly gain little from the added growth and diminished inflation.

All options help the elderly to some degree, but average gains are greatest in those options that are directed specifically at the elderly—options 1 and 2. The poorest elderly gain somewhat in option 1 but are not significantly helped in options 3 and 4. Only option 2, among those simulated, provides a really effective method for addressing the problems of the poorest elderly. However, given the current mood of the electorate, it may be difficult to introduce new transfer initiatives if economic growth is as sluggish as DRI's baseline and option-2 simulations predict.

For this and other reasons, it probably makes sense to consider combinations of policies from the various options, with the aim of improving the overall economy and allowing all the elderly to share fully in that improvement. Chapter 8 addresses possible combinations of the options and the implications of such combinations for the economy and the elderly. For instance, one intriguing finding involves the improved economy resulting from the added older workers in option 1. These workers increase aggregate income enough to create a significant fiscal dividend. In some periods, this dividend actually exceeds the cost of the new tranfers required for a guaranteed minimum income for the elderly in option 2. This result does not strictly mean that option 1 could ever pay for option 2, but it does show that increased participation by older workers could help defray the costs of aiding the poorest elderly. Alternatively, the added economic growth that occurs in options 1, 3, and 4 can be thought of as a "GNP dividend" that could help finance additional transfers such as those described in option 2.

Chapter 8 also presents some speculation regarding the period beyond our simulation horizons, beyond 2005. This period is of particular interest because it includes the years when the postwar-baby-boom generation will reach retirement age.

Note

1. Throughout this book, the term *elderly* refers to individuals aged 65 and over, or to families headed by such individuals, unless otherwise indicated.

2 Summary of Major Themes in the Literature on the Elderly and the Economy

Much has been written about the elderly and the economy. The sheer amount of such material, combined with its often uneven quality, precludes an exhaustive survey of all the literature. Instead, we attempt to investigate some of the major themes that dominate the research. Within each of these themes, we draw on a few prominent studies and present the substance of their discussions. Results from both the published and unpublished literature are reported in order to provide timely and comprehensive information.

This summary is divided into two sections. The first section presents literature regarding the economic status of the elderly in the United States. Research themes include income, wealth and savings, effects of federal policy on labor supply and retirement, and cost of living. The second section discusses some effects of the elderly society on the economy, including themes on labor markets and federal transfer payments.

Economic Status of the Elderly

This section summarizes a sampling of what is known about the economic status of the elderly and how this status is affected by public policy. Many of the questions addressed by this research are not now resolved, but a few major themes are dominant.

Income

The average income of elderly families and single individuals is usually lower than the average income of younger age groups and much lower for certain elderly groups. Growth in this income since the late 1960s has been steady, but as figure 2-1 shows, this growth has only partially restored the elderly to the relative income position they enjoyed in the early 1950s. The period from 1950 to the nadir of relative incomes for the elderly in 1967 was a time of declining labor-force participation among this group and of reductions in real per capita benefits available under social security. Major reforms in social security starting in 1965 acted to reverse this decline, although elderly labor-force participation has continued to fall. Legislated social-security step adjustments raised benefits by more than 70 percent

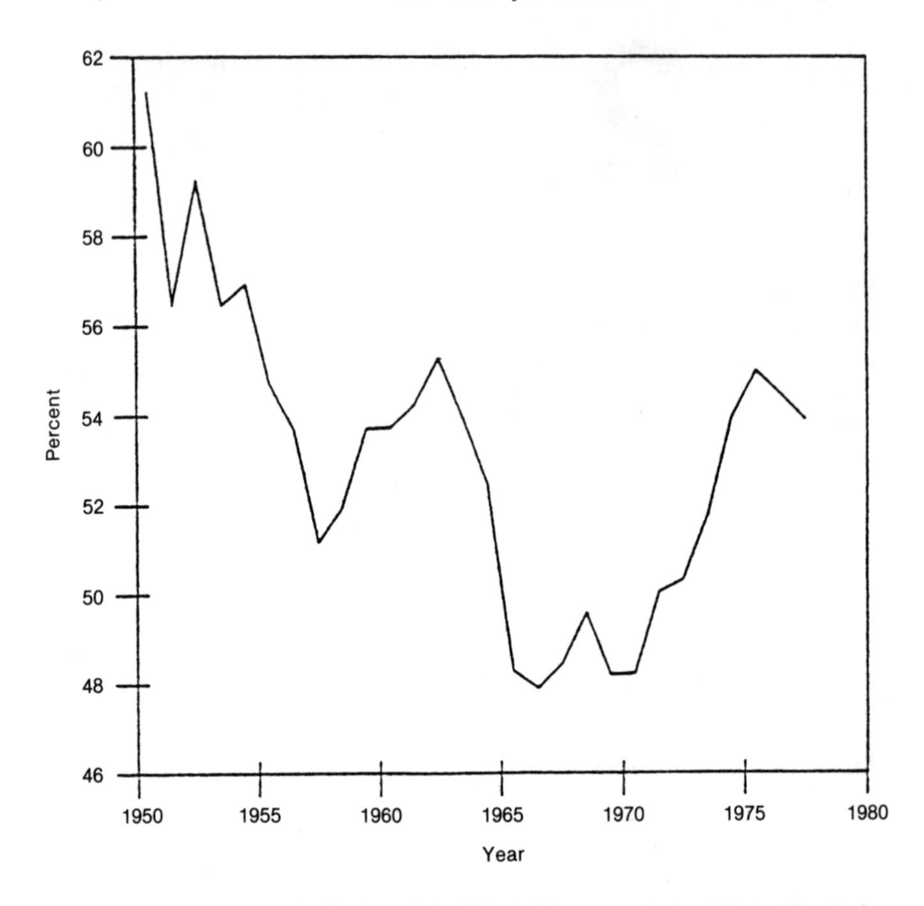

Source: Martin Duffy et al., "Inflation and the Elderly," Report to National Retired Teacher's Association and American Association of Retired Persons (DRI, 1980), p. I-6.

Figure 2-1. Average Elderly Income as a Percentage of Nonelderly Income

from 1968 to 1971, and the effects of the double indexing of benefits (from 1972 through 1978) further contributed to rising relative income for the elderly (Duffy et al. 1980).

One consequence of the rapid recent increase in transfers to the elderly, coupled with their declining activity in the labor market, has been a fall in the share of their income that derives from wage and salary earnings. Table 2-1, which reports tabulations of the Current Population Survey Annual Demographic File, shows that this decline has occurred for all age groups over 55. Improved transfers have contributed to this decline by directly increasing both total income and the fraction that is in transfers and by allowing greater numbers of the elderly to retire.

Table 2-1
Income Shares, by Source
(percentage)

Source	*1967*	*1977*
Age 55-61		
Wages and salaries	76.6	70.9
Social security	1.6	3.1
Asset income	5.2	7.6
All other	16.6	18.4
Age 62-64		
Wages and salaries	67.3	50
Social security	7.6	15.3
Asset income	7.9	11.3
All other	17.2	23.4
Age 65-71		
Wages and salaries	34.3	20.9
Social security	27.6	38
Asset income	14.2	17
All other	23.9	24.9
Age 72 and over		
Wages and salaries	10.9	5.7
Social security	43	48.3
Asset income	19.5	22.9
All other	26.6	23.1

Source: Martin Duffy et al., "Inflation and the Elderly," Report to National Retired Teacher's Association and American Association of Retired Persons (DRI, 1980), p. III-10.

The issue of the adequacy of incomes received by the elderly has also been widely discussed (see, for example, Moon 1977). One can view adequacy either in terms of an absolute standard (such as the cost of a particular market basket of goods and services) or in terms of a relative standard (such as the idea of a replacement rate—that is, the fraction that post-retirement income is of preretirement income).

The poverty standard is a typical absolute income standard since it is based on a cost multiple of an adequate food budget, yet the issue of how many elderly families are truly in poverty is unclear, clouded by the availability of in-kind sources of income. These sources are not normally included in "income" when the concept is applied. A recent study by the Congressional Budget Office (CBO) (1977), for example, asserted that as few as 4 percent of elderly families are in poverty after adjustments for differences in taxes and in-kind transfers. This result can be questioned, however, because, for instance, the study evaluated benefits from government in-kind transfer programs at their full government cost. This was done despite the admitted possibility that it could overstate the value of these benefits. Furthermore, as the following discussion shows, many of the elderly have income just above the poverty standard.

Borzilleri (1980) recently did a study of the effect of in-kind payments on income distributions using imputed market values for in-kind transfers. Borzilleri's results are similar to those in the CBO study with regard to poverty. Considering an adequate budget standard, however, he asserts that the BLS intermediate budget standard is more appropriate than the poverty index. This standard implies that many of the elderly have inadequate income. Even after Borzilleri's adjustments for in-kind income, only about 42 percent of elderly singles and 64 percent of elderly families meet this intermediate standard.

Resolving the continuing controversy surrounding the concept of adding in-kind transfers to income is difficult because conceptual issues are unresolved, and the necessary data for more-accurate studies are not now available.[1] Thus, while attempts to include such transfers may help shed light on the fraction of the elderly in poverty, they are not well enough developed to track changes in income status over time or to simulate changes caused by altered federal policies. As an example of the conceptual issues, the biggest contributors to "full" income in Borzilleri's adjustments are Medicare and Medicaid. These programs increase the adjusted income of the elderly because they usually experience overall poor health (for instance, if poor health raises in-kind transfers, is the Medicare or Medicaid recipient really better off?). Also, since most young persons have access through their employment to private health insurance with comparable total coverage, it is clearly inappropriate when making relative-income comparisons to adjust elderly income for Medicare and Medicaid while not adjusting younger income for the value of private insurance (Borzilleri 1980).

Conversely, relative standards such as replacement rates give a relative method for judging the adequacy of money income (one such relative standard is shown in figure 2-1). Fox (1979) calculates that the median earnings-replacement rate from social-security benefits for married couples with no separate pension income was 49 percent in 1973-1974. For couples with pensions, the replacement rate from social security alone was only 41 percent but, in total, social security and pensions replaced 62 percent of preretirement earnings.

These data illustrate the point made by Schulz et al. (1979) and Grad and Foster (1979) that a critical factor in determining whether the elderly have adequate retirement income is their access to a private or public pension to supplement social security. Grad and Foster report that, in 1976, out of 17.3 million families and singles with elderly heads, 11.2 million had only one retirement-income benefit (social security, private pensions or annuities, government pensions, railroad retirement), and for 10.6 million of these families and singles, that benefit was social security. Families and singles whose only retirement benefit was social security had a median income of only $3,660, while the 4.8 million family/single units with more than one retirement benefit had a median income of $7,800.

Regardless of whether an absolute or relative standard is used to assess adequacy, it is important to understand that the retired have less flexibility in dealing with a changing economy than do the nonretired. This lack of flexibility derives, in part, from employers' unwillingness to allow older people to return to their jobs after they have retired, coupled with penalties on labor income imposed by the social-security-earnings test. Declining health and mobility are also factors (Duffy et al. 1980).

Certain groups within the elderly have very low income, making it difficult to live an adequate life and respond to immediate or prolonged health problems and to a succession of energy crises. The greatest problems with adequacy are concentrated among the oldest age groups and among individuals living alone, particularly elderly women. The study by Duffy et al. (1980) shows that in 1976 nearly half the nation's families and singles in the oldest age group considered, age 72 and over, received a cash income of less than $5,000 (or less than about $100 per week). Among women living alone, this fraction of elderly with less income than $5,000 rises to three-quarters. Moreover, these oldest age groups are precisely the groups that are growing most rapidly in response to declines in mortality rates. The average 65-year-old man today can expect to live about fourteen more years, while the average woman can expect about eighteen more years of life. Retirements today typically occur before age 65, particularly for women. This raises the issue of whether income for some of the elderly will be adequate to meet their minimum needs, especially given continued high rates of inflation.

The income floor provided to the elderly—their guaranteed minimum level of income—is important to insuring income adequacy for the elderly poor. The effective income floor today depends on supplemental security income, the social-security minimum benefit, and levels of adequacy and inflation protection afforded by private pension plans (Moon and Smolensky 1977). This floor, however, especially its pension component, differs markedly among segments of the elderly.

Wealth and Savings

Another source of financial support to help defray the costs of retirement is wealth held by the elderly. The act of retiring involves a transition from a period of relatively high saving to a period in which saving is lower or even negative (Kurz and Avrin 1979; Duffy et al. 1980). Therefore, the stock of wealth held by the elderly, its distribution across segments of the elderly, and the ways wealth is affected by the economy are important topics in the study of the economic status of the elderly. Unfortunately, these topics are the focus of controversies that show no early promise of resolution. Numerous issues of fact and theory remain unresolved. The essentially poor and inconsistent quality of data on the wealth held by the elderly points to a continuation of the controversy.

The focus of many of the studies of wealth and saving is the life-cycle model of economic behavior. This model, originated by Ando and Modigliani (1963), emphasizes that consumption choices over the life cycle reflect a consideration of total resources available over that time. These resources include all income sources such as earnings, social-security benefits, and private pensions as well as gifts and bequests from earlier generations. The original form of the life-cycle model did not include bequests to younger generations. Their subsequent inclusion has cast doubt on some of the simple results of the model because increased resources may result in an increase in the level of bequests rather than higher consumption.

Some authors have asserted that future claims on social security are a form of wealth (see, for example, Feldstein and Pellechio 1979). This concept, which derives from the life-cycle model, remains controversial. To the extent that social-security benefits can be considered as wealth, this stock of wealth differs markedly across generations, both absolutely and relative to payments into the system. The first individuals entering the social-security system received much more than they put in because of the intentional pay-as-you-go structure of the system. Later beneficiaries will receive lower benefits relative to their payments. Also, within each generation, the deliberate redistributive nature of the system leads to higher effective net social-security wealth (that is, a higher total of benefits minus payments into the system) for those with low income as compared to those with high income (Burkhauser and Warlick 1978).

Taking a more-conventional view of retirement assets, the main importance of social security derives from any influence it has on retirement and saving decisions. Feldstein and Pellechio (1979) report that additions to net social-security wealth decrease saving, but Esposito (1978), Barro (1978), and others have cast doubt on this idea. The controversy thus continues. A study now being done by Kurz and others for the President's Commission on Pension Policy will analyze the effect of social security and, analogously, private pensions on saving and retirement behavior (see Kurz 1980). This study may help to resolve the issue of the effects of social security on behavior.

Tables 2-2 and 2-3 present data, differentiated by age, on ownership of various financial assets and on average holdings of assets. These tables report data from the University of Michigan's Survey of Consumer Credit. For most types of assets, a smaller fraction of elderly respondents holds assets as compared to younger groups, but on average the elderly assets involve larger amounts. In part, this is due to a higher percentage of elderly

Table 2-2
Types of Asset Holdings, 1977
(percentage holding each asset)

Assets	*Under 54*	*55-64*	*65 and over*	*All Ages*
Savings account	77	74.8	69.2	75.1
Checking account	82.8	80.9	77	81.4
Stocks	21	24.2	18	21
Certificates of deposit	9.4	19.3	22.8	13.6
U.S. bonds	33.5	30.8	20.1	30.5
State or municipal bonds	1.1	3.3	1.9	1.6
Corporate bonds	1.7	4.7	2.7	2.4
Mutual funds	6.3	9.1	5	6.5
Other real estate	20.8	27.5	17.2	21.2
Number of Respondents	1,651	429	483	2,563

Source: Martin Duffy et al., "Inflation and the Elderly," Report to National Retired Teacher's Association and American Association of Retired Persons (DRI, 1980), p. V-34.

respondents who report owning no financial assets, a full 13 percent of all the elderly respondents (Duffy et al. 1980). This underscores the point that the distribution of assets among the elderly is relatively unequal, as compared with other sources of support for retirement expenses.

The high inflation rates of the 1970s have eroded the value of financial assets held by the elderly. The Duffy et al. study shows that the real value of bank savings, stocks, and bonds has fallen due to inflation in the period since 1967, while home equity (the dominant asset for most elderly households) has increased in value. Losses in the real value of financial assets over the 1970s provide a classic demonstration of the gains to debtors versus creditors caused by unanticipated inflation. Many of the elderly, even those of relatively modest means, have assets exceeding their debts and are thus net creditors. Unanticipated inflation acts to transfer wealth from creditors to debtors and thus to eviscerate retirement savings. The inflation of the 1960s and the 1970s was largely unanticipated, as millions of elderly people can attest. Low rates of economic growth accompanied by high rates of inflation have diminished the prospects for a restoration of losses, particularly in equities. The effect of the higher levels of transfers and lower asset values that occurred in the 1970s has been to frustrate attempts by the elderly to provide for their own retirement and to increase their vulnerability to continued "stagflation" or cutbacks in real-transfer payments.

A clear exception exists, however, to the general decline in real-wealth holdings by the elderly—namely, home equity. The market value of homes has increased relative to inflation. The total value of home equity owned by elderly Americans today has been estimated at $500 billion, and most elderly homeowners have free and clear title to their dwellings (Scholen and Chen 1980). Unfortunately, the money tied up in these homes is largely inaccessi-

Table 2-3
Measures of Asset Holdings, by Age Group, 1977
(dollars for these who hold each asset)

Assets	*Mean*	*Median*
Savings accounts		
Under 54	5,350	1,500
55-64	13,000	6,250
65 and over	16,500	6,250
Total sample	8,100	2,200
Checking accounts		
Under 54	1,330	375
55-64	1,700	750
65 and over	1,550	700
Total sample	1,420	420
Common or preferred stock		
Under 54	22,210	3,000
55-64	38,160	12,800
65 and over	25,230	13,000
Total sample	25,730	4,500
U.S. savings bonds		
Under 54	1,400	300
55-64	2,590	1,200
65 and over	7,760	2,500
Total sample	2,200	400

Source: Martin Duffy et al., "Inflation and the Elderly," Report to National Retired Teacher's Assocation and American Association of Retired Persons (DRI, 1980), p. V-36.

ble for meeting day-to-day or sudden expenses. At the same time, increases in some of the out-of-pocket costs of home ownership (notably fuel, utilities, and real estate taxes) continue at rates exceeding the rate of inflation, often making it difficult for the elderly homeowner to meet out-of-pocket expenses.

Various ideas have been suggested that would allow the elderly to gain access to the asset value tied up in their homes: for example, deferred-payment loans for property taxes or for home repairs and improvements, deferred-payment loans with an annuity, or sale leaseback agreements (Chen 1980). It is beyond the scope of this book to explain these options in detail (see Chen 1980 for more information about their particulars). A point that should be made, however, is that they present considerable difficulties in implementation. Many of the options require coordination between financial institutions. Banks, however, are usually hesitant to accept actuarial risk, while life insurance companies are seldom eager to own dispersed residential real estate. Tax and legal complications also exist, and given the income-tested nature of some existing transfer programs that provide income to the elderly (such as supplementary security income), increased money made available through some of the options might be partially or fully offset by decreases in transfers. Finally, despite low income and difficulty in meeting expenses, many elderly homeowners express reluctance to engage in programs to unlock home equity (Scholen and Chen 1980).

Researchers usually acknowledge the fact that the widespread availability of such programs would be helpful to the elderly if the programs were carefully constructed. Some of the home-equity options have been tested in pilot programs with different levels of success, but given the complications, it will probably be some time before methods for using home equity for retirement expenses are widely available.

Effects of Federal Policy on Labor Supply and Retirement

Since the end of World War II, large increases in transfer payments and pensions have occurred coupled with continuing declines in the percentage of the elderly who work and the fraction of older workers whose jobs are full time. A large body of research has addressed the question of whether these coincident phenomena are causally related.

As an example, it has often been asserted that the social-security-earnings test, which effectively taxes earnings above an exempt amount, depresses the labor supply of the elderly. In 1980, social-security benefits were reduced by $.50 for every $1.00 of earnings above the $5,000 exempt amount until all social-security benefits are exhausted. Pellechio (1980), on the one hand, suggests that the earnings test should lead to a cluster of workers with earnings just below the exempt amount. He finds such a cluster in the 1966 through 1975 period, and in periods when the exempt amount is raised, the cluster moves up immediately to the new level. Sander (1968) and Vroman (1971) reported similar results in earlier studies. On the other hand, Gordon and Schoeplein (1979) find that relatively few workers may be subject to these disincentives. Out of 3.1 million workers aged 65-69 in 1978, they note that over 1 million earned an amount sufficiently below the exempt amount to be unaffected by its work disincentives and that about an additional 500,000 elderly workers earned enough to have exhausted all benefits. Therefore, although investigators usually agree on the existence of work disincentives from the earnings test, they agree less about the magnitude of these effects.

Some private pensions such as the pensions of workers belonging to the United Auto Workers Union also impose direct-earnings tests (Burkhauser 1976). Even pensions that have no direct-earnings test but that require a worker to leave his or her career/job effectively reduce the amount the retired worker can earn relative to his or her market wage in other firms. This reduction in potential remuneration for work, in turn, can lead to lower labor-force participation.

Another component of the retirement-support system that has often been cited for decreasing the labor supply or hastening retirement is the social-security disability program. This program became available to men below age 50 in 1960, and its definition of disability was liberalized in 1965. Over the 1960-1976 period, the number of beneficiaries in this program increased sevenfold as total benefits increased nineteenfold. Leonard (1979) and Parsons (1980) both found evidence of significantly diminished labor-force participation associated with higher levels of available disability benefits. In contrast, Crouch (in Joe and Bogatay, 1980) notes that disincentives for those social-security-disability recipients who face the highest replacement rates may be limited since many of the high-replacement-rate recipients have low enough income to be elibigle for welfare. Further, he argues that many of those elderly with high replacement rates have little education, deficient work skills, or such severe disabilities that their capacity for added work is open to question.

Mandatory-retirement rules can also influence the age at which people retire. Wertheimer and Zedlewski (1980) and Clark, Barker, and Cantrell (1979) find evidence of such an effect. In fact, the latter study suggests that the immediate effect of the 1978 Age Discrimination in Employment Act's prohibiting mandatory retirement will be to increase the labor-force participation of 65-year-old men by about 5 percentage points. Barrington (1980) estimates that, in the long run, the new law will add about 100,000 workers to the U.S. labor force.

Figures 2-2 and 2-3 show labor-force-participation rates by single years of age for men and women from the 1970 census. The sharp decline in participation after age 60 is evident for both sexes, and much of the continuing falloff in participation since 1970 is also concentrated among the over-60 group. These figures underscore the importance of the timing of any future declines in participation and their effect on the average age of retirement. Even relatively small percentage increases in elderly participation can add substantial numbers of older workers to the labor force, and any such increases are in turn mainly a function of the timing of retirement.

Cost of Living

Expenditure patterns differ markedly between the elderly and the nonelderly, with elderly families spending more of their income for food at home, fuel and utilities, and health care. Since these (in addition to shelter) are the categories of expenditures whose price has inflated most rapidly in the 1970s

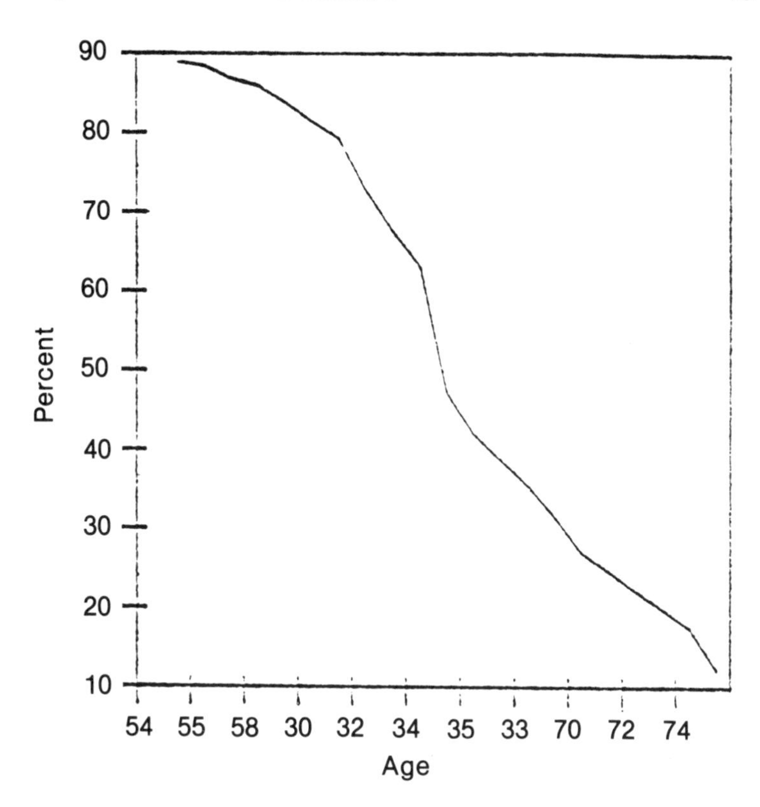

Source: Martin Duffy et al., "Inflation and the Elderly," Report to National Retired Teacher's Association and American Association of Retired Persons (DRI, 1980), p. III-5.

Figure 2-2. Male Labor-Force-Participation Rates, by Age, 1970

[8.3 percent annually from 1970 through 1979 for food at home, 9.4 percent for fuel and utilities, 7.9 percent for health care, compared to 7.2 percent for the BLS all-urban CPI (Duffy et al. 1980)], it is often asserted that the elderly bear a heavy burden from inflation. The evidence supports this view, although differences in the burden of inflation are relatively small.

Duffy et al. (1980, Chapter IV) present a model of expenditures by elderly families and single individuals and use this model to derive historical and forecast CPIs for elderly and younger consumers separated by age (under 55, 55-61, 62-64, 65-71, 72 and over), income class (under $5,000, $5,000-$10,000, $10,000-$15,000, $15,000-$20,000, $20,000-$25,000, $25,000 and over, measured in 1976 dollars), and family status (men living alone, women living alone, families of two or more). The expenditure patterns of elderly consumers in this study are found to be relatively concentrated in food at home, fuel, and health care, and the degree of this con-

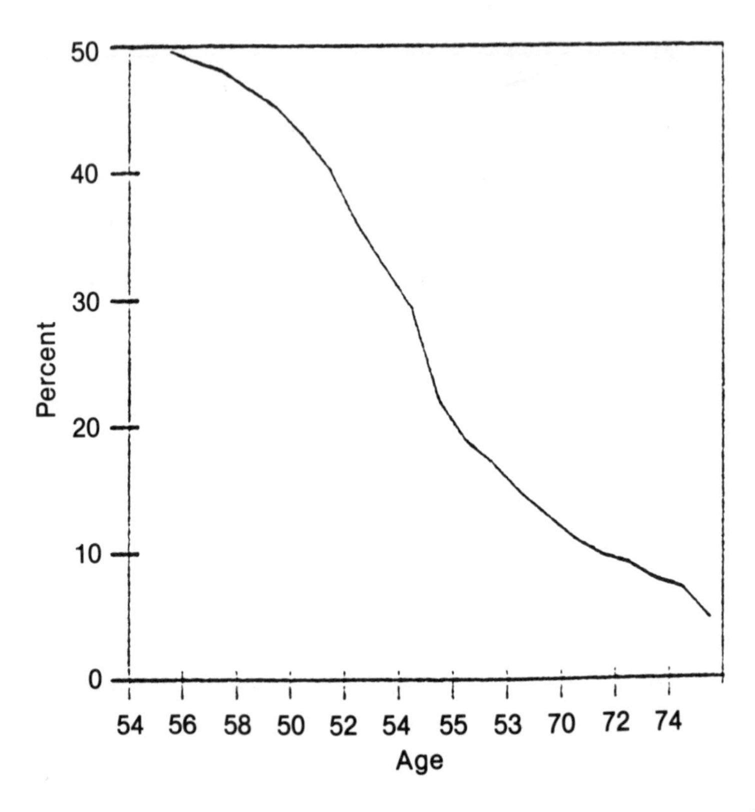

Source: Martin Duffy et al., "Inflation and the Elderly," Report to National Retired Teacher's Association and American Association of Retired Persons (DRI, 1980), p. III-5.

Figure 2-3. Female Labor-Force-Participation Rates, by Age, 1970

centration is greatest for the oldest and poorest among them. Therefore, effective inflation rates are higher for the elderly than for younger consumers, highest for the oldest and poorest among the elderly. These differences, however, are not large. For example, average annual CPI inflation between 1973 and 1975 is estimated at 10.2 percent for consumers under 55 in the highest income class ($25,000 and over, 1976 dollars), compared with 10.7 percent for consumers in the lowest income class and 10.3 percent in the highest income class for those aged 72 and over (Duffy et al. 1980). Since future inflation is also forecast to be concentrated in the "core-necessity" categories (food, fuel, and health care), this disparity is expected to continue. [For example, a study by Freeland et al. (1980) concludes that medical-care prices will continue to grow more rapidly than the general level of prices over the 1980s.] With the CPI indexing of benefits and the low income of the poorest elderly, this evidence (which corroborates an earlier study by Borzilleri 1978) points to the importance of considering the specific inflation borne by particular types of consumers.

These age/status/income CPIs have flaws, but they are relatively invulnerable to two often-raised criticisms: (1) that Medicare and Medicaid obviate the need for elderly consumers to bear a burden from health costs and (2) that fixed-weight CPI indexing overstates true inflation. Borzilleri (1980) notes that the fraction of health costs paid by private health insurance for the population aged 25-64 in 1977 (38 percent) is remarkably comparable to the percentage of the elderly's health bills paid by Medicare (41 percent). Therefore, the main difference across age is the larger health-care bills of the elderly rather than differences in health-insurance coverage, and the elderly are strongly affected by rising health-care costs.

Regarding the argument against fixed-weight indexing, the weights in these age/status/income CPIs are not fixed. They adjust for changes in distributions of consumers across age, family status, and income. Because of data limitations, however, it was not possible to adjust for changes in expenditure patterns in response to changes in the relative prices of expenditure categories, so these CPIs may overstate the absolute effect of inflation on the elderly. Conversely, relative to younger consumers, they may understate the inflationary burden on the elderly. This relative understatement would derive from a lack of flexibility in the purchasing patterns of the elderly caused by low income, restricted mobility, and short time horizons for the investment expenditures (such as a furnace conversion) required for some expenditure adjustments (Duffy et al. 1980). Therefore, differences in the relative burden of inflation across age may be larger than those reported in Duffy et al., and burdens from inflation borne by the oldest and poorest elderly may be understated the most of all. This line of reasoning implies that, on the one hand, while full CPI indexing may moderately overcompensate the elderly for their absolute real-income losses caused by inflation, it is probably insufficient to compensate the average elderly American for inflation-induced losses in income viewed relatively to the losses experienced by younger Americans. The small numbers of high-income elderly, on the other hand, can be expected to respond to price changes with considerable flexibility. Therefore, the full CPI indexing of large pensions could overcompensate those receiving such pensions in both absolute and relative terms (Duffy and Olson 1980).

Effects of an Aging Society on the Economy

The previous section summarized themes regarding the effects of economic and policy changes on the elderly. In this section, we address the effects of increases in the number and population share of the elderly on the economy. The two topics overlap, but this section espouses a more-macroeconomic approach and contains more speculation about the future. Increasing numbers of older people can directly affect the economy because behavior and access to government programs differ by age. Changes in the behavior of the elderly and in programs that serve them can also have an impact on the economy.

The treatment in this section will be relatively brief because detailed literature surveys of the impacts of the elderly on the economy already exist (for example, the Senate Special Committee on Aging 1980) and because the material on our baseline and option simulations covers some of the same ground. Two themes are addressed in this section: the effect of an aging society on labor markets and its effect of federal transfer payments. These themes do not exhaust the list of possible concepts, but they help raise some of the more-important issues. Also, within each theme, we concentrate moderately on effects that are expected beyond the twenty-five-year horizon of our simulations.

Labor Markets

The labor-force-participation rates of older Americans are much lower than those of their younger counterparts. Furthermore, the participation rates for older men have been falling for decades, and the rates for older women have declined moderately in the 1970s, as shown in figures 2-4 through 2-7. These facts, coupled with an increase in the population share of older persons, have exerted downward pressure on economywide rates of participation, particularly in the last decade.

This downward pressure, however, has been completely swamped in the 1970s by the two most dramatic demographic events of the twentieth century: (1) the movement of the baby-boom generation through the age distribution and (2) the unprecedented increase in labor-force participation by adult women. Thus, instead of declining, employment rates grew rapidly between 1970 and 1980. In the years to come, the graying of the population will continue, but the condition of the nation's labor markets will depend on the interaction between the participation levels of older workers, the movement of the baby-boom generation through the age structure, and changes in patterns of participation by women aged 55 and under.

Movements in the overall age structure are relatively easy to predict. The baby boom, which encompasses people born between approximately the years 1947 and 1960, will lead to a bulge that travels through the age structure changing labor markets, relative incomes, housing patterns, and the mix of consumption. The baby-boom children began to enter the labor market around the mid-1960s, providing a decade and a half of large

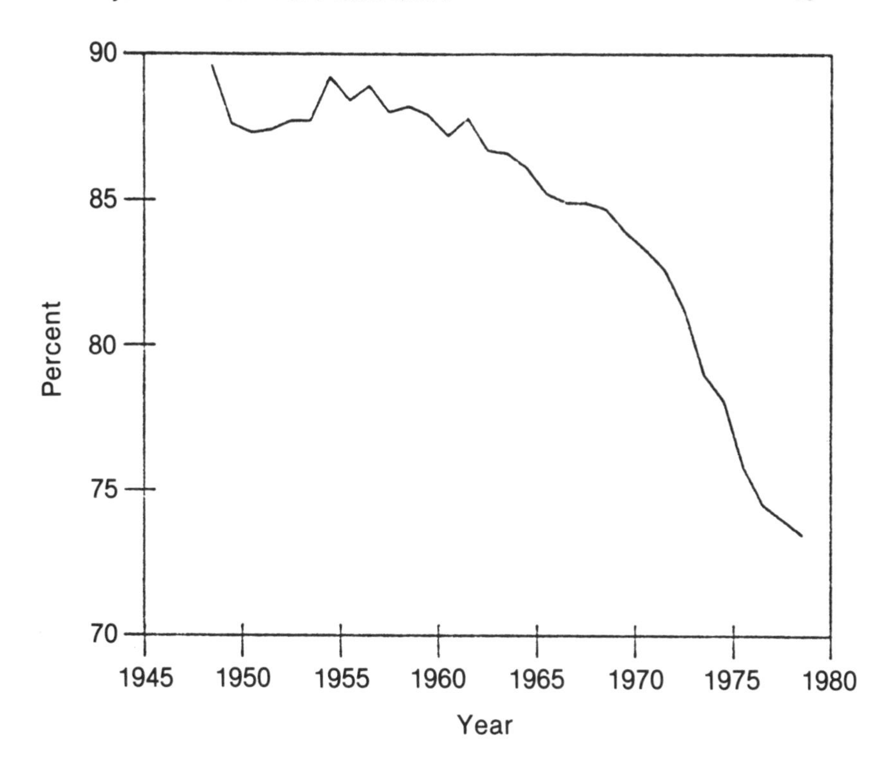

Source: Martin Duffy et al., "Inflation and the Elderly," Report to National Retired Teacher's Association and American Association of Retired Persons (DRI, 1980), p. II-7.

Figure 2-4. Labor-Force-Participation Rates for Men Aged 55 to 64

numbers of new entrants. The future growth of their numbers in the labor force will be slower than in the recent past. These individuals are now in their twenties and early thirties. They will reach their forties and early fifties by the turn of the century and will begin to retire around 2012 and thereafter, unless the age of retirement reverses its decline.

Overall female labor-force-participation rates are likely to rise less rapidly in future years than in the recent past although the general agreement seems to be that participation will continue to increase (see, for example, Anderson 1980). The important question, then, deals with participation rates by older age groups. Higher participation by these groups may help to fill the gap in labor-force growth caused by slower increases in the number of young workers and female workers in the 1980s and 1990s. In the twenty-first century, higher levels of participation by older baby-boom workers could help diminish the labor-market disruption that could occur if they all retired within a short time span.

Unfortunately, there is no general agreement at this time on the likely

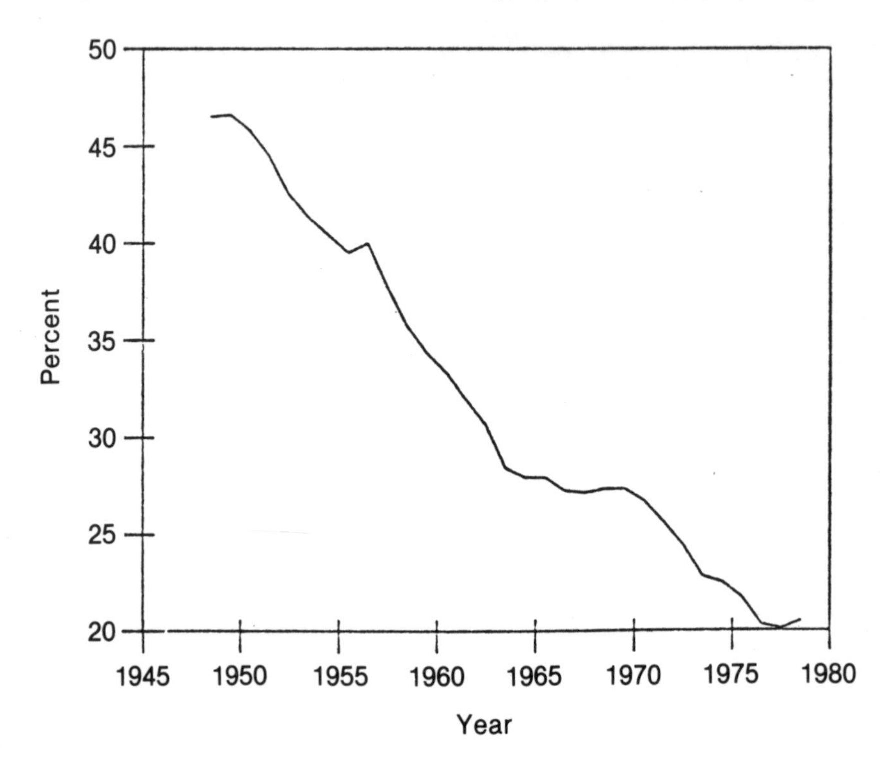

Source: Martin Duffy et al., "Inflation and the Elderly," Report to National Retired Teacher's Association and American Association of Retired Persons (DRI, 1980), pp. II-4, II-9.

Figure 2-5. Labor-Force-Participation Rates for Elderly Men

path of work-force participation and retirement by older Americans. Past trends point to decreased participation and earlier retirement, at least for men. Various factors, however, may contribute to a reversal of these trends, including the Age Discrimination in Employment Act, renewed interest by policymakers in methods for inducing more elderly participation, and the attempts by older Americans to protect themselves from the effects of high and uncertain rates of inflation. At the present time, evidence on this point is mixed and opinions differ.

A critical factor for understanding the effects of the changing numbers and age mix of workers is the degree to which workers of different ages are substitutable for one another in production. The traditional simplification in economics—which treats labor as a single, homogeneous input—has been replaced in the literature by the idea that workers of different ages and sexes can interact in diverse ways with one another and with capital inputs.

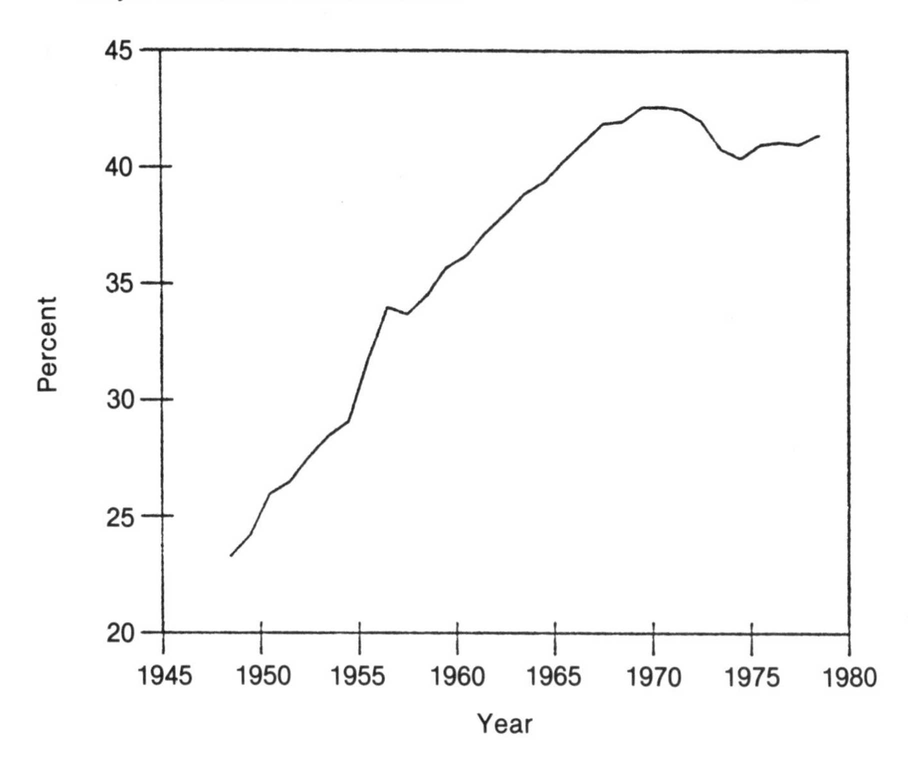

Source: Martin Duffy et al., "Inflation and the Elderly," Report to National Retired Teacher's Association and American Association of Retired Persons (DRI, 1980), p. II-8.

Figure 2-6. Labor-Force-Participation Rates for Women Aged 55 to 64

Anderson (1978; 1980) and Freeman (1979) have studied the degree of substitutability across workers of different ages in the labor force. The overall finding of these studies is that the degree of substitutability across ages is somewhat limited, implying that an increase in the relative size of any one age group may depress that group's returns from labor relative to the others. Thus, the inrush of baby-boom children into the labor market appears to have diminished their average earnings and elevated their rate of unemployment (Anderson 1978).

Limited substitutability may be less of a problem for older men since what is being addressed is a possible turnabout in the decline of their participation and a return to participation rates that have been sustained in the past. For women, especially women over 45, the evidence appears to show a greater degree of substitutability. Anderson (1978) finds evidence that women aged 45 and over can substitute for older men and for all female age groups so that increases in numbers of older women in the labor force may

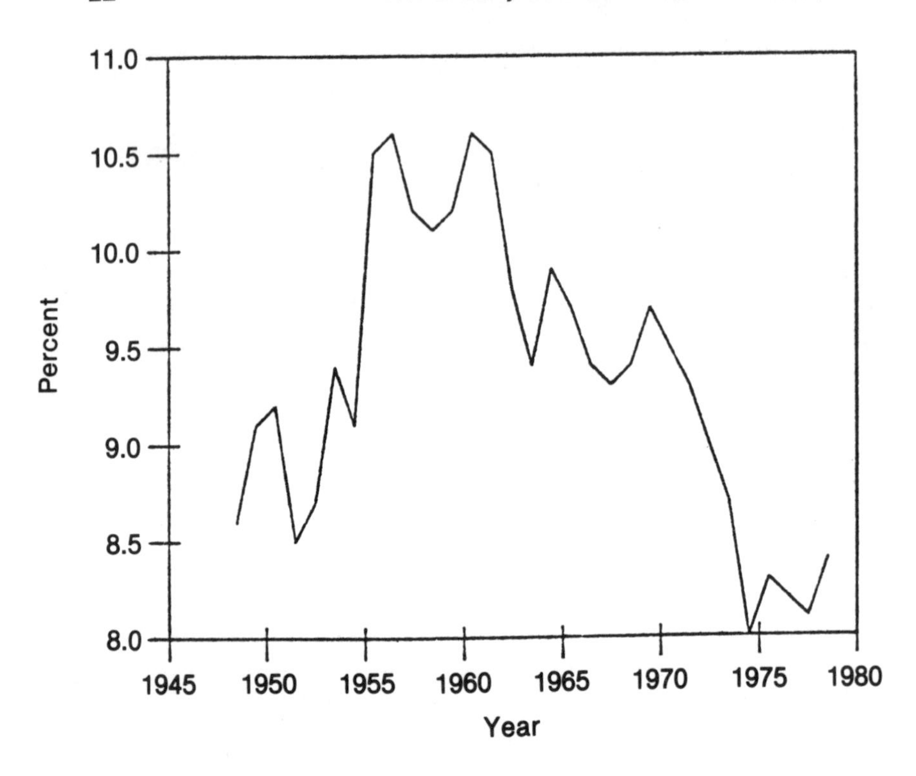

Source: Martin Duffy et al., "Inflation and the Elderly," Report to National Retired Teacher's Association and American Association of Retired Persons (DRI, 1980), p. II-10.

Figure 2-7. Labor-Force-Participation Rates for Elderly Women

help offset the declining numbers of young, female, new entrants. Freeman (1979) also reports higher levels of substitution among younger and older women than among younger and older men, although the degree of this substitutability can be expected to fall as women's attachment to the labor force becomes more similar to that of men.

Federal Transfer Payments

The flow of resources from the working to the retired populations is determined by the relative sizes of older and younger age groups, the average age of retirement, the amounts the retired can provide from their own resources and from funded pensions, and whether retirement income maintains a relative status vis-à-vis younger Americans or an absolute level. The period since the mid-1960s has shown rising population shares in the older age groups, an increasing prevalence of early retirement, declines in the value of financial assets held by the elderly and by fully funded pension funds, and increases in the relative income of the elderly after a fifteen-year decline. Increasing transfer payments to the elderly have caused a heightened level of concern about present and future burdens on the younger population, especially with regard to transfers by the federal government.

Clark and Menefee (1978) chart increasing federal expenditures on the elderly, including federal retirement programs, social security, Medicare, Medicaid, supplementary security income, special aid to those aged 72 and over, housing subsidies, food stamps, and the social and employment services. They estimate that total federal expenditures on the elderly grew from $27 billion in 1960 to $112 billion in 1978, in constant 1978 dollars. This fourfold increase represents a near doubling in the share of the federal budget, from 13 percent to 24 percent, and a more than doubling in the GNP share, from 2.5 percent to 5.3 percent. Clark and Menefee find that most of this increase derives from explicit policy changes designed to improve the quality of the retirement years, and they conclude that the growth of benefits in the future is largely controllable. They estimate also that maintenance of absolute benefit levels could be borne out of a stable or declining fraction of GNP. In contrast, maintenance of relative benefit levels (for example, indexing to average wage rates) increases the proportion of the GNP required in direct relation to changes in the population age structure.

Feldstein and Pellechio (1979) project an increase in the ratio of social-security-benefit payments to total covered wages from 10.7 percent in 1980 to 17.7 percent in 2025, based on wage indexing of initial benefit levels. Wage indexing of initial benefits, as stipulated in current law, maintains a constant initial replacement rate from social-security benefits. If price indexing is used to determine the initial benefit level, this ratio increases only slightly, to 12 percent.[2] Price indexing would maintain the absolute level of initial benefits.

Substantial public support exists for the notion of keeping the income of the elderly constant with the younger population in relative terms and even for further increases in relative income. Increased costs of what older people buy, losses in asset values, and usually low levels of income point to significant problems still to be addressed if old age is to be a pleasanter period of life. The current indexation of transfer payments means that income has been transferred to the nonworking population. Additional transfers to raise income support to the elderly in relative terms could lead to increasing opposition and tension between generations. The debate will be even sharper if future economic growth is more sluggish than expected, if the decline in the age of retirement does not slow or reverse, or if the relatively conservative fertility- and mortality-rate assumptions incorporated in census population projections end up understating the growth in the elderly's population share (see Bayo, Richie, and Faber 1978).

Finally, any discussion of the burden of transfers should consider the younger dependent population and private transfers within the family. The lower birth rates that have been the rule since about 1960 reduce the population share of dependent children. Decreases in education and other expenditures necessary to support this other dependent population can partially offset rising burdens caused by increases in the elderly population. Therefore, the overall dependency rate in the United States should continue to decline until at least the end of this century.

The problem with this formulation is on the one hand, that many people view transfers to the elderly as maintenance expenditures, as opposed to transfers to children that are usually thought of as investments. On the other hand, both the decline in transfers caused by decreasing numbers of young people and the increase going to the elderly are often overestimated. A larger share of *total* transfers to children occurs through the family—and is, therefore, not counted in the NIA—while the declining importance of extended families and the increasing tendency of older people to live alone tend to cause a larger proportion of transfers to the elderly to pass through public channels and be counted. Considering the elderly, therefore, at least part of the increase in public transfers may simply be compensation for declines in private, intrafamily transfers.

Notes

1. For example, "as of 1980, there is no official estimate of the number of persons currently in possession of a valid Medicaid card and no estimate of the number of persons currently eligible for program benefits, should a major and costly illness occur that would result in their being deemed 'medically needy': *In view of these constraints, it should be clearly understood that the estimates provided here are best considered as a 'rough order of magnitude' rather than precise.*" (Borzilleri 1980, pp. 8-9, emphasis in the original).

2. See Bayo, Richie, and Faber (1978) for detailed projections of flows into and out of the OASDI trust fund based on a range of long-term economic and actuarial assumptions. Considering a midrange projection, this study anticipates a system in close actuarial balance under current law until about 2011 and in deficit over the subsequent few decades. The study cautions, however, that the law is likely to change. Historically, such changes have increased average benefits.

3 Data Resources, Inc.'s Baseline Twenty-Five-Year Simulation of the Economy and the Income of the Elderly

As we enter the last two decades of the twentieth century, many questions arise about how our economy is changing, how well it can provide for the elderly and how the elderly and programs devised to help them affect the economy. DRI's baseline twenty-five-year simulation, which assumes a continuation of current economic and behavioral trends, attempts to answer some of these questions.

The outlook is for some improvement for the elderly, but with slower economic growth and continued high inflation, the rapid income gains enjoyed by the elderly in recent years are projected to moderate. Also, the projected ongoing decline in labor-force participation by older age groups tends to exacerbate the main cause of slower aggregate growth—fewer young new entrants into the labor force.

Because many of the questions raised here are inherently long term, a twenty-five-year horizon, the longest period for which DRI simulations are performed, is used. Results are derived from twenty-five-year simulations of the DRI Macroeconomic Model and the DRI Demographic-Economic (DECO) Model of the Elderly in order to provide a comprehensive and detailed picture of the future. Current behavioral and governmental trends are assumed so the baseline simulation can provide a benchmark to which the policy simulations in chapters 4-7 can be compared.

If governmental policy toward the economy and the elderly does not change over the next quarter-century, the future is expected to bring the following:

Real-GNP and consumption growth will slow from the rates achieved in the 1960s and the 1970s.

Inflation will moderate only slowly.

Real-income growth of the elderly will slow.

The relative income position of the elderly will deteriorate.

Gains in the income adequacy of elderly will be attained but at a much reduced pace as compared with the recent past.

Income differentials between segments of the elderly (defined by age, sex, and family status) will diminish but less rapidly than in recent years.

Outlook for the Overall Economy

DRI's baseline outlook for the overall economy projects a continuation of current economic trends in the absence of new initiatives to aid the elderly. Under these conditions, the outlook shows slow but steady improvement of the economy from its current recessionary state, with renewed growth and declining inflation. This growth is projected to be less than the growth that occurred historically, however, and gains against inflation are painfully slow. Thus, Consumer Price Index (CPI) inflation averages 8.1 percent from 1980 to 1990 and is still a high 6.8 percent from 2000 to 2005.

The smaller numbers of young people entering the labor force are a principal constraint on growth. Thus, in sharp contrast to recent years, future increases in employment act as a drag on economic growth.

Specification of the Baseline Macroeconomic Simulation

The baseline macroeconomic simulation discussed in this book is DRI's TRENDLONG2005 twenty-five-year simulation. This simulation was prepared in September 1980.[1] The baseline simulation assumes population growth consistent with the Bureau of the Census Series II projection in which, from 1980 to 2015, the fertility rate increases from its current level of 1.7 to 2.1. The census projection also assumes some small improvement in mortality as well as net immigration of 400,000 per year. Total U.S. population is 244 million by 1990 and 268 million by 2005. The baseline projection assumes a significant slowing in labor-force growth, primarily reflecting slower growth in the prime-age population and in participation rates.

Since 1970, the proportion of the population over age 18 has increased from 66 percent to 72.1 percent, swelled by the peristaltic movement of the postwar baby boom through the nation's age distribution. However, given that the last baby-boom children were born around 1960, the number of new entrants to the prime age group is already slowing and will continue to do so for many years. Thus, average annual increases of only 1.1 percent in the prime-age population are assumed from 1980 to 1990. A further slowing to 0.8 percent is projected for the period 1990 to 2005.

The aggregate labor-force-participation rate rose from 57.8 percent in 1970 to 62.2 percent in 1980, a ten-year increase of 4.4 percentage points. This surge in participation partly reflects the pattern of postwar births discussed previously. It also reflects the rise in female participation from 38.6 percent in 1965 to 50.4 percent in 1980. Women have accounted for close to 60 percent of the increase in the labor force in the last fifteen years. However, in spite of continued projected high rates of female participation, the aging of the baby-boom generation constrains growth in overall labor-force participation to a total of 3.1 percentage points in the 1980s and only 1.3 percentage points from 1990 to 2005.

While growth in the participation rate of the whole civilian labor force slows, the baseline projection assumes that the participation rate of the elderly will continue to decline as it has for several decades. From 1980 to 2005, the participation rate for elderly men falls from 18 percent to 11 percent. During the same period, the participation rate of elderly women drops from 8 percent to 6 percent. The participation rate of near-elderly men (aged 55 to 64) also declines within the projection period from about 72 percent in 1980 to about 56 percent in 2005. The participation rate of near-elderly women falls during the twenty-five-year period from about 40 percent to about 37 percent. The net result of these assumed trends in population growth and labor-force participation is that growth in the labor force slows from an annual average of 2.5 percent in the last decade to 1.5 percent in the 1980s to only 0.9 percent from 1990 to 2005.

In the formulation of baseline assumptions concerning fiscal policy, several conflicting forces likely to operate on the public sector were postulated, including public resistance to further increases in taxes, perceived political needs for increased defense spending, lower growth in demand for state and local services, and the continuing need to provide some measure of an adequate-living standard for government-transfer recipients. Under these conflicting forces, the portion of GNP that passes through the federal budget is projected to fall slightly from 23.6 percent in 1981 to 22.4 percent in 1990 before stabilizing at close to 23 percent for the remainder of the 1980s and beyond 2000. Transfers to persons average 3.5 percent real annual growth from 1980 to 2005, somewhat in excess of the economy's overall growth and considerably less than the 8 percent average real growth in transfers recorded between 1965 and 1980. As a percentage of GNP, transfer payments rise from 9.7 percent in 1980 to 11.8 percent in 2005. As a percentage of the total federal budget, they rise from 41.6 percent to 51.3 percent (see figure 3-1). Defense spending as a percentage of GNP also rises, from 5 percent in 1980 to 5.8 percent by 1990, and then remains roughly at that level for the remainder of the projection period.

On the receipts side of the federal ledger, the baseline projection assumes a tax cut of $32 billion, enacted in mid-1981. This cut includes a personal-income-tax reduction of $25 billion and $7 billion in corporate investment incentives. The corporate-tax cuts are assumed to be enacted retroactively to January. It is further assumed that discrete personal-income-tax cuts are enacted every second year, beginning in 1984. Despite these cuts, the effective federal personal-income-tax rate is projected to rise from 14.2 percent in 1980 to 15.9 percent in 1990 to 17.6 percent in 2005.

With respect to state and local governments, from 1980 to 1985 expenditures are expected to decline as a percentage of GNP in response to declin-

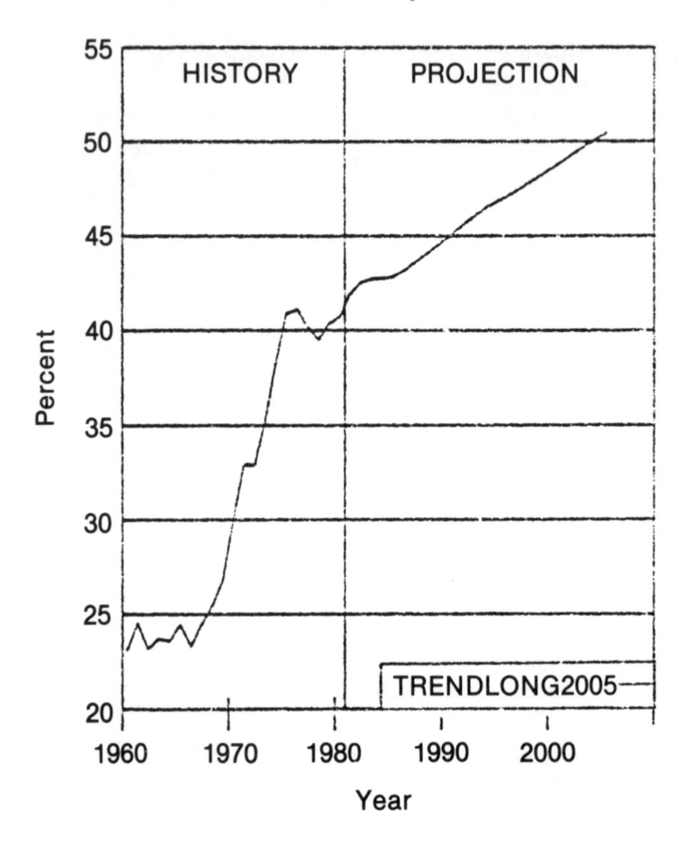

Figure 3-1. Personal Transfer Payments as a Percentage of the Federal Budget: Baseline

ing growth in grants and property-tax revenues. The situation reverses itself in the late 1980s as rising income standards and a growing school-age population generate increased demands for services. It is further assumed that as a percentage of GNP, federal grants-in-aid decline from 3.3 percent in 1980 to 2.8 percent in 1985 to 2.6 percent by 2005. State and local governments are assumed to rely more heavily on corporate- and personal-income taxes and less heavily on property taxes.

The baseline projection assumes that oil supplies will continue to be tight throughout the next quarter-century. Thus, throughout this period, energy prices are projected to rise some 3-4 percent faster than the overall rate of inflation. Despite considerable conservation, energy scarcity constrains overall economic growth.

Implicit in the baseline scenario is the overall assumption that

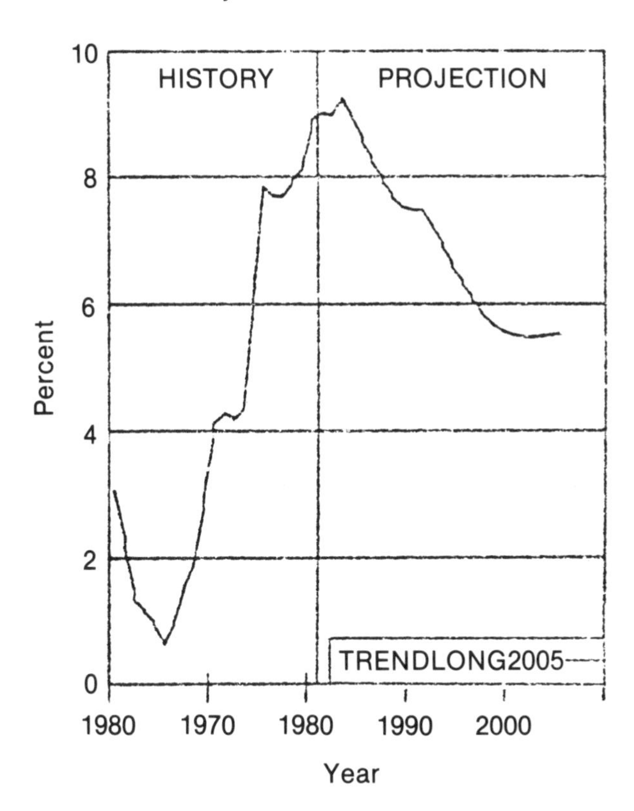

Figure 3-2. The Core Rate of Inflation in the Implicit GNP Deflator: Baseline

throughout the projection period, the economy suffers no major disruptions such as further severe oil-price shocks; untoward swings in monetary, fiscal, and regulatory policy; excessively rapid runups in demand; crop shortages; and so forth. The baseline projection is therefore best described as depicting the mean of possible paths the economy would follow if subject to none of these major disruptions. The key characteristics of the economy under the baseline scenario are

A slowdown in economic growth. Annual growth in real GNP averages only 2.5 percent from 1981-2005, compared with 3.1 percent in 1955 to 1980.

A mild, gradual improvement in the rate of inflation (see figure 3-2). Inflation as measured by the GNP deflator falls from 9.6 percent in 1981 to 6 percent by 1995. Energy prices remain considerably higher, however, largely because of tight supplies of imported oil. The wholesale price index for fuels, related products, and power in 1985 is expected to be more than triple its 1979 value.

A slight decline in the proportion of the nation's resources devoted to the public sector. Transfers grow, but less rapidly than in recent history. Defense spending accelerates.

Detailed Macroeconomic Outlook

Key differences between the performance of the economy projected in the baseline scenario over the next twenty-five years and its actual performance over the past twenty-five years are captured in table 3-1. Average annual growth in real GNP is projected to slow from 3.1 percent to 2.5 percent. After a period of moderate growth coinciding with recovery from the downturn of 1980 and 1981, the growth rate declines continuously from 4.8 percent in 1982 to 1.8 percent in 1993. Although improvements in productivity and inflation permit some subsequent acceleration in growth, the annual growth rate never exceeds 2.5 percent for the remainder of the projection period.

Table 3-2 gives historical and projected rates of increase of potential output for the last two decades and for the remainder of this century. Since it also shows the appropriately weighted contributions of factor inputs to these growth rates, it highlights the degree to which these declining rates are a function of declining labor-force growth. The slowing growth in the 1970s was due to shrinking contributions from all factors except the labor force. In the next two decades, while nonlabor inputs can be expected to grow at least as rapidly as in the past decade, labor-force growth can be expected to

Table 3-1
Some Key Economic Parameters, Past and Future: Baseline

Parameters	*1955-1980*	*1981-2005*
Average real GNP growth	3.1	2.5
Average inflation (implicit GNP deflator)	4.5	6.9
Average unemployment rate	5.5	6.3
Average growth in industrial production	3.7	3.6
Average labor-force growth	1.9	1.1
Average fuel-import bill (percentage of GNP)	0.9	3.7
Average tax burden (percentage of GNP)	29.5	34.1

slow significantly (see figures 3-3 and 3-4). Thus, labor's contribution to growth in potential output shrinks relative to that of other factor inputs.

Thus, the economy in the 1990s can be expected to grow at only a little more than half the rate that characterized the 1960s. Potential GNP per head rose by an annual average of 2.6 percent between 1960 and 1970. By the mid-1990s, this figure is projected to be at about 1.6 percent (figure 3-5 shows growth in aggregate potential output, a concept that increases somewhat more rapidly than output per head because of population growth). This rate, of course, means not only that market growth will be slow but also that expectations of real-income increases that match those that have been achieved historically are likely to be frustrated.

The silver lining in this rather pessimistic scenario is that inflation improves. However, the improvement is very modest. The projected rate of increase in the implicit GNP deflator falls from 9.6 percent in 1981 to 7.7 percent in 1990 to 6 percent from 1995 on. What little improvement does occur can be traced mostly to improved productivity of labor. The greater the quantity of goods and services produced by the average worker, the lower are the labor costs per unit of output and consequently the lower is the price that firms must charge to cover those costs. Recent DRI research has shown that a 1 percent improvement in the rate of growth of output per hour can eventually reduce the rate of inflation by about 2 percent (Caton and Probyn 1979).

Productivity improves because labor grows more slowly than capital. In effect, each worker can produce more because he or she has more plant and equipment at his or her disposal. Improvement in management techniques fostered by relatively stable economic conditions also enhances productivity.

Capital grows more rapidly than labor because, while growth in the latter slows for demographic reasons, growth in the former is stimulated by investment tax incentives. Stable economic conditions also encourage investment by nurturing business confidence. As a percentage of GNP, business fixed investment rises from an average of 10.2 percent in the 1970s to an

Table 3-2
Average Annual Contributions to Potential Output Growth: Baseline
(percentage points)

Factors of Production	*1960-1970*	*1970-1980*	*1980-1990*	*1990-2005*
Labor	0.97	1.32	0.84	0.52
Business fixed capital	1.62	0.79	0.89	0.89
Energy	0.21	0.06	0.06	0.07
R&D stock	0.45	0.16	0.17	0.27
Residual	0.68	0.71	0.49	0.44
Potential growth	3.93	3.04	2.45	2.19

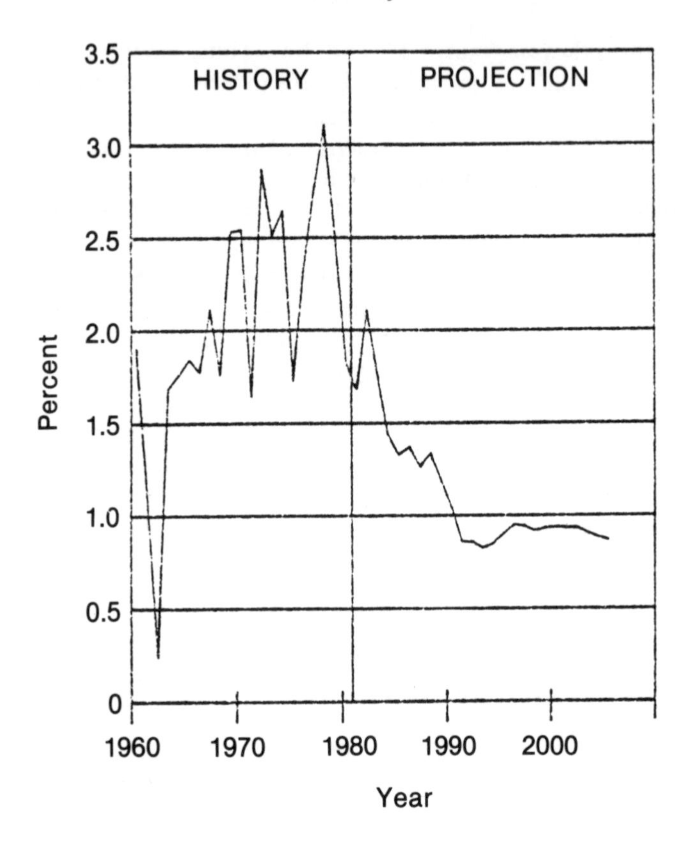

Figure 3-3. Percentage Rate of Labor-Force Growth: Baseline

average of 10.8 percent in 1985-1990. This percentage increases steadily throughout the remainder of the simulation period so that by 2000-2005 it averages 11.7 percent.

Overall inflation improves only marginally in the baseline projection because inflationary expectations are so deeply imbedded in the economy. These expectations have contributed to the acceleration of inflation over the last fifteen years by accelerating the core, or underlying, rate of inflation. The core rate of inflation is determined by the rate of increase of the factor costs, which is itself determined by an expectational mechanism derived from the recent history of actual inflation. This mechanism has the effect of embedding inflation, once generated, into the system. The rising trend of inflation in recent years has resulted from the interaction of this expectational mechanism with two unusual events. First, the economy has been run, on average, at an unusually high rate of utilization. Second, the "shocks" to the inflationary system in the last fifteen years have been overwhelmingly unfavorable. For example, energy- and food-price shocks,

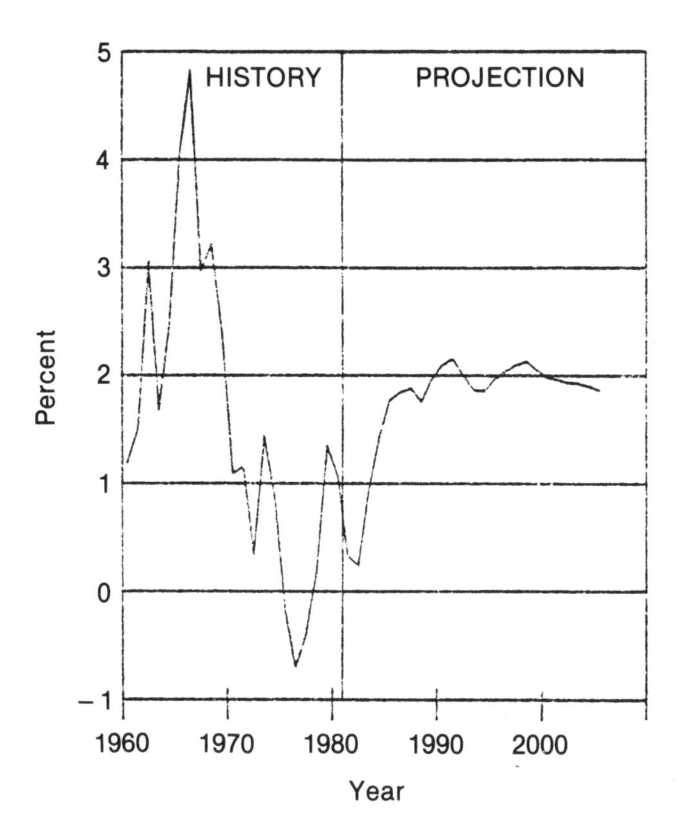

Figure 3-4. Percentage Rate of Growth in Capital/Labor Ratio: Baseline

social-security and minimum-wage increases, and exchange-rate movements have imparted an upward momentum to actual inflation and have then been built into the core rate of inflation. They thus have a final effect on inflation that far exceeds their initial, or impact, effect.[2]

Such an analysis implies that the underlying rate of inflation can be improved only slowly, with even this slow improvement requiring several years of relatively slow real growth, a better productivity performance than that seen in recent years, and relatively good luck with respect to shocks to the system. DRI's projection incorporates each of these elements and thus allows a steady, but very slow, improvement in inflation. Simulation exercises with DRI's Macroeconomic Model suggest that more-dramatic improvement could be obtained only by draconian measures or uncommonly good luck. For example, it has been estimated that, other things equal, it could require as long as five years of running the economy with enough slack to hold the unemployment rate close to 8 percent to reduce the core rate of inflation to 7 percent.

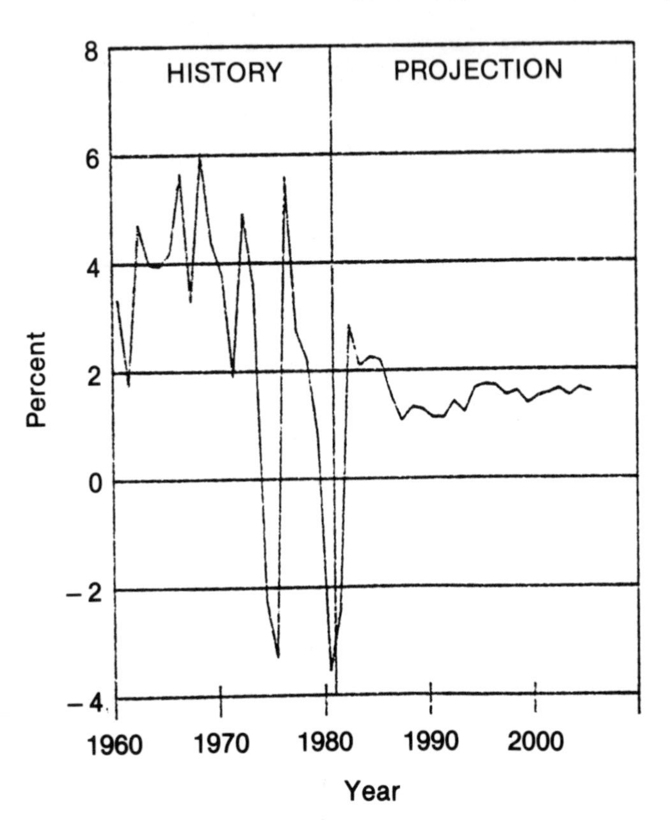

Figure 3-5. Percentage Rate of Potential Output Growth: Baseline

Of course, inflation could be far worse. More-pessimistic scenarios such as a core rate of inflation that continues to climb for the next decade cannot definitely be ruled out. Such an outcome would have considerable, though difficult-to-quantify, repercussions for many categories of spending (particularly investment), saving behavior, the financing of economic activity, productivity growth, the balance of payments and the exchange rate, the tax system, the burden of federal transfer payments, and ultimately for the viability of the entire economic structure.

It should be pointed out that the U.S. economy has successfully extricated itself from past episodes of double-digit inflation. For example, the implicit price deflator for GNP rose by 15.7 percent in 1946, by 13.1 percent in 1947, but improved to 6.9 percent in 1948. In 1949, this deflator actually fell by 1 percent. However, inflationary expectations were not so firmly entrenched then, and implicit or explicit indexation of wages and other incomes was neither widespread, nor were real energy price increases likely to be so persistent and severe. In the near-term, energy prices are projected to increase much more rapidly than are prices in general. Also, given the likelihood of further large OPEC increases and the effects of domestic decontrol, the average acquisition price of imported oil is expected to increase at an annual rate of 12.4 percent through 1985 and then to average 11.8 percent annual increases through to 1990 and 10.8 percent thereafter. These increases put the average acquisition price per barrel at $500 by 2005.

The increase in domestic-energy prices is even more rapid. The wholesale price index for fuels, related products, and power in 1985 is expected to be more than triple its 1979 value. The annual rate of increase of this index slows to 14 percent by 1985 but is pushed up to 15 percent by 1990, reflecting the assumed phasing in of natural-gas deregulation over a five-year period. From 1990 to 2000, some deceleration takes place, but this index is still increasing at a 9 percent annual rate in 2000.

Energy-price rises experienced by consumers, consistent with the previous considerations, can be expected to average about 12 percent between 1980 and 1990 and 9 percent between 1990 and 2000. Some further conservation is possible, but the share of total consumption spending (on a National Income Accounts basis) devoted to energy-intensive consumption (gasoline, fuel oil and coal, electricity and natural gas) can be expected to rise from 10 percent in 1980 to 14 percent by 2000.

Compared to energy-price rises, inflation in food prices is projected to be considerably more moderate. Food- and beverage-price increases exhibit a gradual downward trend throughout the twenty-five-year-simulation period. They rise only marginally faster than do total consumer prices, which is consistent with the historical record.

The continued relative-price increases for energy are caused largely by a persistent tightness of imported-oil supplies. These price increases will spur conservation efforts (see figure 3-6) that will be sufficient to hold the elasticity of energy usage with respect to real GNP at about 0.6 (that is, for every 1 percent increase in GNP energy usage will increase by 0.6 percent). This elasticity is consistent with total usage in the year 2000 of 101 quads.

Thus, slow growth, only slight improvement in inflation, moderation in the growth of the public sector, and tight supplies of energy highlight the macroeconomic outlook in the baseline scenario (see table 3-3). Further aspects of this outlook are referred to in the discussions of the four options. A complete, detailed discussion of the baseline scenario is provided in appendix A.

Outlook for Income and Its Distribution

This section reports on the TRENDLONG2005 baseline simulation of DRI's DECO Model of the Elderly. This model projects trends in elderly and nonelderly income differentiated by age (under 55, 55-61, 62-64, 65-71, 72 and over), family status (men living alone, women living alone, families of two or more), and income level. The baseline simulation of this DECO

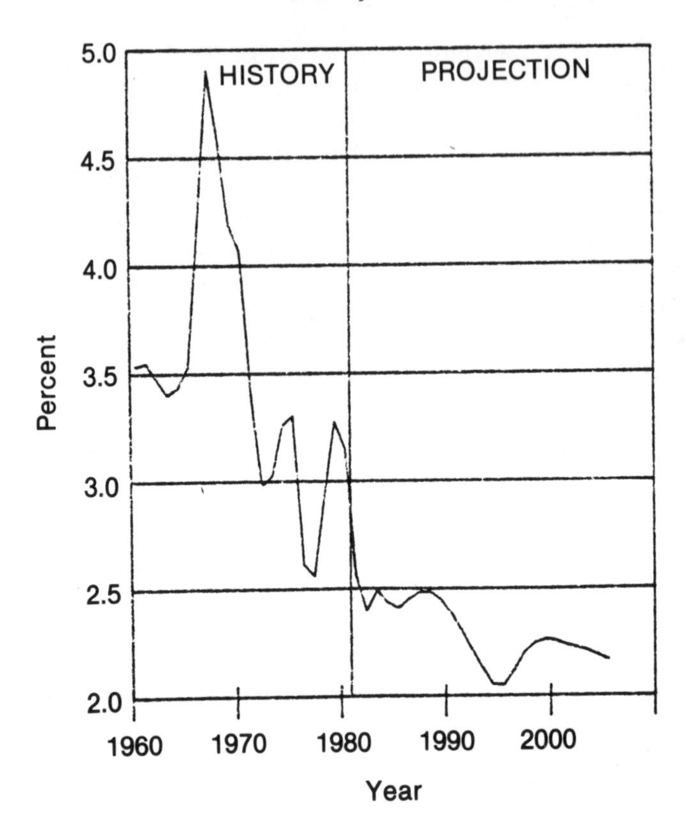

Figure 3-6. Percentage Rate of Growth in Energy Usage (Quads): Baseline

Model shows the implications of the baseline macroeconomic scenario for various groups within the elderly population, both in absolute terms and relative to younger age groups. Over the next twenty-five years, findings point to a continuation, although at a slower pace, in the growth of real income received by the elderly. Compared to the growth of the average income of the nonelderly population, however, the income of the elderly population is projected to lose ground.

Three of the most important factors in this outlook are (1) changes in the age distribution, (2) trends in labor-force participation, and (3) the outlook for transfer payments. These are discussed in turn. Next we present the average outlook for elderly income, both absolute and relative to the nonelderly. Finally, we discuss projected changes in the distribution of income within elderly groups, showing how the low-income elderly are expected to fare relative to elderly families and singles at higher-income levels.

Age Distribution

Figure 3-7 shows the population shares of adult age groups over the past and projected for the future. The values in this figure are derived from census data and Series II projections, with minor adjustments to account for differences in population coverage between the census and the Current Population Survey. Figure 3-7 demonstrates the influence of the baby-boom generation, as illustrated by the successive population waves at ten-year intervals. The cohort that preceded the baby boom is known as the "depression dent" because its members were born during the low-birth-rate years of the Great Depression. This group gives rise to the successive troughs immediately preceding the baby-boom waves. The over-65 population will continue to grow, primarily because of declining mortality, except for some reduction in its share of total population that will occur during the late 1900s and early 2000s when the depression-dent generation reaches ages 65 and over.

The sharp upturn in the 55-64-year-old age group in the mid-1990s presages a similar movement among the 65-and-over population beyond our forecast horizon as the baby-boom generation reaches retirement age. It is easy to see why the future, particularly the period from about 2012 to 2030, is worrisome for policymakers. The combination of a large birth cohort's reaching old age, improvements in mortality rates, and low rates of elderly labor-force participation augur for big increases in the relative size of the older, dependent population unless a significant change occurs in behavior and policy.

Table 3-4 shows the share of the population aged 65 and over. This share has increased from 9.2 percent in 1960 to 11.2 percent today. This imbalance of growth will continue over the next twenty-five years—that is, the elderly population will increase by 30.5 percent, while the total population will grow by only 20.5 percent.

Table 3-5 shows numbers of single men, single women, and families of two or more within each of the elderly age groups as projected by the DECO Model of the Elderly. All groups will increase over the twenty-five-year-projection horizon. For example, the number of elderly women, living alone is projected to increase by about 45 percent, elderly single men by 19 percent, and elderly families by 22 percent. The oldest group of women living alone is expected to grow even more rapidly, by approximately 48 percent, reflecting declining mortality rates among women. The rapid growth of this group has important consequences for public policy since very old elderly women living alone have the lowest average income of all of the elderly age groups.

Table 3-3
Capsule Summary of the Baseline Macroeconomic Outlook

	History				*Baseline*				
Parameters	*1960-1965*	*1965-1970*	*1970-1975*	*1975-1980*	*1980-1985*	*1985-1990*	*1990-1995*	*1995-2000*	*2000-2005*
Composition of real GNP (average annual rates of change)									
GNP	4.7	3	2.3	3.2	3.2	2.7	2.2	2.3	2.3
Final sales	4.5	3.2	2.5	3.1	3	2.7	2.2	2.3	2.3
Total consumption	4.3	3.7	3	3.4	2.8	2.7	2.4	2.1	2.2
Nonresidential fixed investment	7.7	2.9	0.6	4.9	3.1	3.5	2.6	3.4	2.9
Equipment	8.5	3.7	2.6	4.6	4.2	3.7	3.3	3.9	3.4
Nonresidential construction	6.6	1.6	−2.8	5.4	0.8	3.1	1.1	1.9	1.3
Residential fixed investment	4.3	−1.5	−0.8	2.4	8.9	1.4	−2.2	0.4	2.4
Exports	6.5	6.4	6.1	7.3	3.7	4.2	3.6	4.3	4.2
Imports	6.2	9.9	0.5	8.4	3.4	3.3	3.7	3.7	3.8
Federal government	2	2	−2.7	2.1	3.6	2.5	1.8	1.8	1.7
State and local government	5.9	5	3.6	0.9	1.7	2.2	1.9	1.7	2
Shares of nominal GNP (percent)									
Consumption	63.1	62	62.9	64	64.2	62.8	62.7	62.6	62.1
Business investment	9.4	10.4	10.1	10.3	10.3	10.8	11	11.4	11.7
Residential construction	4.7	3.7	4.4	4.4	4.9	5.2	4.7	4.3	4.5
Government purchases	20.6	22.2	21.6	20.7	20.5	20.6	21	21	20.9
Prices and wages (average annual rates of change)									
Implicit price deflator	1.6	4.2	6.8	7.3	8.5	7.8	6.6	5.9	5.8
CPI all urban consumers	1.3	4.3	6.8	8.9	8.6	8.1	7.3	6.8	6.7
Wholesale price index	0.4	2.7	9.6	9	10.3	9.3	7.4	6.7	6.8
Compensation per hour	3.7	6.4	8	8.7	10.1	9.4	8.4	7.7	7.4

Production and other key measures									
Industrial production (average percentage change)	6.3	3.7	1.8	4.1	4.8	3.6	2.8	3.4	3.5
Housing starts (million units)	1.5	1.4	1.8	1.7	2	2.2	1.9	1.8	1.9
Retail car sales (million units)	7.6	9	10.1	10.4	10.9	11.4	11.4	11.8	12
Unemployment rate (percentage)	5.5	3.9	6.1	6.8	7.4	6	6.3	5.9	5.9
Federal budget surplus (National Income Accounts	−2.1	−4.9	−25.5	−39	−43	−15.3	−40.7	−69.9	−120.9
Money and interest rates									
Money Supply (M1-B) (average percentage change)	3.5	5	6.1	6.8	8.2	8.3	7.3	6.3	5.7
New AA corporate utility rate (percentage)	4.5	6.9	8.4	9.8	11.8	11.1	10.2	9.1	8.8
New high-grade corporate bond rate (percentage)	4.4	6.8	8	9.4	11.3	10.7	9.8	8.8	8.5
Federal funds rate (percentage)	3.1	6.1	6.8	8.3	10.3	9.3	8	7.2	7.2
Prime rate (percentage)	4.5	6.7	7.5	9.8	11.2	10.6	9.3	8.6	8.6

Note: Demand deposits + currency + other checking accounts (including NOW accounts) = new corporate utility bonds with a rating of AA.

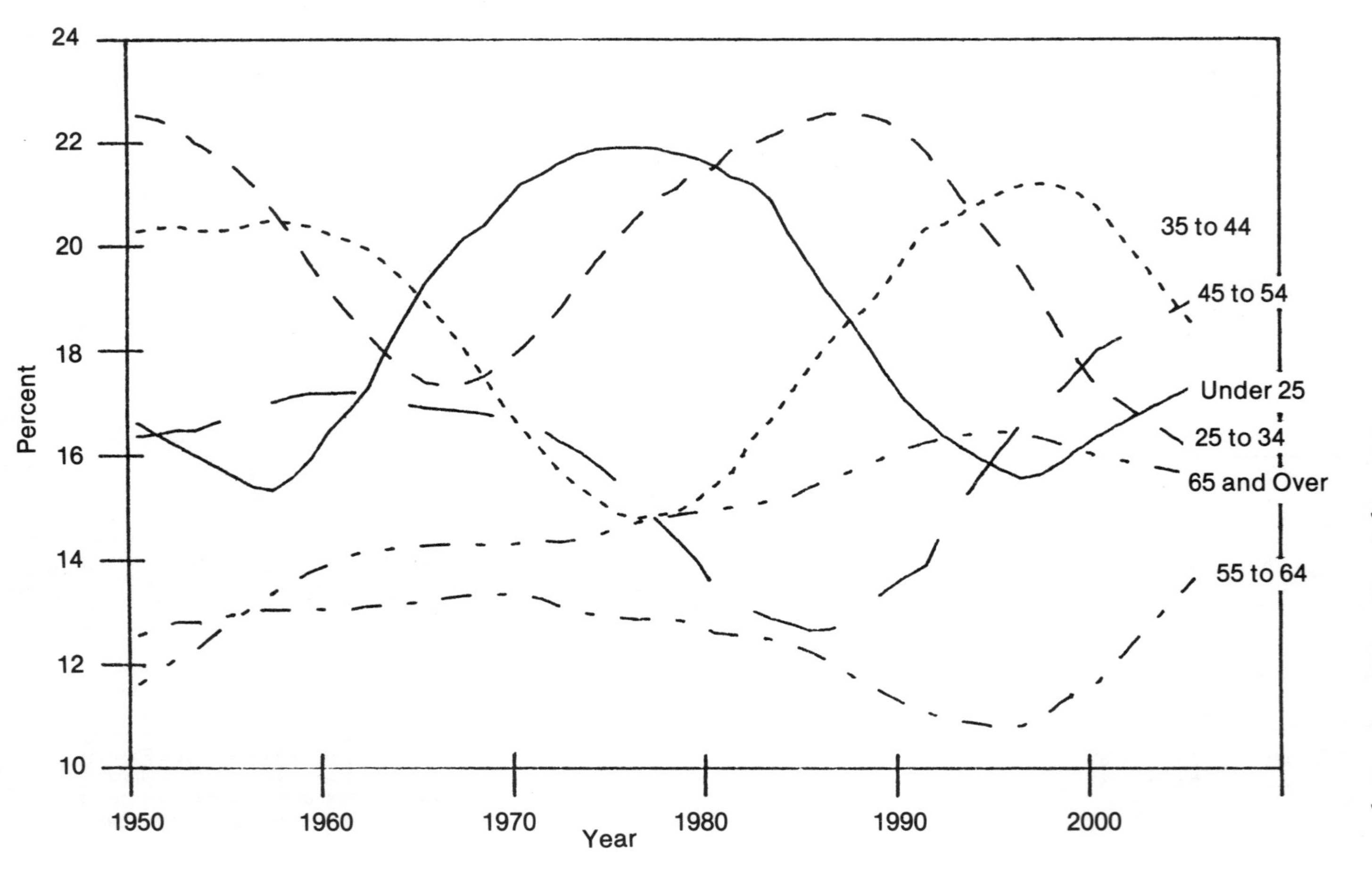

Figure 3-7. Age Composition: Percentages of the Adult Population

Table 3-4
Population
(millions of persons)

Year	*Total Population*	*65 and over*	*Percentage Share*
1960	181.1	16.7	9.2
1970	205.1	20.1	9.8
1980	222.4	24.9	11.2
1990	243.8	29.8	12.3
2000	260.6	31.8	12.2
2005	267.9	32.5	12.1

Source: Series II projections from "Projections of the Population of the Untied States: 1977 to 2050," *Current Population Reports,* series p. 25, no. 704 (July 1977).

Labor-Force Participation

The work and retirement patterns of the elderly have changed dramatically since World War II. The labor-force-participation rate for elderly men is now less than half of its 1950 value. For women, the current labor-force-participation rate is only slightly lower than in the 1950s. The decline of elderly-female labor-force participation since the early 1960s more than offsets increases that occurred in the 1950s.

At about 18 percent and 8 percent respectively, the 1980 labor-force-participation rates for elderly men and women indicate that the preponderant majority of the elderly population is not in the labor force (see figures 3-8 and 3-9). Projections of future participation behavior by the DECO Model of the Elderly anticipate a continuation of this decline over the next twenty-five years but at a slower pace than has been true in the recent past. In part, an attenuated decline is expected because the current rates are already so low that they leave little room for further diminution. Also, DRI expects a somewhat slower expansion in the incentives to retire than has occurred in the past. This change reflects the uncertainty created by continued inflation matched with slower growth in transfer payments. Furthermore, the recent prohibitions on mandatory retirement before age 70 may contribute to prolonging the average work life.

With slower economy-wide growth, mounting pressures on the federal budget to control the "uncontrollable" elements in the budget, and decreasing mortality, more emphasis will be placed on private solutions to the social problem of support for the elderly. These considerations may signal a further shift in government policy toward providing increased incentives for older workers to stay in the labor force, although our baseline projection incorporates no such policy changes. It is also possible that the decline in elderly labor-force participation may reverse in the absence of new policy initiatives, but as yet no convincing evidence exists of any such change.

Table 3-5
Number of Elderly Families and Singles, by Age Group
(thousands)

Age	*1970*	*1975*	*1980*	*1985*	*1990*	*1995*	*2000*	*2005*
Single Men								
65 to 71	581.1	633.1	729.2	794.7	855.5	880.7	883.5	908.5
72 and over	828.9	843.9	954.7	1,010.1	1,061.1	1,078.7	1,078.2	1,101.7
Total	1,410	1,477	1,683.9	1,804.9	1,916.6	1,959.5	1,961.7	2,010.1
Single Women								
65 to 71	1,767.8	2,138.3	2,411.5	2,723.6	3,023.6	3,190.1	3,262.1	3,361
72 and over	2,630.2	3,236.7	3,817	4,397	4,961.7	5,312.2	5,484.9	5,645.8
Total	4,398	5,375	6,228.5	7,120.6	7,985.3	8,502.3	8,747	9,006.8
Families								
65 to 71	3,710.3	4,392.9	4,618.4	5,047.3	5,487.9	5,829.6	5,814	5,872.1
72 and over	3,464.7	3,770.1	4,014.2	4,277.7	4,548.3	4,758.2	4,748.6	4,784.3
Total	7,175	8,163	8,632.5	9,324.9	10,036.2	10,587.8	10,562.7	10,656.4

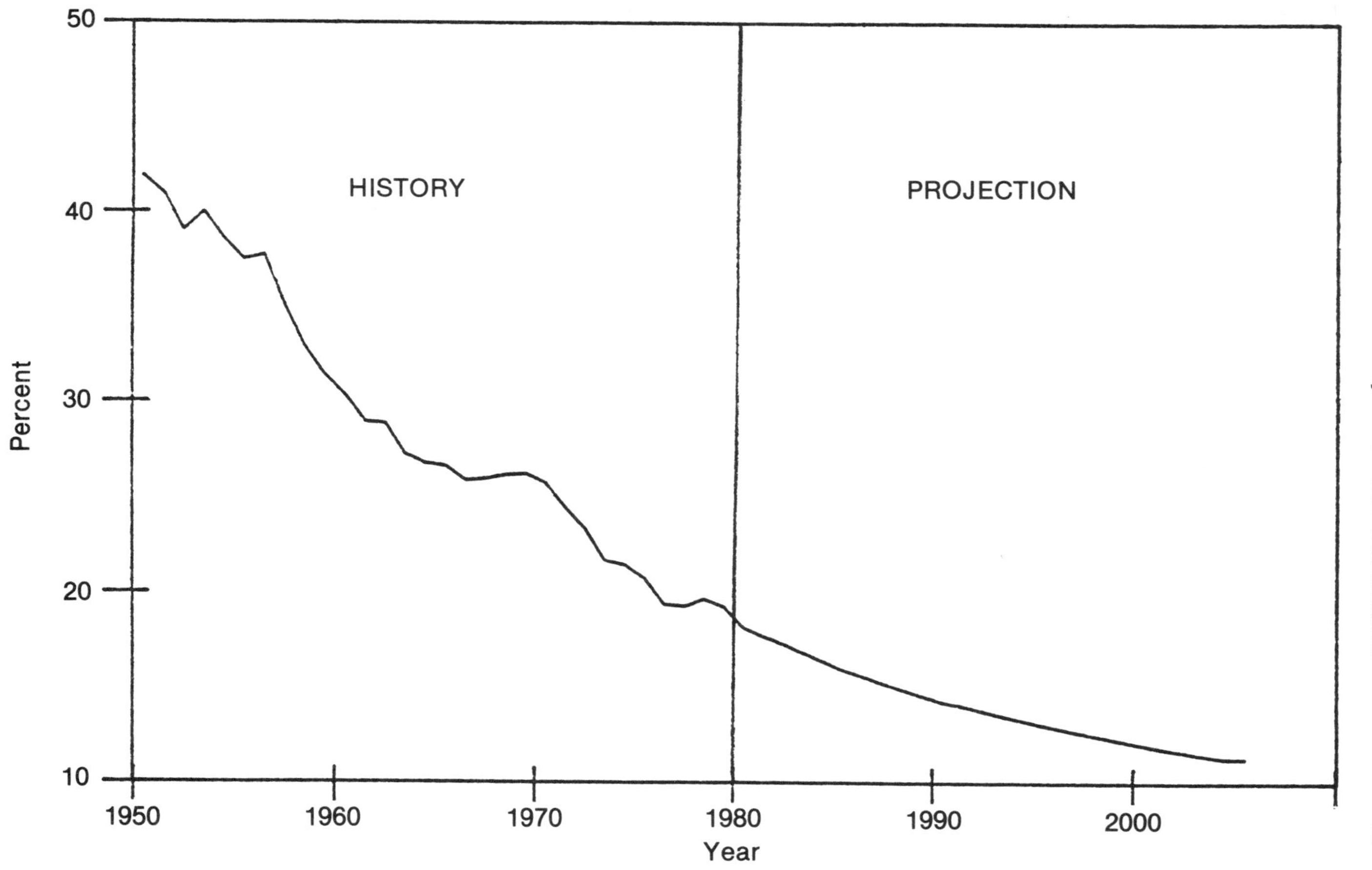

Figure 3-8. Labor-Force-Participation Rate for Elderly Men: Baseline

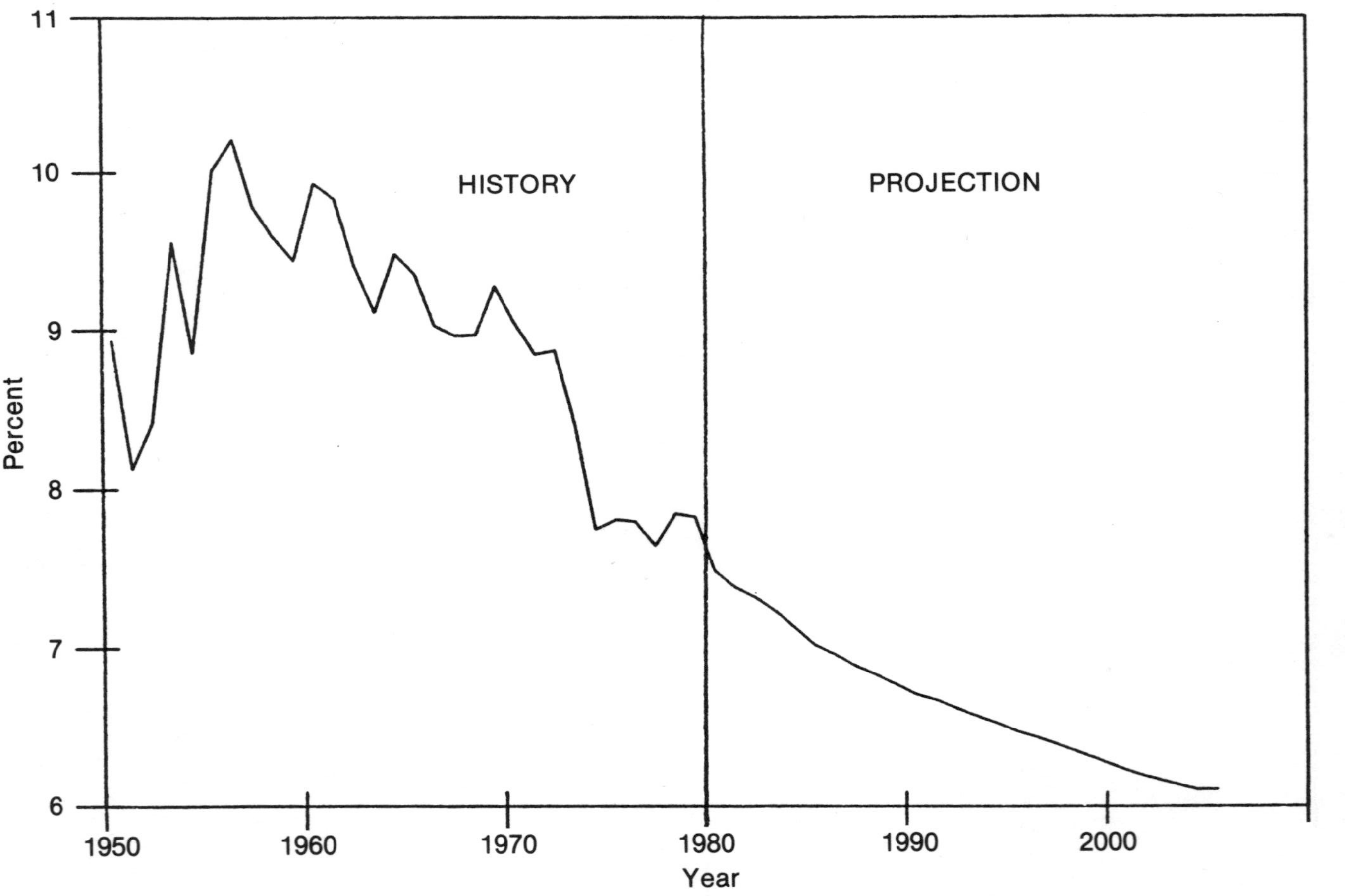

Figure 3-9. Labor-Force-Participation Rate for Elderly Women: Baseline

Transfer Payments

This section is brief because the reasons for a more-moderate growth in transfers were discussed before in conjunction with the other macroeconomic projections. From 1953 to 1979, the average annual growth rate in transfers to persons was 8.5 percent in real terms. Table 3-6 shows the share of personal income that derives from transfers. The approximately 70 percent total growth of this share in the decade of 1970s is expected to diminish over the simulation horizon. In the twenty-five years between 1980 and 2005, the transfer share is expected to grow by only about one-quarter.

Real and Relative Income

The average income of the elderly has increased substantially over the past fifteen years. As figure 3-10 shows, continued gains in real income are expected but at much lower rates than have occurred in the recent past. Real-income growth for the elderly is expected to average only about 0.8 percent per year over the simulation horizon, about one-third of the 2.4 percent annual growth since 1967. Because of the recession, the income of the elderly is expected to decline slightly in 1980 and 1981 and then to rebound in the subsequent recovery. Over the projection period, the continuation of the trends toward declining labor-force participation by the elderly, diminishing growth in the rate of accumulation of retirement assets, and continued but reduced growth in real transfer payments should contribute to slower, but steady, increases in the real income of the elderly.

While these projections indicate that elderly income will continue to increase, they provide incomplete information about how the income of the elderly can be expected to fare relative to that of younger age groups. One measure of this relative economic status is the ratio of the mean income of

Table 3-6
Transfer-Payment Share of Personal Income
(percentage)

Year	*Share*
1970	6.8
1980	11.5
1990	12.4
2000	13.6
2005	14.2

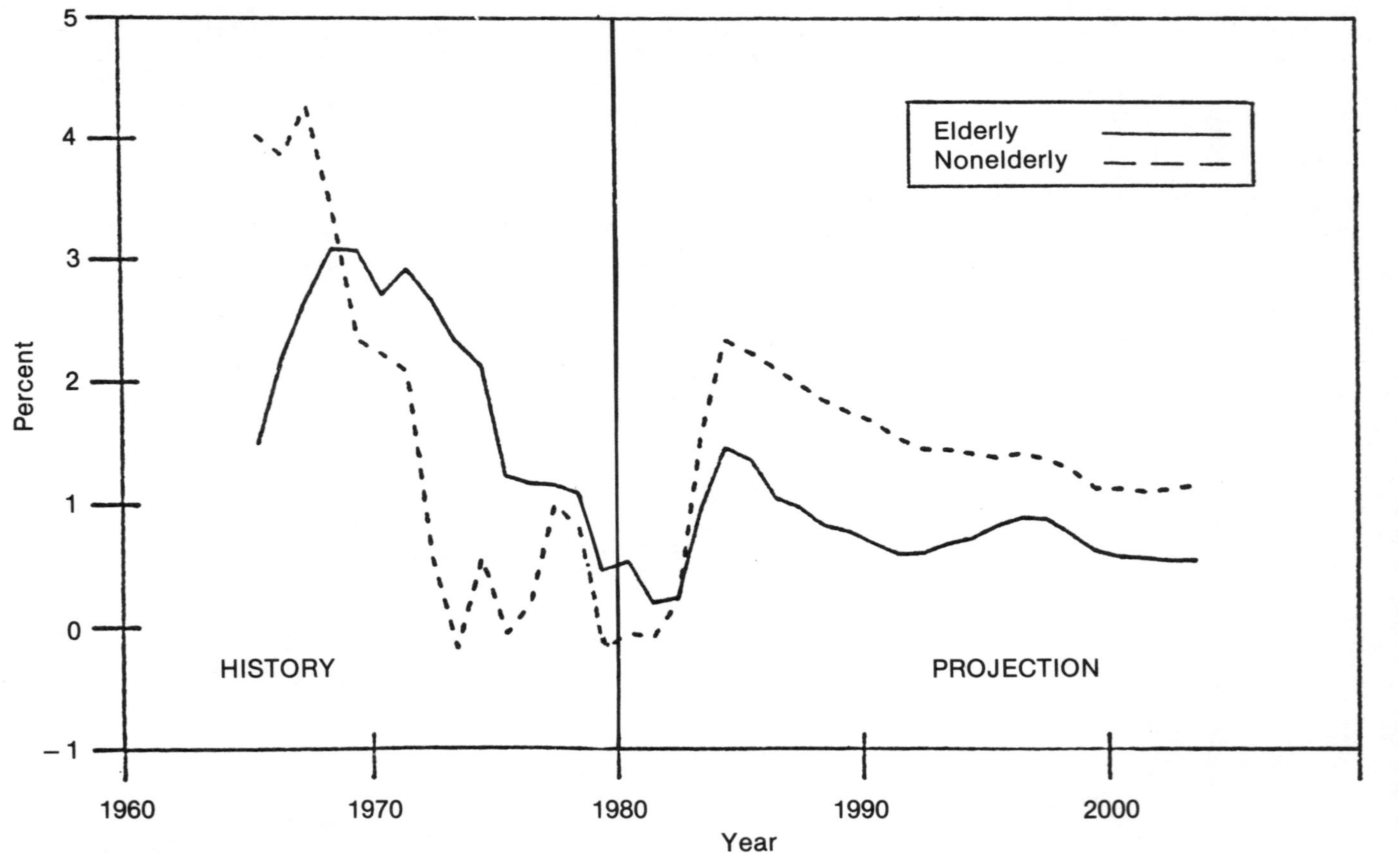

Figure 3-10. Five-Year Moving Average of Percentage Rate of Growth in Average Elderly and Nonelderly Income: Baseline

the elderly to the mean income of the under-65 age group. Figure 3-11 presents historical changes since 1965 and DECO Model projections of future changes in relative income.

The projected real rate of growth of elderly income is not sufficient to maintain its relative status over the next few decades. This is in marked contrast to rapid increases of recent years, which have been due mainly to rapid increases in real transfer payments. Due to the combination of recession (primarily visited on the younger working population) and social-security indexing (primarily visited on the elderly), 1980 and 1981 witness moderate increases in the relative income of the elderly. After this time, the situation is expected to reverse.

Beginning in 1982, the ratio of elderly to nonelderly mean income is projected to undergo a long, gradual decline.[3] This fall-off reflects a number of factors. Declining labor-force participation, slower growth in transfer payments, and the poor performance of most assets have already been discussed. Changes in the composition of the elderly and nonelderly population are also important. As the baby-boom generation matures over the next twenty-five years, they will advance into the most productive and remunerative periods of their working lives. This disproportionately large age group with its rapidly growing income profile will boost the average income of the under-65 group. The important issue to remember in this relative-income comparison is that change is occurring for both the numerator (elderly income) and the denominator (nonelderly income), with the net effect favoring a relatively rapid increase in the average income accruing to the younger segment.

Over the same period, the share of the elderly in the population will continue to increase and the older age groups among the elderly will advance as a proportion of the elderly. The result of this "aging" within the elderly group will be to increase demands on government resources since the very old among the elderly have limited resources outside of transfers. Furthermore, within each elderly age group, the rapid growth of individuals living alone, especially single women, will influence negatively the average income of all the elderly. Between 1980 and 2005, the DECO Model of the Elderly projects a 1.5 percent annual growth in the numbers of elderly women living alone, compared to only 0.7 percent for single men. Similarly, individuals as a group should increase at about a 1.3 percent rate, while yearly growth in the number of elderly families is expected to average only 0.8 percent. These demographic changes among the elderly will exert a negative influence on their relative economic status.

Finally, note that future economic growth will primarily benefit the younger, working population. For those who are currently retired, the die has already been cast. With a more-restrictive federal policy on government

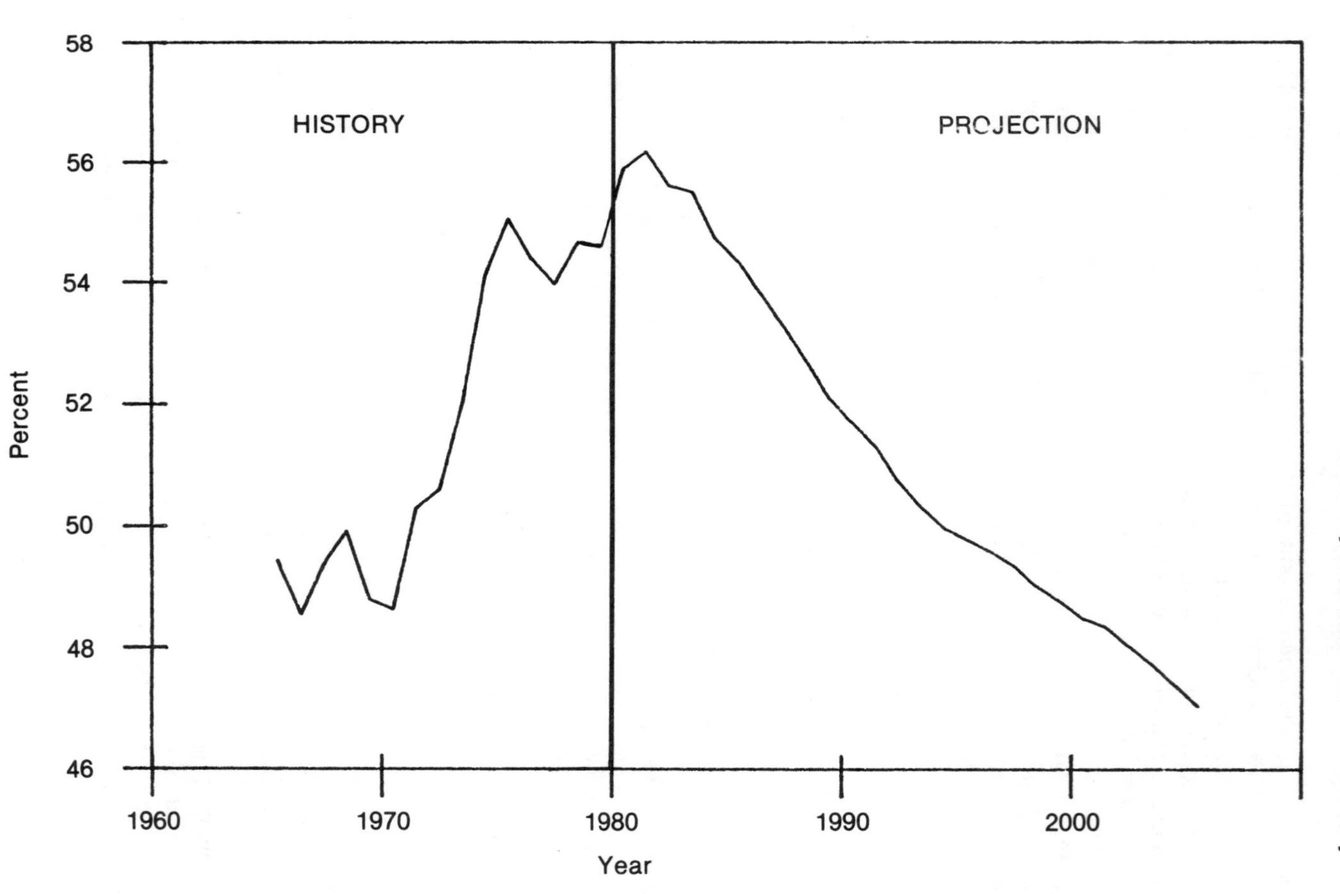

Figure 3-11. Average Elderly Income as a Percentage of Nonelderly Income: Baseline

expenditures (arising, for example, from taxpayer resistance), future income gains for the elderly will accrue less from transfers and more from personal sources such as private pensions, IRAs, and other assets. The importance of private-capital formation that will be supportive of elderly income gains is underscored in this scenario.

The total income position of the elderly is summarized in table 3-7. Although the real income of the elderly increases by about 60 percent over the next quarter-century, their share of total income falls from 11.6 percent to 9.6 percent, a 17 percent decline. Of course, not all demographic subgroups within the elderly population are in the same income position. Table 3-8 illustrates the large differences in income across the family-status dimension. The low income of women living alone relative to that of men living alone is particularly notable. Elderly single women in the oldest age group have the lowest annual income of all—averaging only $6,255 (or about $120 a week) in 1980. Our projections imply a moderate narrowing of the gap between the average income of elderly single men and women as more and more women have their own labor-force experience and as men continue to leave the labor force earlier. The large number of women in their 40s and 50s who have recently entered the labor force have begun to accumulate assets, pensions, and their own social-security eligibility. Thus, the increases projected for this group in the 1990s and 2000s are in part an echo of changes experienced by younger groups in the 1960s and 1970s. Despite this movement toward equality, elderly men should continue to enjoy higher income throughout the projection horizon.

Income Adequacy and Distribution

On average, elderly income has risen since the mid-1960s, in both absolute and relative terms. The outlook is for further, but slower, real-income increases and for a decline in their relative position as compared with that of

Table 3-7
Total Income Received by Elderly Families and Singles, and Percentage of All Income: Baseline
(billions of 1980 dollars)

	1980	*1985*	*1990*	*1995*	*2000*	*2005*
Income	198.1	228	259.9	285.6	301.8	318.6
Percentage share of total income	11.6	11.1	10.8	10.6	10.1	9.6

Table 3-8
Average Income of Elderly Families and Singles, by Age Group: Baseline
(real 1980 dollars)

Age Group	*1980*	*1985*	*1990*	*1995*	*2000*	*2005*
Men						
65 to 71	8,369	8,697	9,078	9,369	9,780	10,094
72 and over	7,454	7,754	8,101	8,375	8,750	9,042
All elderly	7,850	8,169	8,537	8,822	9,214	9,517
Women						
65 to 71	7,297	7,646	7,989	8,276	8,676	8,998
72 and over	6,255	6,464	6,885	7,392	7,981	8,528
All elderly	6,658	6,916	7,303	7,724	8,240	8,703
Families						
65 to 71	18,019	19,032	19,925	20,637	21,549	22,270
72 and over	14,984	15,878	16,675	17,314	18,186	18,874
All elderly	16,608	17,585	18,452	19,144	20,037	20,746

the younger population. Clearly, however, these averages obscure much that has occurred for particular demographic and income groups within the total elderly population. Have the elderly with lower-than-average income done better or worse than those with average income? How have the elderly with higher-than-average income fared? How are these differences projected to change over the next twenty-five years?

Basically, income distributions have been becoming more equal among the elderly in recent years, and this move toward equality is projected to continue. The lowest income elderly have improved their economic status relative to younger groups and relative to the average across the elderly since 1967. This is true both in total (across all of the elderly) and also within each of the six older age/status groups, three status groups (men living alone, women living alone, and families; the 65-71 and 72-and-over age groups). During this same period, the elderly with the highest income have lost some ground relative to the average. These changes arise from the increasing importance of transfer payments, a decline in the importance of wage and salary earnings, and an inflation-induced redistribution of wealth from creditors (who usually have high income) to debtors (who usually have low income). Increasing transfers have also tended to protect those elderly with the lowest income from cyclical downturns. Thus, in the 1974 and 1975 recession, the income of the low-income elderly gained in relation to the average and above average.

The DECO Model of the Elderly projects continued, although more-moderate, improvement in the relative income of the lowest income elderly. The relative improvement of the low-income elderly as compared with middle-income elderly is expected to proceed at a rate only about half as rapid as that in the period since 1967 as transfer payments continue to grow relative to national income but at a much slower pace. The baseline simulation also projects a very slight income improvement for the higher-than-average-income elderly as compared to the middle-income elderly as the economy begins to function more effectively in the later years of the simulation.

The elderly population's ability to cope can be quantified using the concept of an income-adequacy standard. Adequacy is a controversial area, and no consensus as to the correct standard exists. One possible adequacy standard, however, is the Bureau of Labor Statistics (BLS) Intermediate Budget for a Retired Couple for elderly families and an analogous measure for retired individuals. This BLS standard is an absolute, fixed-consumption-bundle standard used to measure income adequacy by many researchers (see, for example, Borzilleri 1980). The latest such standard for couples is $8,562 for 1979.

To generate an approximately equivalent standard for a single retired person, we use a rough BLS rule of thumb that the consumption expenditures of such a person are about 55 percent of the expenditures of a retired couple at a similar living standard. In 1979, consumption expenditures accounted for 94 percent of the total budget for a retired couple at the intermediate level. According to a BLS representative, no attempt is made to estimate the amount of "other expenditures" (the remaining 6 percent) made by a single retired person. We therefore assume that the intermediate-budget level for a single retired person is 55 percent of the consumption expenditures plus 100 percent of the "other expenditures" of a retired couple. This leads to a standard of $4,941 in 1979, about 58 percent of the standard for a retired couple. Various inquiries to federal employees and others who work in the adequacy field resulted in comments to the effect that this standard seemed reasonably consistent with the couples' standard.

Another issue concerns the appropriate index to use for changing nominal to real in these adequacy comparisons. By bringing all the income distributions to 1979, we avoid having to index the adequacy standard. There was also no need to discount the income distributions. DECO simulations are performed in real terms, deflating all relevant concepts by the National Income Accounts (NIA) implicit deflator for personal-consumption expenditures. Thus, the distributions are *defined* in real terms. This still leaves somewhat open the question of whether the personal-consumption deflator is the appropriate real-income index. On the one hand, this deflator adjusts implicitly for aggregate changes in consumption patterns, while the adequacy standard includes a fixed bundle of goods (a different bundle than is used in the CPI). On the other hand, it is highly unlikely that the items in this standard will remain fixed over a twenty-five-year period, particularly since standards that adjust for changes in consumption are under study by the BLS.

Given these difficulties, adequacy figures provide at most a rough guide to the performance of the income of the elderly relative to a particular adequacy standard. Furthermore, the degree of precision is clearly smaller the further out in the future one goes.

Based on the intermediate-budget standard, large percentages of the elderly now have too little income to enjoy this standard of living in their old age. As indicated in table 3-9, percentages with less-than-adequate income (as defined by this standard) are lowest for families—that is, about 29 percent for those with head aged 56-71, 41 percent for those with head aged 72 and over—in 1979. The next-lowest incidence of inadequacy is for single men—that is, approximately 45 percent of those aged 65-71, 50 percent for the oldest group. Single women have the largest fraction with inadequate income—that is, 50 percent for the younger elderly group, fully 59 percent for the oldest group. These fractions are high enough to raise serious concern, especially since the BLS intermediate standard hardly allows a lavish existence.

Nevertheless, the DECO Model projects gradual improvement for all groups over the next twenty-five years, reducing the percentages with inadequate income as measured by the BLS standard. Also, the largest increases in real income are projected to be concentrated among the poorest groups of the elderly and among the poorest members of each group. Single individuals are projected to experience faster growth than are families, elderly single women should do relatively better than elderly single men, and those in the lower tail of the distributions should receive more-rapid gains than those with higher income.

Perhaps the most striking change has been discussed in other contexts—the expected improvement for the oldest group of single women. Over the twenty-five-year horizon, the percentage of this group with inadequate in-

Table 3-9
Elderly with Inadequate Income, by Family Status and Age: Baseline
(percentage)

Age/Status Group	*1979*	*1990*	*2005*
Individuals			
Men, 65-71	44.6	42.1	36.4
Women, 65-71	49.6	45.8	38.8
Men, 72 and over	49.8	46.6	39.3
Women, 72 and over	59	52.1	38.1
All elderly individuals	53.7	48.7	38.3
Families			
Head, 65-71	29.1	24.1	18.6
Head, 72 and over	41.4	35.5	28.5
All elderly families	34.8	29.3	23

come is projected to decline from the current level of about 59 percent to approximately 38 percent.[4] The great majority of this decline is projected for the 1990-2005 period when women with more labor-force attachment retire and when the DRI Macroeconomic Model projects improvements in the functioning of the economy.

Figure 3-12 shows the gains to this poorest group in another way—that is, as an upward march of their percentage income distribution. The height of the distribution curves represents the percentage of the group receiving income in the relevant $1,000 interval. The area under any particular segment of each curve represents the total percentage with income in that

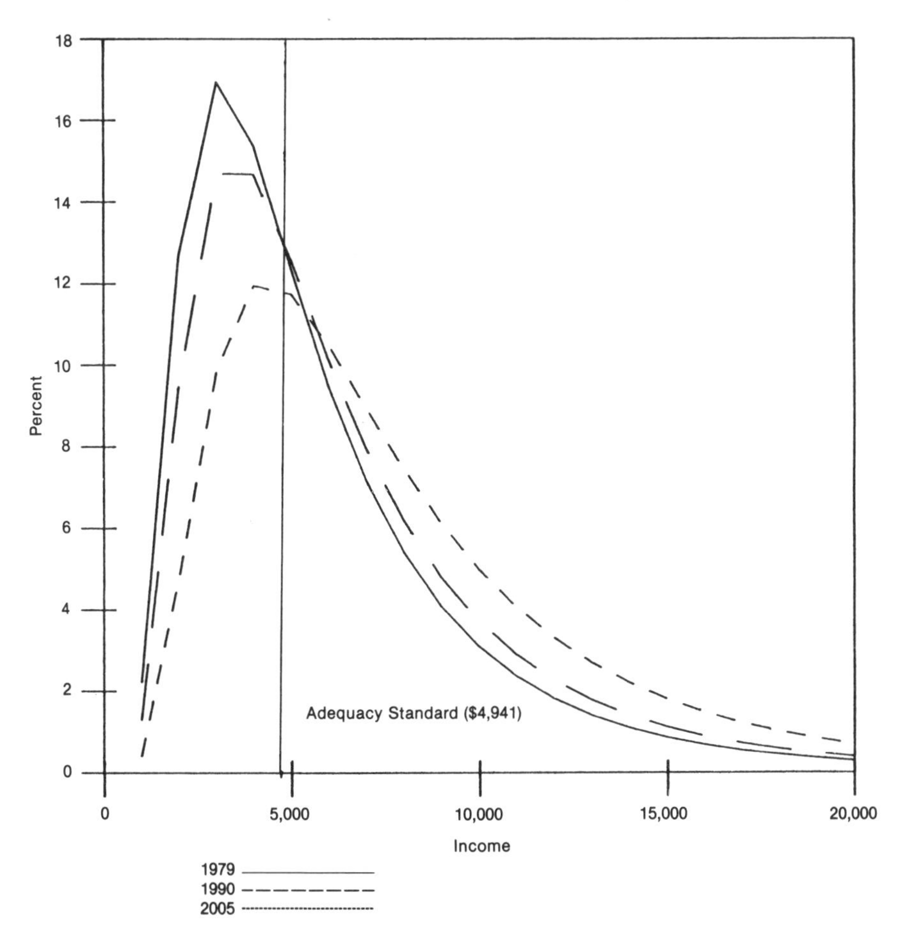

Figure 3-12. Percentages of Income Distribution (1979 Dollars) for Female Individuals Aged 72 and over: Baseline

range. Thus, the rapid shrinkage of the area to the left of the adequacy line reflects projected growth in the income of these poorest elderly. (Similar figures for other elderly groups are presented in appendix B.)

Even with the growth reflected in table 3-9 and figure 3-12, many of the elderly will continue to have inadequate income. Among the 65-71-year-old age group, the data project that approximately 23 percent of all families and about 38 percent of all single individuals will have inadequate income in 2005. This fraction is even higher for families in the 72-and-over age group, about 29 percent. Beyond our projection horizon, the clarity of the outlook dims, but important indications of future trouble exist, resulting from the aging of the baby-boom generation.

Income-distribution tables can serve to expand on the notion of adequacy by highlighting the percentage of the elderly population in each of six income classes. The tables, then, can show income changes in the low-income groups in greater detail and can facilitate a comparison of changes at low levels with those at higher levels. Tables 3-10 through 3-18 show numbers and income distributions, in real 1980 dollars, for families and singles in the under-55, 55-61, 62-64, 65-71, and 72-and-over age groups. For the four older age groups, the singles are also differentiated by sex. The tables present DECO Model projections for the years 1980, 1990, and 2005. The reader is cautioned against too literal an interpretation of the information in these tables, particularly as regards the exact percentages in particular income classes. This caution is especially important when interpreting the percentages at the extreme high or low tails of the distribution.

Tables 3-10 through 3-14 relate to families as compared with singles. The families in the 55-61 age group enjoy a slightly better income position than do the under-55 group, with smaller percentages in the lowest income

Table 3-10
Numbers and Income Distributions for Families and Singles under Age 55: Baseline
(percentage within real 1980 income classes)

	Families of Two or More			*Singles*		
Income Distribution	*1980*	*1990*	*2005*	*1980*	*1990*	*2005*
$0 to $2,500	3.511	2.626	2.046	11.166	7.938	5.895
$2,500 to $5,000	2.697	1.819	1.244	11.064	8.287	5.808
$5,000 to $7,500	3.852	2.596	1.746	13.029	10.521	7.911
$7,500 to $10,000	5.036	3.450	2.319	13.028	11.434	9.347
$10,000 to $20,000	28.226	21.383	15.133	36.306	38.195	36.807
$20,000 and over	56.678	68.127	77.511	15.406	23.625	34.231
Number (thousands)	41,708.857	49,971.838	54,093.006	15,419.634	21,978.559	26,113.182

Table 3-11
Numbers and Income Distributions for Families and Singles Aged 55 to 61: Baseline
(percentage within real 1980 income classes)

	Families of Two or More			*Singles*		
Income Distribution	*1980*	*1990*	*2005*	*1980*	*1990*	*2005*
$0 to $2,500	2.400	1.275	0.693	10.119	7.085	4.324
$2,500 to $5,000	2.467	1.480	0.844	16.180	12.748	9.259
$5,000 to $7,500	3.640	2.321	1.378	16.711	14.542	11.979
$7,500 to $10,000	4.788	3.227	2	14.152	13.369	12.030
$10,000 to $20,000	26.167	20.125	14.084	30.068	32.867	34.331
$20,000 and over	60.538	71.572	81.002	12.770	19.389	28.077
Number (thousands)	7,000.337	6,775.089	8,933.183	2,214.078	2,230.154	3,145.447

class and larger percentages in the highest class. This difference is projected to persist throughout the projection period.

Starting with the age group 62-64, each older group has smaller proportions in the highest income class in all periods than its next-younger predecessor. The percentages in the lowest class do not rise uniformly with age, however. In some cases they decline. This reflects an increasing reliance of older Americans on transfer payments as an income source. Transfers are relatively equally distributed, and the system, as now constituted, has the effect of building a floor below which few of the elderly are found. For example, notice that essentially none of the families in the 72-and-over age group receives less than $2,500, and relatively small percentages are found in the next income class. The oldest singles, however have large numbers in the lowest and next-lowest income class—a clear majority of these singles

Table 3-12
Numbers and Income Distributions for Families and Singles Aged 62 to 64: Baseline
(percentage within real 1980 income classes)

	Families of Two or More			*Singles*		
Income Distribution	*1980*	*1990*	*2005*	*1980*	*1990*	*2005*
$0 to $2,500	2.774	1.856	1.274	10.529	6.063	1.751
$2,500 to $5,000	4.191	2.904	1.931	25.596	22.869	18.164
$5,000 to $7,500	6.191	4.502	3.078	20.022	19.971	19.703
$7,500 to $10,000	7.634	5.847	4.167	13.446	14.177	14.952
$10,000 to $20,000	32.705	28.425	22.899	22.284	25.310	28.872
$20,000 and over	46.504	56.467	66.651	8.124	11.610	16.558
Number (thousands)	2,593.945	2,454.800	3,787.943	1,141.162	1,094.109	1,530.452

Table 3-13
Numbers and Income Distributions for Families and Singles Aged 65 to 71: Baseline
(percentage within real 1980 income classes)

Income Distribution	Families of Two or More			Singles		
	1980	1990	2005	1980	1990	2005
$0 to $2,500	0.236	0	0	6.589	2.008	0
$2,500 to $5,000	5.918	2.520	0.288	40.251	39.958	32.737
$5,000 to $7,500	12.268	9.936	5.977	21.610	22.955	25.976
$7,500 to $10,000	13.594	12.979	11.461	11.348	12.168	13.998
$10,000 to $20,000	38.099	39.936	41.679	15.268	16.818	19.528
$20,000 and over	29.885	34.628	40.595	4.935	6.092	7.760
Number (thousands)	4,618.359	5,487.917	5,872.101	3,140.664	3,879.170	4,269.474

are projected to receive less than $5,000 (1980 dollars) in 1981. This group is projected to drop to about 32 percent in 2005.

In all periods and in all groups, families have larger percentages in the highest income class and smaller percentages in the lowest income class than do singles. This is true, in particular, for the two elderly age groups. In contrast, for the future, DRI's DECO simulation projects much larger decreases in the percentage in the lowest income class for singles as compared with families. Since the oldest singles are also the poorest group of all, this projected change, which derives mainly from the "deepening" of social security and pensions, is welcome.

Tables 3-15 through 3-18 disaggregate the information for singles by sex. Single women are routinely worse off than are single men with larger concentrations in the lowest income class and smaller concentrations in the

Table 3-14
Numbers and Income Distributions for Families and Singles Age 72 and over: Baseline
(percentage within real 1980 income classes)

Income Distribution	Families of Two or More			Singles		
	1980	1990	2005	1980	1990	2005
$0 to $2,500	0	0	0	8.109	2.530	0.144
$2,500 to $5,000	8.790	3.428	0.225	46.093	46.783	31.713
$5,000 to $7,500	19.702	17.388	11.591	22.002	23.588	30.160
$7,500 to $10,000	17.289	17.881	17.652	10.238	11.128	14.906
$10,000 to $20,000	34.833	38.494	43.055	10.403	12.099	17.616
$20,000 and over	19.387	22.809	27.477	3.155	3.872	5.461
Number (thousands)	4,014.170	4,548.314	4,784.306	4,771.709	6,022.728	6,747.424

Table 3-15
Numbers and Income Distributions for Singles Aged 55 to 61: Baseline
(percentage within real 1980 income classes)

Income Distribution	Men 1980	Men 1990	Men 2005	Women 1980	Women 1990	Women 2005
$0 to $2,500	9.150	7.081	5.189	10.681	7.088	3.650
$2,500 to $5,000	11.343	8.686	6.344	18.985	15.420	11.530
$5,000 to $7,500	13.220	10.724	8.282	18.736	17.052	14.860
$7,500 to $10,000	12.905	11.214	9.246	14.875	14.786	14.199
$10,000 to $20,000	34.311	34.864	33.480	27.608	31.554	34.995
$20,000 and over	19.070	27.431	37.459	9.116	14.100	20.766
Number (thousands)	812.650	884.720	1,377.586	1,401.428	1,345.435	1,767.861

highest class. Considering the 1980 values for the two elderly groups (see tables 2-17 and 2-18), these differences are smaller for the 65-71 age group, larger for the 72-and-over group.

Tables 3-19 and 3-20 repeat the information in tables 3-11–3-14 at a more-aggregate level for families and singles aged 55-64 and 65 and over.

Conclusion

The baseline simulation demonstrates that the U.S. economy faces a number of serious difficulties in coming years: slow growth in output, fewer new entrants into the labor force, rapid and necessity-focused inflation, rising transfer payments, and increasing friction over the public/private-sector split. These problems have unpleasant consequences for the elderly: continuing excess relative burdens from inflation, slowly rising real income

Table 3-16
Numbers and Income Distributions for Singles Aged 62 to 64: Baseline
(percentage within real 1980 income classes)

Income Distribution	Men 1980	Men 1990	Men 2005	Women 1980	Women 1990	Women 2005
$0 to $2,500	9.789	6.273	3.210	10.834	5.976	1.144
$2,500 to $5,000	18.838	15.177	11.076	28.385	26.071	21.110
$5,000 to $7,500	17.542	15.989	13.760	21.044	21.628	22.173
$7,500 to $10,000	13.674	13.572	12.933	13.352	14.429	15.792
$10,000 to $20,000	26.873	30.188	33.002	20.391	23.279	27.155
$20,000 and over	13.283	18.800	26.018	5.995	8.616	12.627
Number (thousands)	333.329	321.628	449.268	807.833	772.481	1,081.184

Table 3-17
Numbers and Income Distributions for Singles Aged 65 to 71: Baseline
(percentage within real 1980 income classes)

Income Distribution	Men			Women		
	1980	1990	2005	1980	1990	2005
$0 to $2,500	6.296	2.443	0	6.677	1.885	0
$2,500 to $5,000	36.380	35.925	30.488	41.421	41.100	33.345
$5,000 to $7,500	21.014	22.051	24.103	21.790	23.211	26.482
$7,500 to $10,000	11.800	12.483	13.895	11.212	12.079	14.026
$10,000 to $20,000	17.650	18.733	20.877	14.547	16.277	19.164
$20,000 and over	6.860	8.366	10.637	4.353	5.449	6.983
Number (thousands)	729.170	855.523	908.478	2,411.495	3,023.647	3,360.996

Table 3-18
Numbers and Income Distributions for Singles Aged 72 and over: Baseline
(percentage within real 1980 income classes)

Income Distribution	Men			Women		
	1980	1990	2005	1980	1990	2005
$0 to $2,500	7.080	4.110	0.879	8.366	2.192	0
$2,500 to $5,000	40.413	38.886	33.016	47.514	48.472	31.459
$5,000 to $7,500	23.089	23.959	26.125	21.731	23.509	30.948
$7,500 to $10,000	11.836	12.685	14.777	9.839	10.795	14.931
$10,000 to $20,000	13.013	14.951	18.726	9.750	11.489	17.400
$20,000 and over	4.570	5.410	6.477	2.801	3.543	5.263
Number (thousands)	954.688	1,061.071	1,101.657	3,817.020	4,961.656	5,645.767

Table 3-19
Numbers and Income Distributions for Families and Singles Aged 55 to 64: Baseline
(percentage within real 1980 income classes)

Income Distribution	Families of Two or More			Singles		
	1980	1990	2005	1980	1990	2005
$0 to $2,500	2.501	1.430	0.866	10.258	6.749	3.481
$2,500 to $5,000	2.933	1.859	1.167	19.383	16.079	12.174
$5,000 to $7,500	4.330	2.901	1.884	17.837	16.328	14.508
$7,500 to $10,000	5.558	3.924	2.645	13.912	13.635	12.987
$10,000 to $20,000	27.934	22.332	16.709	27.421	30.380	32.544
$20,000 and over	56.744	67.555	76.729	11.190	16.828	24.306
Number (thousands)	9,594.282	9,229.888	12,721.125	3,355.240	3,324.263	4,675.899

Table 3-20
Numbers and Income Distributions for Families and Singles Aged 65 and over: Baseline
(percentage within real 1980 income classes)

	Families of Two or More			Singles		
Income Distribution	*1980*	*1990*	*2005*	*1980*	*1990*	*2005*
$0 to $2,500	0.126	0	0	7.505	2.325	0.088
$2,500 to $5,000	7.254	2.931	0.260	43.774	44.109	32.110
$5,000 to $7,500	15.725	13.313	8.498	21.847	23.340	28.539
$7,500 to $10,000	15.312	15.200	14.240	10.679	11.536	14.554
$10,000 to $20,000	36.580	39.283	42.297	12.334	13.948	18.357
$20,000 and over	25.003	29.272	34.705	3.861	4.742	6.352
Number (thousands)	8,632.528	10,036.230	10,656.407	7,912.373	9,901.898	11,016.897

but falling relative income, and perhaps some intergenerational conflict as the population share of the elderly continues to rise.

A host of proposals have been raised to address the problems of the elderly and the economy, but only a few of these proposals have been simulated. Chapters 3 through 6 present simulations of four such policies. Each chapter includes a description of a particular simulation and a comparison of the performance of the economy under that option and under the baseline assumptions.

Notes

1. A twenty-five-year simulation of the DRI Macroeconomic Model is a solution to the model's 1,000-plus equations over that period, consistent with a particular, predefined path for certain exogenous variables (that is, variables determined outside the model). Each simulation thus embodies all the historical information contained in the model regarding levels and interactions of variables, together with knowledge about political realities and well-defined assumptions on any anticipated policy changes such as tax cuts. DRI normally creates a group of twenty-five-year simulations once a year, including a baseline or control simulation and alternative simulations reflecting different assumptions about the shape of the future economy. Such alternatives can include policy simulations that reflect particular changes in variables caused either by explicitly assumed economic policies or by different underlying assumptions about future behavior. Each simulation of the DRI Macroeconomic Model can, in turn, become the basis for

simulating other DRI Models such as the DECO Model of the Elderly. These second-tier simulations can then reflect changed circumstances or assumptions in two ways: (1) either through the models (reflecting historical reactions to similar changes) or (2) outside the models (reflecting assumed changes in historical patterns). See Caton (1980) and appendix A for additional details on the TRENDLONG2005 simulation.

2. For further details of this approach to the inflationary experience of the past fifteen years, see Eckstein (1981).

3. The size of the 1970s relative increase for the elderly is somewhat overstated and the future decline is understated. As demonstrated in chapter 2, the elderly bear a moderately greater burden of inflation than do the nonelderly because their expenditures are focused on the core necessities—food, fuel, and health care—the cost of which has recently inflated and is projected to continue to inflate at unusually high rates. Also, this relative excess burden of inflation if greatest for the oldest and poorest elderly.

4. The fraction of this group with inadequate income even falls below the projected fraction for men aged 72 and over. However, it would strain the precision of the model to pretend that this difference carried any information except that men and women in this age group will experience some convergence in their income experience.

4 Option 1: Increased Labor-Force Participation by Older Americans

This simulation examines the effect of a reversal in the labor-force decline among elderly and near-elderly men and women. Compared to the baseline projection of continued declines, moderate increases in participation are shown to have beneficial effects on the elderly and the near elderly while also improving the growth and functioning of the overall economy.

Recent years have witnessed reductions in labor-force participation by four groups of older Americans—men aged 55-64, women aged 55-64, men aged 65 and over, and women aged 65 and over—with the most rapid declines occurring among the two male groups. As pointed out initially, the baseline projects continuing declines for these four groups, and a reduced labor-force increase from younger groups is projected to be a major drag on economic growth (see figure 4-1). It was decided to analyze an increase in participation among each of the older groups beginning in 1981, raising them by 1990 to the rates at which they had participated in 1970. Rates are then held at their 1970 levels for the remainder of the projection period.

A return to the 1970 participation levels was considered feasible in reaction to any of a range of policies that could be adopted to encourage older workers to participate—subsidies or tax inducements, changes in the social-security-earnings test, increases in the normal and early retirement ages under social security, and so forth. It is also possible that the rates may reverse their decline in the absence of new policy initiatives as a reaction to the 1978 Age Discrimination in Employment Act's prohibition on mandatory retirement below age 70 or to high and uncertain rates of inflation. No explicit new policy was assumed in the simulation as a cause of the increased participation in order to preserve the greatest generality in the results.

Compared with the baseline, option 1 has the following key results:

Extra workers add significantly to unemployment in the next few years because of the current period of stagnant growth, but total employment is increased in all years.

Real GNP increases an additional 3.9 percent by 2005. Consumption increases 3.7 percent. The per-year difference in GNP growth is about 0.2 percentage points.

Inflation is lower by 0.2 percentage points per year.

A significant fiscal dividend arises from somewhat higher growth.

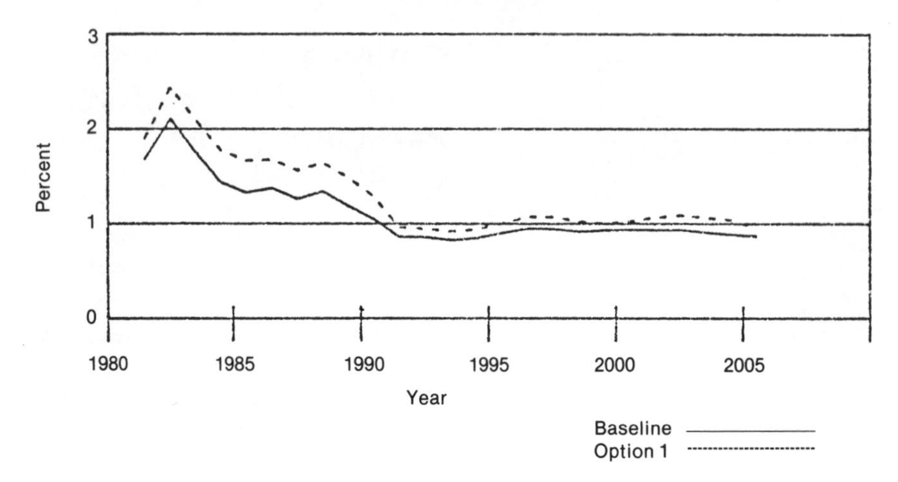

Figure 4-1. Percentage Rate of Labor-Force Growth: Option 1 Compared with Baseline

The real income of the near elderly and elderly increases.

The relative income of the elderly increases but still remains on a downward trend from its peak in the early 1980s.

Adequacy improves as wage income to the elderly increases.

Macroeconomic Effects

The macroeconomic effects of this option are shown to be generally positive, following an initial period during which the economy experiences difficulty in absorbing the new workers. Once the economy gets on track, the new workers help to offset declines in labor-force growth among the young. They raise GNP and personal income while reducing inflation and creating a fiscal dividend.

In the near future, the simulation shows that many of the new elderly participants will not find work because, for cyclical reasons, the economy will be unable to absorb them. At present, the economy is incapable of absorbing all labor willing to work, let alone new labor-force participants, as indicated by the high current unemployment rate (7.3 percent as of March 1981). The influx of new elderly participants will push this rate even higher, to 8.8 percent in 1981, as the labor force grows faster than employment, but the bulk of this new unemployment will be borne by the elderly and near-elderly net new entrants. By comparison, in the baseline the unemployment rate is 8.6 percent in 1981. By 1985, this rate is 0.7 of a percentage point higher than its baseline value (see figure 4-2).

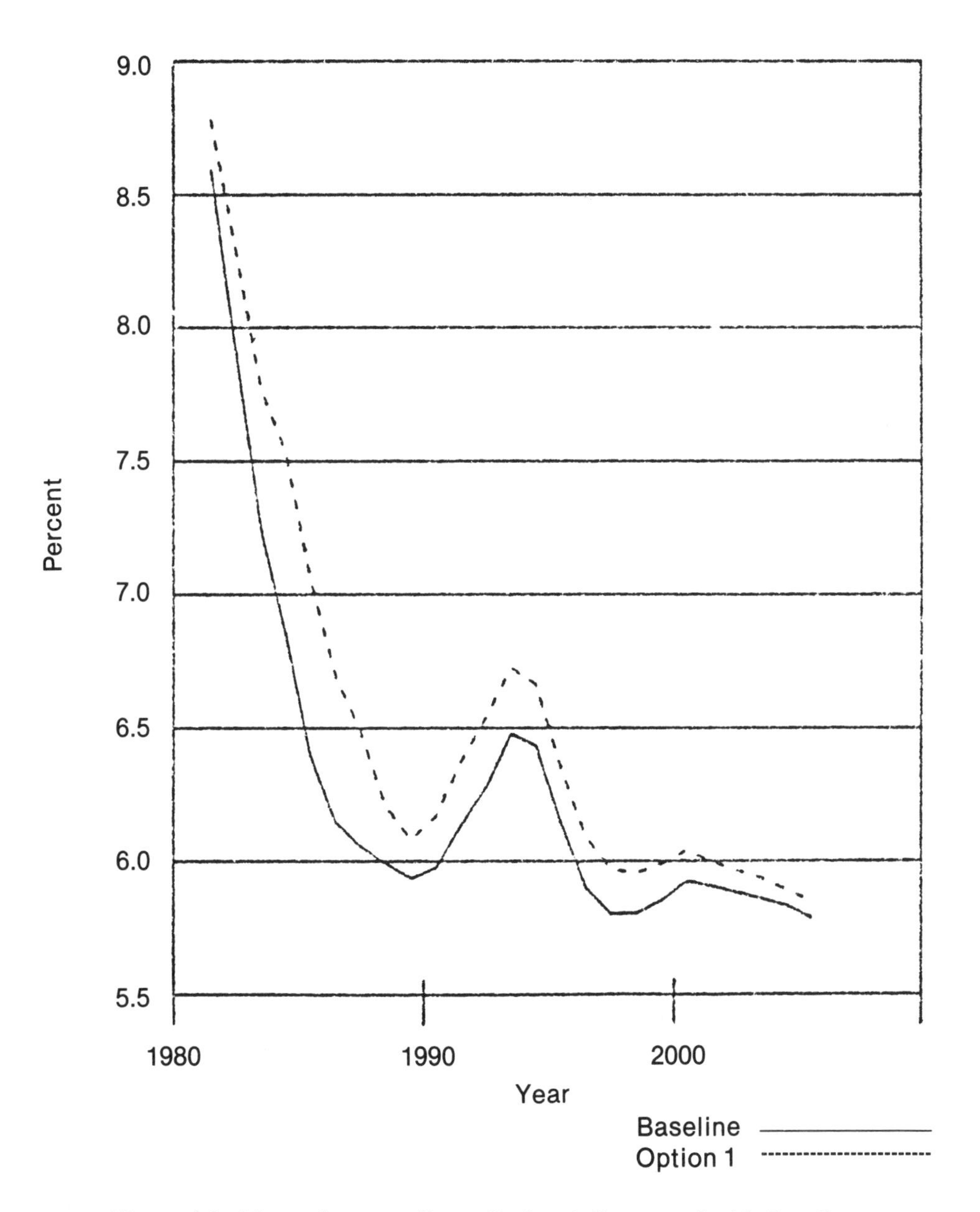

Figure 4-2. Unemployment Rate: Option 1 Compared with Baseline

By the late 1980s, however, the economy is shown to be vigourous enough to absorb most of the new participants, just as it has successfully absorbed the large influx of new prime-age female participants over the past fifteen years. With a larger labor force at its disposal, in the long run the economy will therefore expand more than in the baseline.

The average annual rate of growth in real GNP is raised to 2.7 percent, compared with 2.5 percent in the baseline (see figure 4-3). The disaggregation of this extra growth by component of GNP and by time period can be seen in table 4-1. The average annual rate of growth in real consumption rises to 2.6 percent, compared with 2.4 percent in the baseline. This extra growth is fairly uniformly distributed across categories of consumption. By 2005, durable consumption is raised by 4.3 percent relative to the baseline, nondurable consumption by 3.2 percent, and consumption of services by 3.7 percent. In the same year, a disposable-income growth of 2.6 percent is recorded, compared with 2.4 percent in the baseline, and real household net worth is 1.8 percent above the baseline.

Business fixed investment is shown to be stimulated by the increased rate of growth of end markets—that is, it grows by an average annual 3.3 percent in real terms, compared with 3.1 percent in the baseline. This may seem a surprisingly strong performance, as one might postulate that the larger supply of labor could induce some substitution of labor for capital by depressing the cost of the former relative to that of the latter. Indeed, some substitution does occur, indicated by a decline in the ratio of capital to labor. In the year 2005, while the labor force is 4.7 percent greater than its baseline value, the capital stock is only 3.8 percent greater. Nevertheless, the economy as a whole is so much larger that both the labor force and the capital stock are larger than in the baseline.

Housing does not benefit as much as other components of final demand, mainly because the major gainers in this option, the elderly who go out to work, tend already to have filled their housing needs. The sector does make some gains, caused mainly by higher growth in consumer income, but only enough to raise the stock of houses by 900,000 (0.8 percent) by 2005.

The simulation shows that federal fiscal dividend results from the expanded economy (see figure 4-4). This dividend does not become significant until the mid-to-late 1980s since it takes until then for the economy to be able fully to absorb the increased elderly labor force. Nonmilitary purchases, grants-in-aid to state and local governments, and transfer payments are all raised, relative to the baseline, by 3.7 percent in real terms by 2005. In addition, the deficit reduction observed in this option permits some lowering of the personal-tax rate—federal personal taxes rise to only 17.1 percent of income in 2005, compared with 17.6 percent in the baseline. The tax burden (defined as the ratio of total taxes to GNP) is reduced from a mean of 34.1 percent to one of 33.8 percent. The personal-income-tax rate

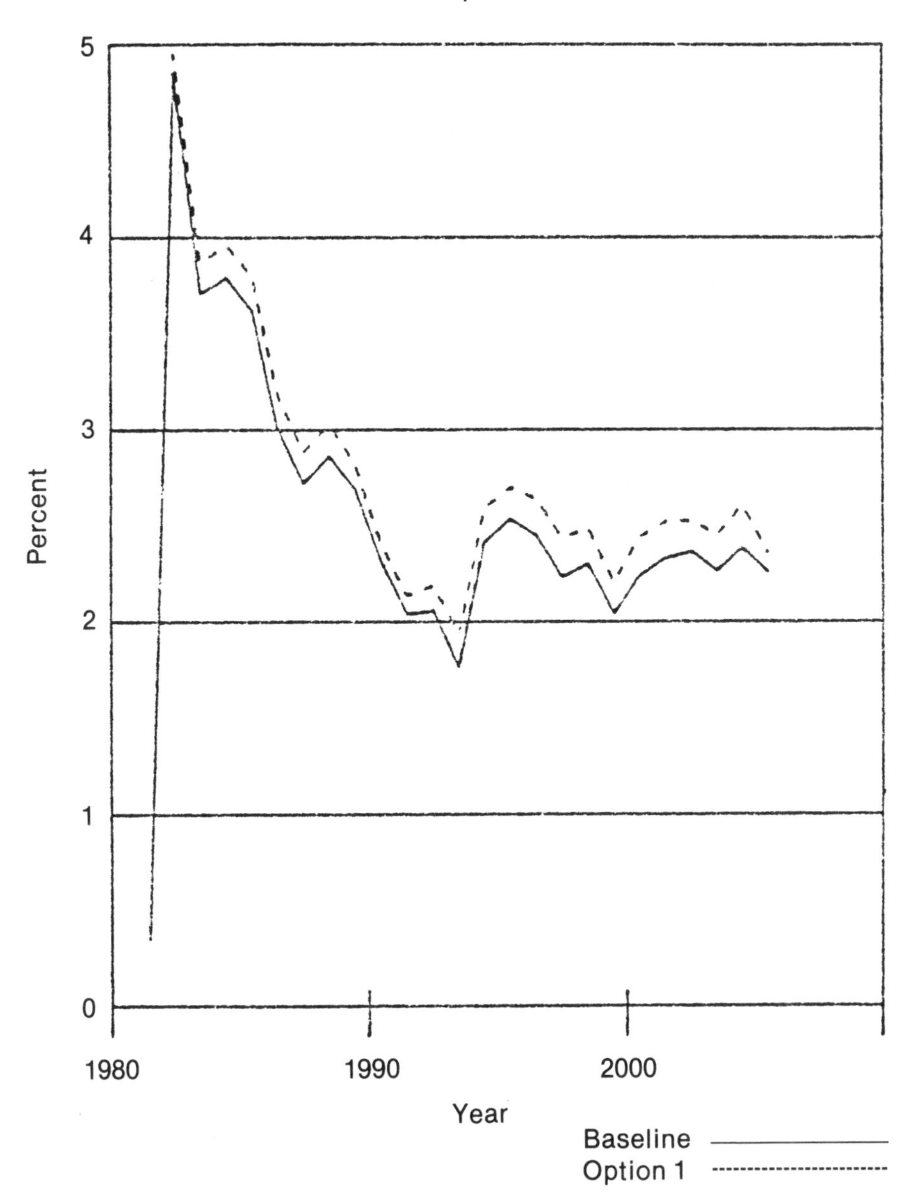

Figure 4-3. Percentage Rate of GNP Growth: Option 1 Compared with Baseline

(total personal-income taxes as a fraction of personal-income net of transfer payments) decreases from an average of 20.2 percent to 19.9 percent.

Table 4-1
Macroeconomic Effects of Option 1
(averages over entire simulation period)

Effects	*Baseline 1981-2005*	*Option 1 1981-2005*
Average annual growth rates		
GNP	2.5	2.7
Consumption	2.4	2.6
Investment	3.1	3.3
Government spending	2.1	2.2
Disposable income	2.4	2.6
Industrial production	3.6	3.7
Shares of output (percentage)		
Consumption	62.9	63
Investment	16.5	16.6
Government	20.8	20.5
Other economic aggregates		
CPI inflation	7.5	7.3
Unemployment	6.3	6.5
Share of personal income in GNP (percentage)	81.9	81.8
Share of transfers in personal income (percentage)	14.8	15.2

State and local governments appear to benefit from the increase in grants, and also from increased tax receipts due to the larger economy, further raising the total fiscal dividend. As a consequence, state and local spending is raised significantly. In 2005, for example, it is 3.7 percent above its baseline value. It could also have been assumed that expenditures remained the same, with the state and local units balancing their books via tax reductions.

Potential output (which the economy could produce at high and stable capacity utilization and at a low stable rate of unemployment) grows about 0.2 percent faster than in the baseline, thus being raised by 4.1 percent in 2005. Since so much of this increase in potential comes from greater assumed growth of the labor force, there is no significant deviation from the baseline in output per man-hour.

Inflation is about 0.2 percent lower than in the baseline (see figure 4-5). The higher unemployment rate in the early 1980s constrains growth in wages, which in turn moderates subsequent inflationary expectations. Furthermore, the greater growth in total output reduces inflation by closing the gap between aggregate supply and aggregate demand.

As mentioned, the unemployment rate is substantially higher in the early years, by as much as 0.7 of a percentage point in 1984 and 1985, with most of this added unemployment falling on the elderly and near-elderly net

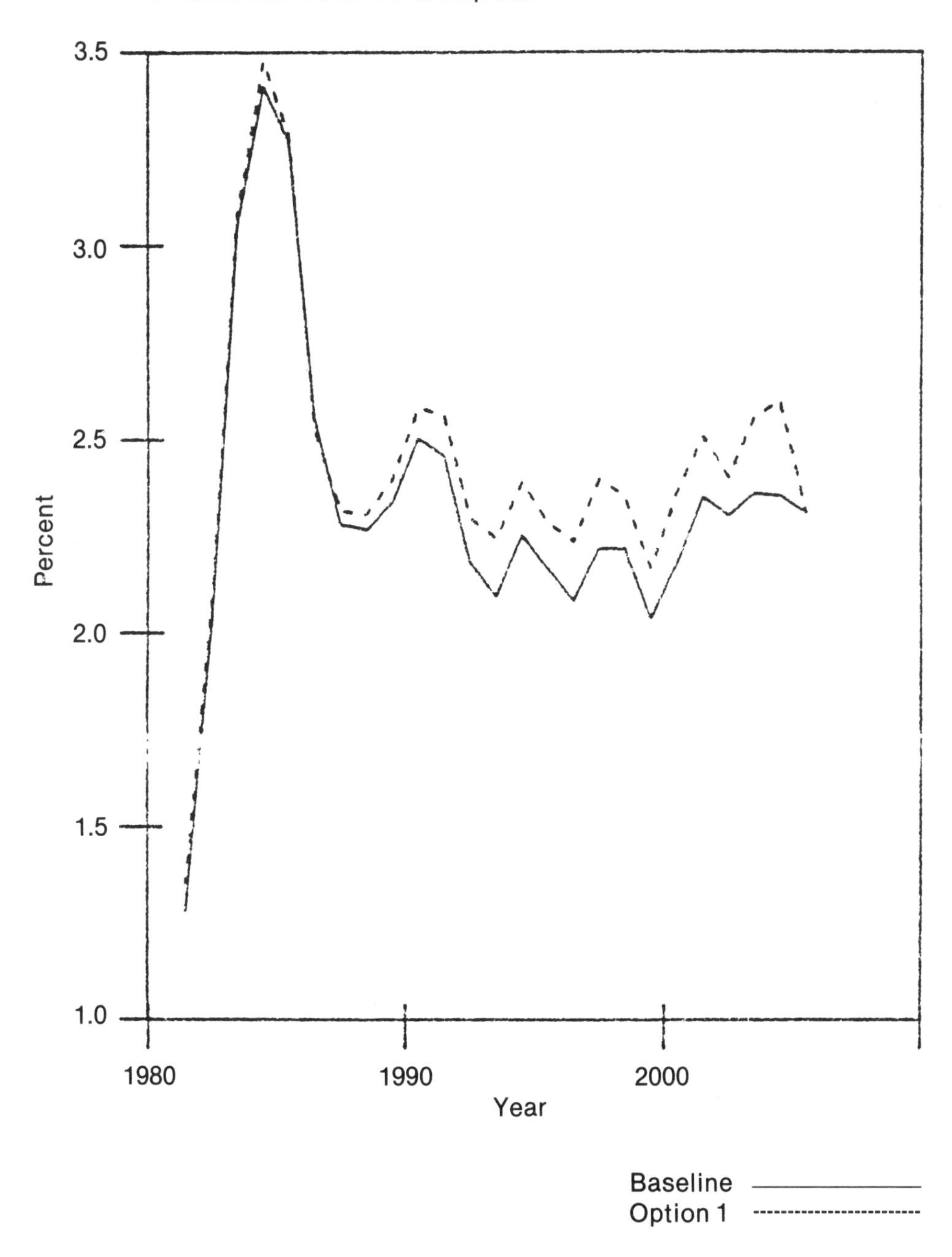

Figure 4-4. Percentage Rate of Growth in Real Government Spending: Option 1 Compared with Baseline

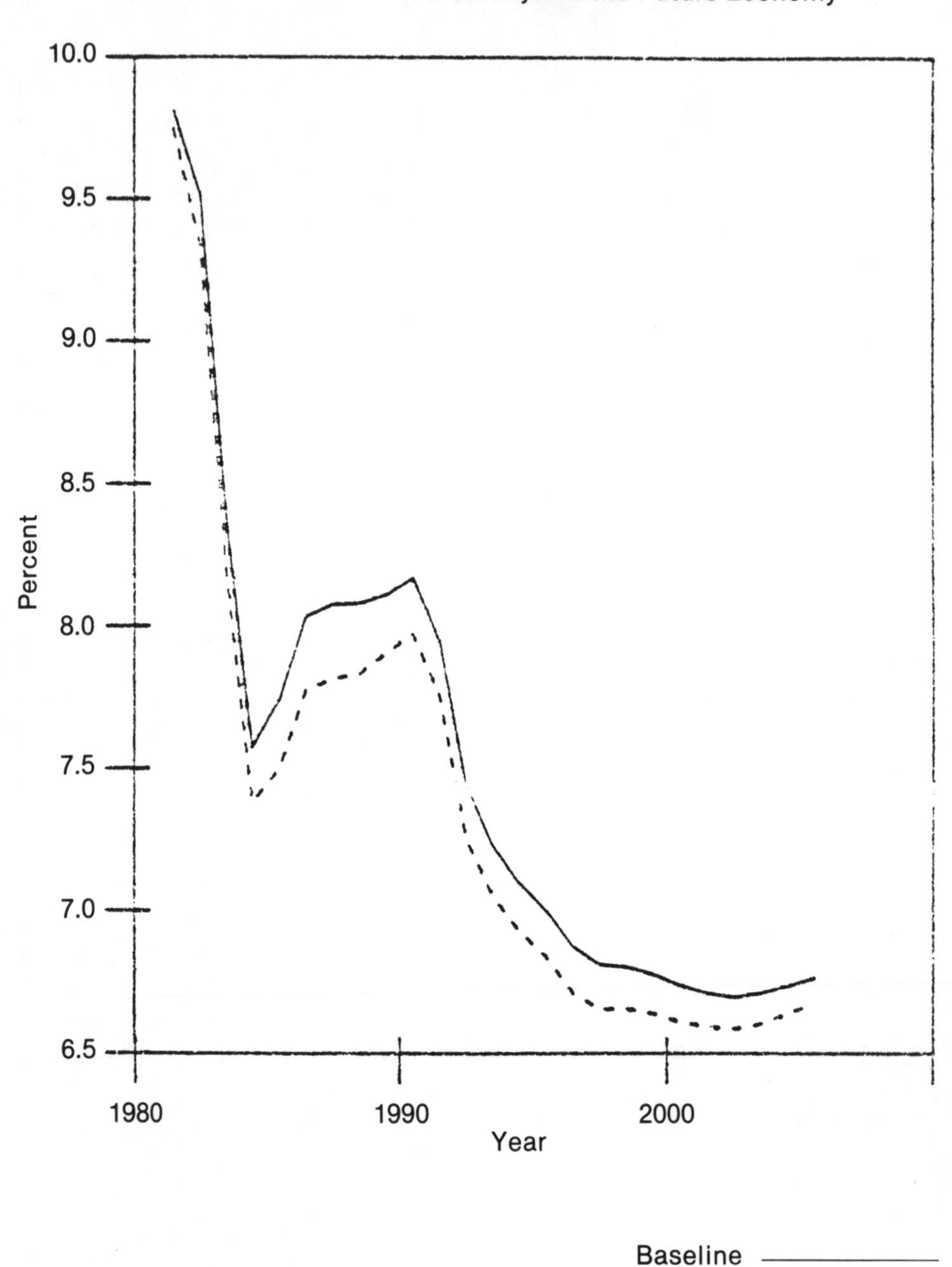

Figure 4-5. CPI Inflation Rate: Option 1 Compared with Baseline

new participants. This effect could be offset by, for example, a government-jobs program or a tax cut to stimulate demand. However, these offsetting measures would themselves have costs such as greater deficits or higher inflation.

The added unemployment is less of a burden than it might appear because employment is shown to increase significantly in all simulation years. Aggregate employment is raised by 4.7 percent by 2005, only marginally less than the increase in the labor force. The long-run fungibility of labor implies that the composition of this extra employment reflects more the composition of extra final demand than it does that of occupational categories of the elderly. In other words, even if all of the extra elderly workers were employed in the service sector, this would be difficult to discern in the aggregate-employment result. Other jobs would be created for the displaced service workers in, say, durable manufacturing, which experiences increased demand for its output. Thus, gains in employment in 2005 range from 0.7 percent (100,000 workers) in mining (one can safely assume that few elderly miners would elect to continue working and that the increase in elderly participation can be accounted for by less physically demanding occupations) to 5.2 percent (40,000 workers) in rubber and plastics.

The ratio of personal income to GNP is not shown to be significantly affected, surprising given the significant increase in the labor force. Indeed, the simulations show that the share of personal income in GNP is marginally reduced. Wages, salaries, and supplements average 63 percent of GNP, compared with 63.1 percent in the baseline. This result is, in fact, in line with the historical record—that is, the share of labor income in GNP tends not to vary systematically with labor-force growth (witness the 1970s, for example), in part because the extra supply of labor initially tends to depress real wages. Relative to the baseline, the shares of dividends, interest income, and transfers in personal income are changed only marginally.

The faster growth of the economy requires a significant increase in oil imports, which are 1 million barrels per day higher than in the baseline by 2005 (see table 4-2). Nevertheless, performance vis-a-vis our non-OPEC-trading partners is improved by the better U.S.-inflation result. The exchange value of the dollar is marginally higher, by 1.4 percent, in 2005—that is, on average each dollar buys 1.4 percent more of foreign currency than in the baseline.

Effects on Income and Its Distribution

The net additions to the labor force in option 1 (as compared with the projected declines in the baseline) are shown to increase the economy's labor income while directly benefiting the elderly and near elderly. The real and

Table 4-2
Capsule Summary of Option 1

	History					Difference from Baseline				
Parameters	*1980-1985*	*1985-1990*	*1990-1995*	*1995-2000*	*2000-2005*	*1980-1985*	*1985-1990*	*1990-1995*	*1995-2000*	*2000-2005*
Composition of real GNP (average annual rates of change)										
GNP	3.4	2.9	2.3	2.4	2.5	0.1	0.1	0.1	0.2	0.2
Final sales	3.2	2.9	2.3	2.5	2.5	0.1	0.1	0.1	0.2	0.2
Total consumption	3	2.8	2.5	2.3	2.3	0.1	0.1	0.2	0.2	0.2
Nonresidential fixed investment	3.4	3.8	2.8	3.6	3.1	0.2	0.2	0.2	0.2	0.2
Equipment	4.5	4	3.4	4.1	3.6	0.3	0.3	0.2	0.2	0.2
Nonresidential construction	1	3.2	1.2	2.1	1.4	0.2	0.1	0.1	0.1	0.1
Residential fixed investment	9	1.5	−2.2	0.4	2.4	0.2	0.1	0.1	0	0
Exports	3.8	4.4	3.8	4.5	4.5	0.1	0.3	0.1	0.3	0.3
Imports	3.4	3.4	3.9	3.9	4	0	0.1	0.2	0.2	0.2
Federal government	3.6	2.6	1.9	1.8	1.8	0	0	0.1	0	0
State and local government	1.8	2.4	2.1	2	2.2	0	0.2	0.1	0.2	0.2
Shares of nominal GNP (percentage)										
Consumption	64.2	62.8	62.8	62.9	62.5	0	0	0.1	0.2	0.4
Business investment	10.3	10.9	11.2	11.6	11.9	0	0.1	0.1	0.2	0.2
Residential construction	4.9	5.2	4.7	4.3	4.5	0	0	0	0	−0.1
Government purchases	20.4	20.4	20.7	20.6	20.5	−0.1	−0.2	−0.3	−0.4	−0.4

Prices and wages (average annual rates of change)										
Implicit price deflator	8.3	7.5	6.4	5.7	5.6	−0.2	−0.3	−0.2	−0.2	−0.2
CPI all urban consumers	8.4	7.9	7.2	6.7	6.6	−0.2	−0.2	−0.2	−0.1	−0.1
Wholesale price index	10.1	9.1	7.2	6.5	6.7	−0.2	−0.3	−0.2	−0.2	−0.1
Compensation per hour	9.8	9	8.1	7.5	7.2	−0.3	−0.4	−0.3	−0.2	−0.2
Production and other key measures										
Industrial production (average percentage change)	4.9	3.6	2.9	3.6	3.7	0.1	0.2	0.2	0.2	0.2
Housing starts (million units)	2	2.2	2	1.8	2	0	0	0	0	0
Retail car sales (million units)	10.9	11.6	11.6	12.2	12.5	0.1	0.2	0.2	0.4	0.5
Unemployment rate (percentage)	7.9	6.3	6.5	6	5.9	0.5	0.3	0.2	0.1	0.1
Federal budget surplus (National Income Accounts	−44.7	−10.6	−36.9	−63.7	−117.3	−1.7	4.7	3.8	6.2	3.6
Money and interest rates										
Money supply (M1-B) (average percentage change)	8.3	8.7	7.6	5.9	5.7	0.1	0.3	0.3	−0.4	0
New AA corporate utility rate (percentage)	11.3	10.7	9.8	8.8	8.6	−0.5	−0.5	−0.4	−0.3	−0.2
New high-grade corporate bond rate (percentage)	10.9	10.2	9.4	8.5	8.3	−0.4	−0.5	−0.3	−0.3	−0.2
Federal funds rate (percentage)	10.2	9.3	7.9	7.1	7.3	0	0	−0.1	0	0
Prime rate (percentage)	11.1	10.6	9.3	8.6	8.6	−0.1	0	−0.1	−0.1	0

Note: Demand deposits + currency + other checking accounts (including NOW accounts) = new corporate utility bonds with a rating of AA.

relative income of these groups increases. To the extent that net new labor-force members would have had inadequate income, problems of adequacy are also reduced. The oldest and poorest are helped relatively little by gains in labor participation by the elderly, however. They are largely unable to work, and the improved economy confers few direct benefits to them.

Figures 4-6 through 4-9 show the option's assumptions about labor-force participation of the elderly and near elderly, together with baseline projections. Since most of the recent declines in participation have been among men, the largest total gains and relative-to-baseline increases are in male participation. Between 1980 and 1990, participation of men aged 55-64 increases by 8.4 percentage points (compared with the baseline's 6.8-point decline). Participation of men aged 65 and over increases by 7.7 points (as opposed to a 3.8-point decline in the baseline). Participation by near-elderly women goes up by 1.8 percentage points, rather than declining 1.7 points, and for elderly women a 1.5-point increase replaces a 0.8-point decline.

Table 4-3 shows the numbers of employed elderly and near-elderly workers in option 1 and in the baseline, as well as net differences. Between 1980 and 2005, the number of these workers grows by 7.4 million in option 1, reflecting increases in the elderly and near-elderly population coupled

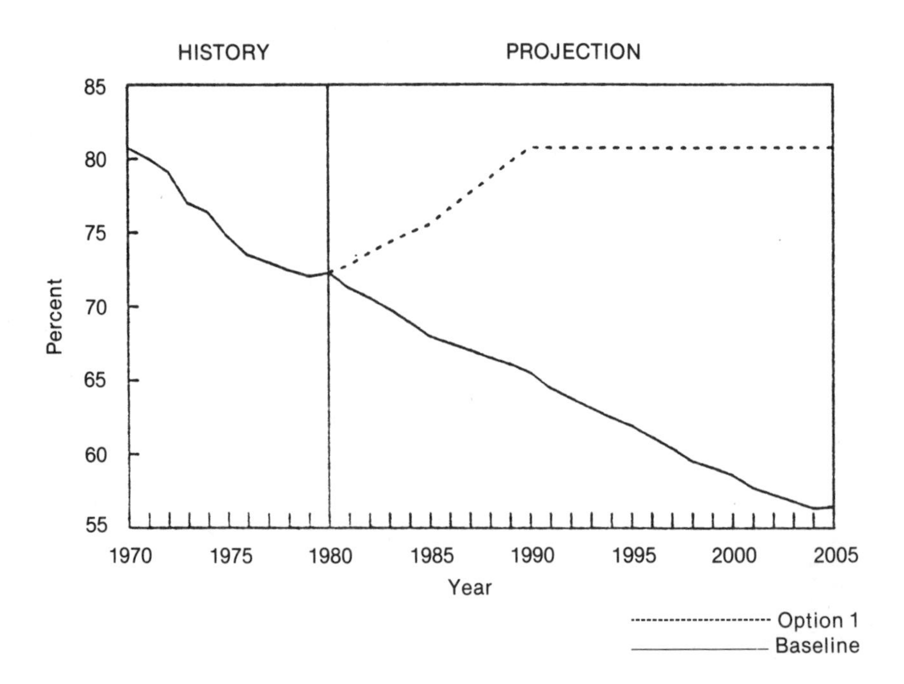

Figure 4-6. Labor-Force-Participation Rate for Men Aged 55 to 64: Option 1 Compared with Baseline

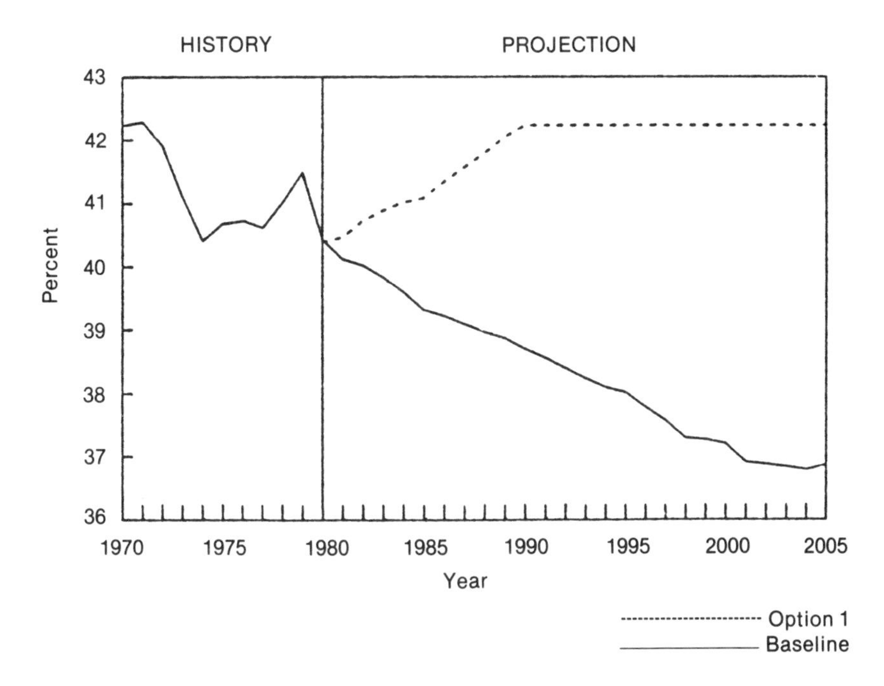

Figure 4-7. Labor-Force-Participation Rate for Women Aged 55 to 64: Option 1 Compared with Baseline

with the moderate rise in participation rates assumed by the option. The falling participation rates of the baseline, in contrast, lead to only about a 1.2-million-worker increase. Thus, the projection in option 1 foresees about 6.3 million more employed elderly and near-elderly workers by 2005 than does the baseline projection, out of an additional 6.5 million elderly and near-elderly net new labor-force members. Therefore, almost all of the net new participants are eventually employed. This success in finding employment reflects the relatively low unemployment rates of older workers (for example, 4 percent in 2005 for males aged 65 and over in option 1 versus 3.6 percent for this group in the baseline and 5.8 percent for the economy wide option 1 unemployment rate).

As assumed the simulation is structured, most of the net additional workers are men.[1] Also, since the most likely form for the net added participation is through a delay in retirement, these added participants are concentrated in the age groups surrounding the traditional retirement age—62-64 as opposed to 55-61 and (especially) 65-71 as opposed to 72 and over.

The DECO option 1 simulation uses input from a special simulation of the ICF Inc. Econometric-Demographic Model, to help gauge the effects of

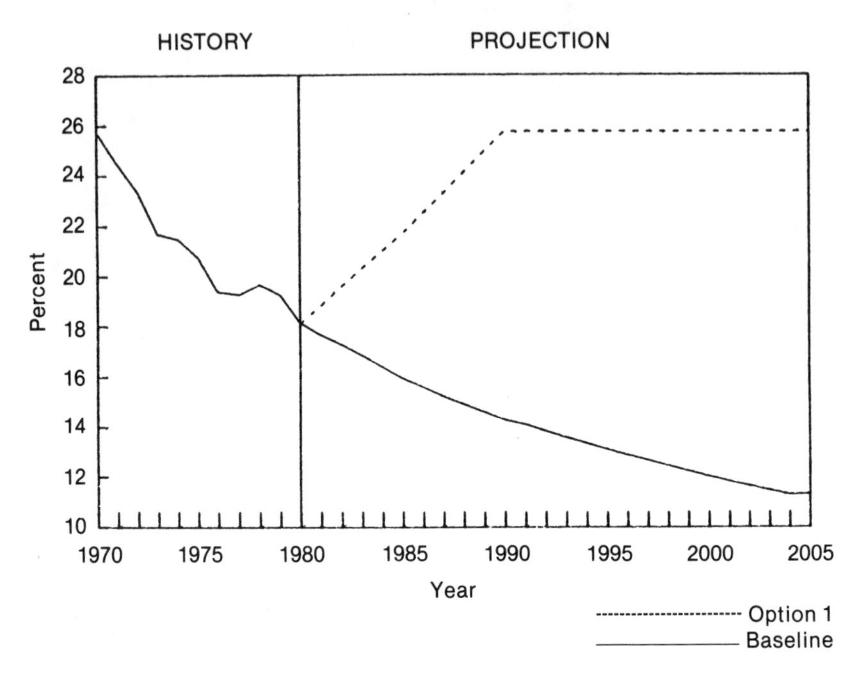

Figure 4-8. Labor-Force-Participation Rate for Elderly Men: Option 1 Compared with Baseline

the net new entrants on the relative wage and employment experience of younger and older men and women. (The ICF simulation was performed by Joseph Anderson.) The ICF Model demonstrated that the negative effects of the new participants would fall mainly on the age/sex groups to which they belong. This occurs because the historical record evidences only moderate levels of substitutability between age groups, especially for men. We also performed a special simulation of DRI's DECO Wage and Salary Model to provide data on how movements in economic aggregates over the next twenty-five years will affect the earnings distribution of the net new entrants. Information from the ICF and DECO Wage and Salary Model simulations was then incorporated judgmentally into the option 1 simulation of the DECO Model of the Elderly.

Real and Relative Income

The simulation indicates that both the elderly and near elderly experience significant gains in real and relative income in this option but that these

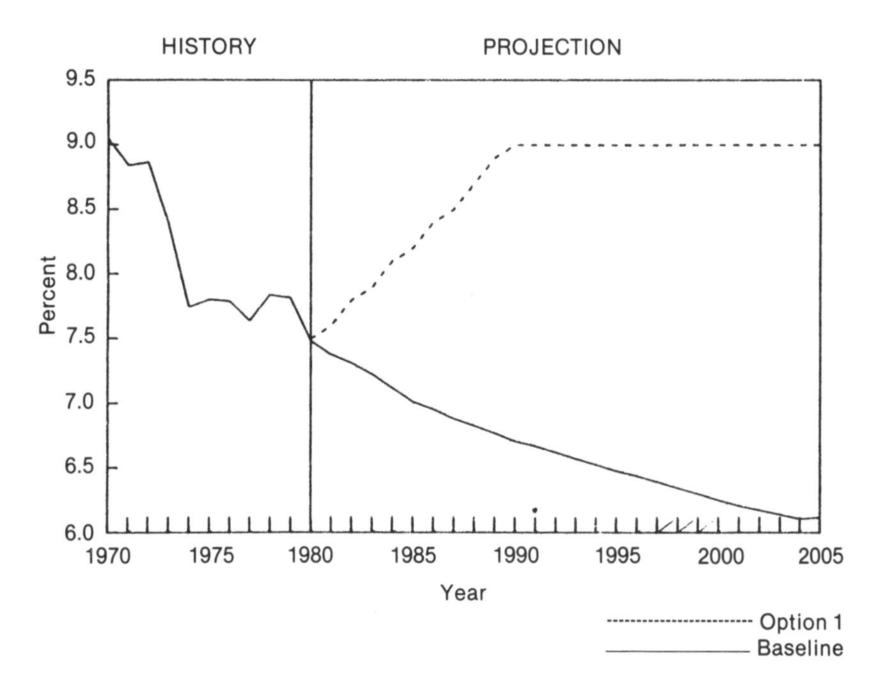

Figure 4-9. Labor-Force-Participation Rate for Elderly Women: Option 1 Compared with Baseline

gains are larger for men than for women and for the younger groups among the elderly than for those aged 72 and over.

Figure 4-10 shows changes in mean income for those under age 55, aged 55-64, and aged 65 and over in the form of differences from baseline means. The elderly gain significantly in this option, almost $500 (1980 dollars) on average by 2005, with the great majority of this gain accruing to the net new labor-force entrants. The near elderly experience even larger average gains, about $1,050 by 2005, reflecting both the higher earnings of these younger net new workers and their greater numbers. The increased labor income to the near elderly can help them in their later years by providing new opportunities to save, to qualify for a pension, or to secure entitlement to social security.

The simulation shows that younger age groups gain less but that the improved economy eventually benefits them as well by raising their average income by over $100 in 2005. Since these gains are less than those of the older groups, figures 4-11 and 4-12 show an improved relative position for the older groups. The elderly still lose out relatively, however, because their option 1 gains are still smaller than the average gains enjoyed by the nonelderly.

Table 4-3
Number of Employed Elderly and Near-Elderly Workers: Net Difference between Option 1 and Baseline
(thousands)

Workers	*1980*	*1985*	*1990*	*1995*	*2000*	*2005*
Men, 55-64						
Option 1	6,934.7	7,478.9	7,767.6	7,682.7	8,688.1	10,627.7
Baseline	6,934.7	6,770.9	6,307.8	5,898.2	6,310	7,428.9
Net difference	0	708	1,459.8	1,784.5	2,378.1	3,198.8
Women, 55-64						
Option 1	4,315.3	4,447.8	4,379.3	4,326.9	4,906.5	5,971.7
Baseline	4,315.3	4,307.6	4,041.5	3,928.9	4,352.8	5,232.6
Net difference	0	140.1	337.7	398	553.8	739
Men, 65 and over						
Option 1	1,744.7	2,250.5	2,941.1	3,080	3,122	3,185.3
Baseline	1,744.7	1,677.6	1,643.6	1,581.3	1,472.1	1,412
Net difference	0	572.9	1,297.6	1,498.7	1,649.9	1,773.3
Women, 65 and over						
Option 1	1,062.6	1,265.3	1,542	1,620.7	1,654.4	1,694.2
Baseline	1,062.6	1,097.4	1,151.5	1,170.7	1,151.7	1,150.2
Net difference	0	167.8	390.4	450	502.8	544.1
Total						
Option 1	14,057.3	15,442.4	16,630	16,710.3	18,371.2	21,479
Baseline	14,057.3	13,853.6	13,144.4	12,579.1	13,286.5	15,223.8
Net difference	0	1,588.8	3,485.6	4,131.2	5,084.6	6,255.2

Table 4-4 shows the total income received by the elderly and how this figure differs from the baseline. The eventual gain reaches $10 billion in 2005. The elderly's share of total income nonetheless declines, but less rapidly than in the baseline.

Table 4-5 shows how average income gains are distributed across age/status groups among the elderly. The greatest gains accrue to 65-71-year-old single men because they have the largest number of net new participants among the elderly and they also earn the highest amount when they do work. Gains to single men in the 72-and-over age group are smaller since it was assumed that most of the net new entrants would be in the younger groups. Single women show a similar pattern but with smaller average gains because the assumptions of the option imply fewer new female workers than male workers. Gains to families fall between those of single men and single women.

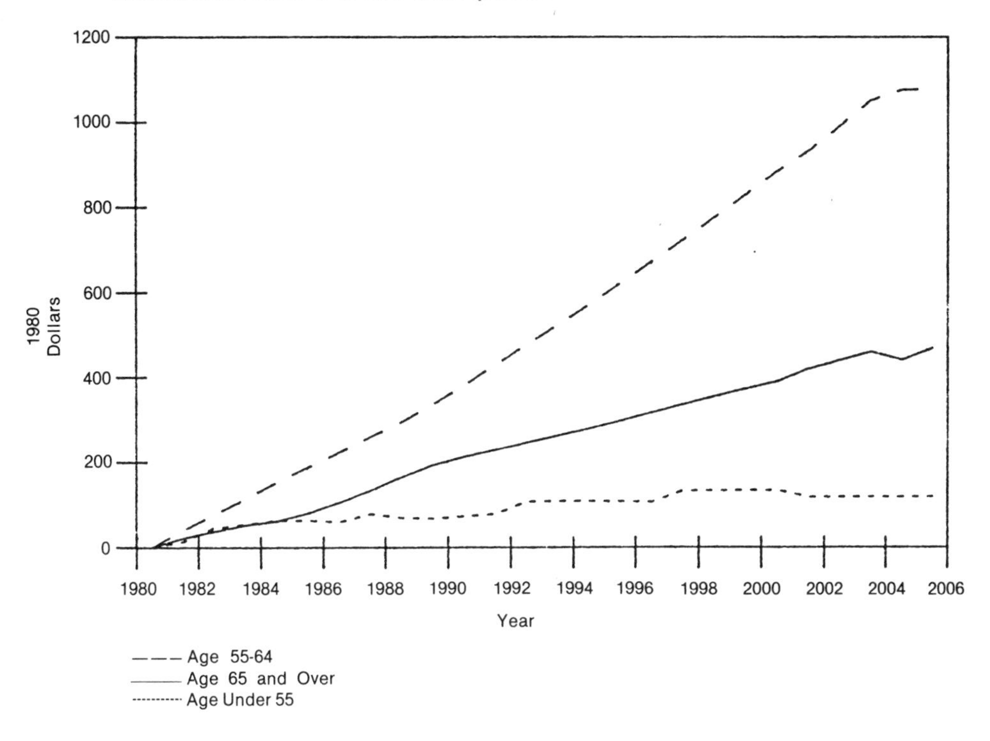

Note: Values shown are (1) option 1 average income per family/single unit minus (2) the identical concept in the baseline simulation.

Figure 4-10. Increase in Average Income for Those over 65, 55-64, and under 55: Option 1 minus Baseline

Income Adequacy and Distribution

All elderly and near-elderly groups are shown to experience significant gains spread across their income distributions, but these gains accrue mainly to those relatively few younger and more-vigorous elderly who are able to work. Adequacy gains for the elderly are also significant. Table 4-6 shows percentages for each elderly group with inadequate income in option 1 and the change from the baseline. (We do not attempt to posit an adequacy standard for the nonelderly, so problems of income adequacy are addressed only for the elderly.) All groups experience significant gains, reflecting the assumption that some of the net new participants would have otherwise had inadequate income. Gains are marginally larger for single men than for

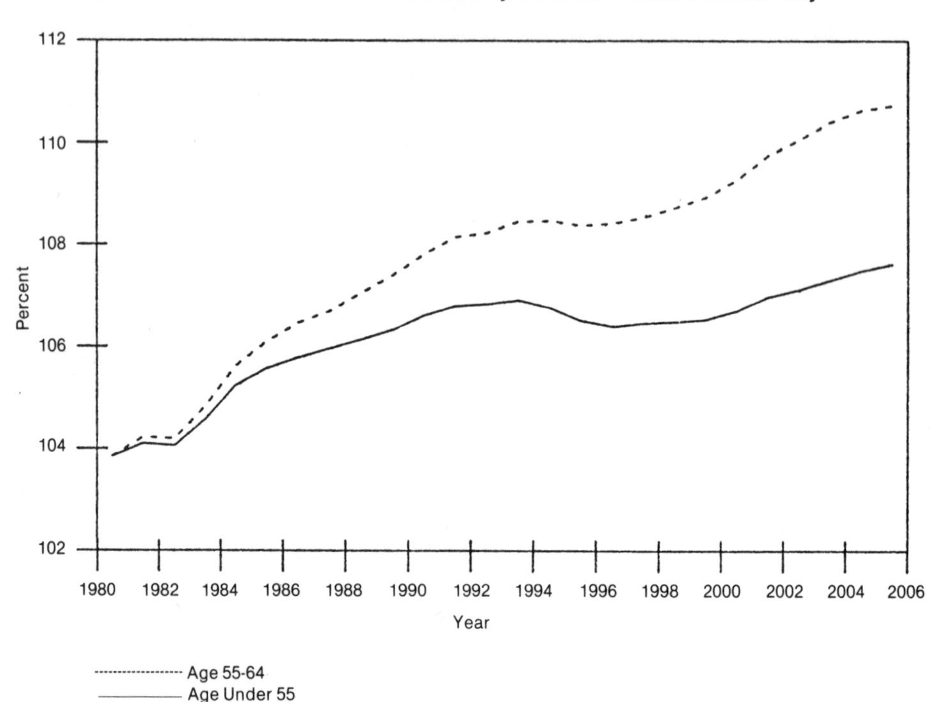

Figure 4-11. Average Income of Those 55 to 64 as a Percentage of Income of Those under Age 55: Option 1 Compared with Baseline

single women and for the 65-71-year-old groups than for the 72-and-over age groups.

Tables 4-7 and 4-8 show changes in income distributions for families and individuals aged 55-64 and 65 and over.[2] Gains are notable for individuals aged 65 and over (and for men within that group) by 2005, reflecting the low average income of that group in the baseline and thus the large gains from having more of the group employed. Also, the higher income classes that contain most of the 55-64-year-old groups are defined with wider limits, so it takes more additional income to move a given percentage of the group to a higher income class.

It should be noted that, although all elderly and near-elderly groups experience significant distributional and adequacy gains in this option, these gains are not all evenly distributed. Rather, those few members of each group who are net new entrants experience large gains, while many of the remaining members (especially among the oldest and poorest elderly) gain relatively little. In fact, some low-income elderly may actually lose ground

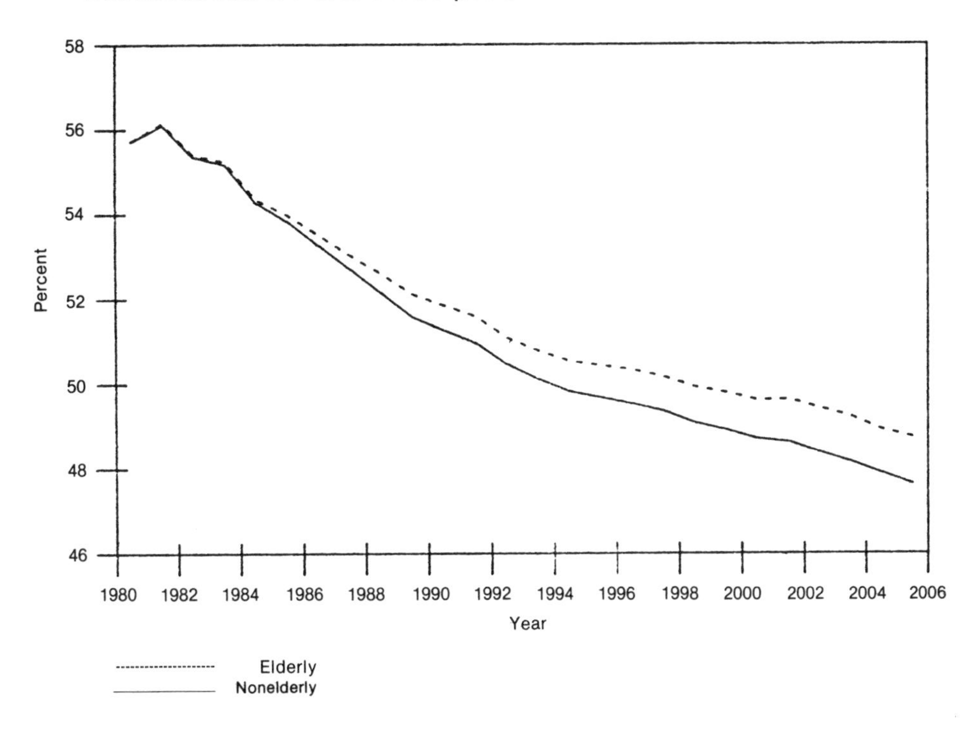

Figure 4-12. Average Elderly Income as a Percentage of Nonelderly Income: Option 1 Compared with Baseline

in the simulation's early years if competition from the net new entrants makes it more difficult for them to secure employment. Therefore, the option leaves largely unsolved the problems of many of the oldest, poorest, and frailest of the elderly (who rely heavily on transfers to meet their expenses), unless new transfer initiatives are undertaken. The fiscal dividend that this option provides might make such initiatives more likely, thus providing indirect help for some of those elderly who experience little direct benefit.

Table 4-4
Total Income Received by Elderly Families and Singles and Percentage of All Income: Option 1
(billions of 1980 dollars)

	1980	1985	1990	1995	2000	2005
Income	198.1	229.4	264.1	291.9	310.1	328.7
Percentage share of total income	11.6	11.2	10.9	10.7	10.2	9.8
Difference from baseline	0	1.5	4.2	6.3	8.3	10.1

Table 4-5
Average Income of Elderly Families and Singles, by Age Group: Option 1
(real 1980 dollars)

Age Group	1980	1985	1990	1995	2000	2005
Men						
65 to 71	8,369	8,833	9,603	10,042	10,603	11,134
72 and over	7,454	7,828	8,950	8,678	9,112	9,478
All elderly	7,850	8,271	8,910	9,291	9,784	10,226
Women						
65 to 71	7,297	7,729	8,258	8,634	9,144	9,599
72 and over	6,255	6,479	7,027	7,567	8,197	8,809
All elderly	6,658	6,957	7,493	7,968	8,551	9,104
Families						
65 to 71	18,019	19,155	20,176	21,034	22,102	22,927
72 and over	14,984	15,964	16,817	17,519	18,450	19,137
All elderly	16,608	17,691	18,653	19,454	20,460	21,226
		Difference from Baseline				
Men						
65 to 71	0	136	525	673	823	1,040
72 and over	0	74	249	303	362	436
All elderly	0	102	372	469	569	709
Women						
65 to 71	0	83	269	358	468	601
72 and over	0	16	142	176	217	281
All elderly	0	41	190	244	311	401
Families						
65 to 71	0	123	250	396	553	656
72 and over	0	87	141	205	264	263
All elderly	0	106	201	310	423	480

Table 4-6
Elderly with Inadequate Income and Change from Baseline, by Family Status and Age: Option 1
(percentage)

	Elderly with Inadequate Income			Change from Baseline	
Age/Status Groups	*1979*	*1990*	*2005*	*1990*	*2005*
Individuals					
Men, 65-71	46.6	39.2	31.9	−2.9	−4.5
Women, 65-71	49.6	43.9	35.3	−1.9	−3.5
Men, 72 and over	49.8	44.5	36.4	−2.1	−2.9
Women, 72 and over	59	50.5	35.7	−1.6	−2.4
All elderly individuals	53.7	46.8	35.3	−1.9	−3
Families					
Head, 65-71	29.1	23.5	17.4	−0.6	−1.2
Head, 72 and over	41.4	35	27.6	−0.5	−0.9
All elderly families	34.8	28.7	22	−0.6	−1

Table 4-7
Numbers and Income Distributions for Families and Singles Aged 55 to 64: Option 1
(percentage within real 1980 income classes)

	Families of Two or More			Singles		
	1980	*1990*	*2005*	*1980*	*1990*	*2005*
Income Distribution						
$0 to $2,500	2.501	1.432	0.730	10.258	6.442	2.840
$2,500 to $5,000	2.933	1.827	1.056	19.383	15.907	11.427
$5,000 to $7,500	4.330	2.839	1.745	17.837	16.264	14.394
$7,500 to $10,000	5.558	3.834	2.488	13.912	13.611	12.993
$10,000 to $20,000	27.934	21.877	16.101	27.421	30.472	32.853
$20,000 and over	56.744	68.190	77.880	11.190	17.305	25.492
Difference from Baseline						
$0 to $2,500	0	0.002	−0.136	0	−0.307	−0.641
$2,500 to $5,000	0	−0.032	−0.111	0	−0.173	−0.746
$5,000 to $7,500	0	−0.062	−0.139	0	−0.065	−0.113
$7,500 to $10,000	0	−0.089	−0.157	0	−0.024	0.007
$10,000 to $20,000	0	−0.455	−0.608	0	0.092	0.309
$20,000 and over	0	0.636	1.151	0	0.476	1.185
Number (thousands)	9,594.282	9,229.888	12,721.125	3,355.240	3,324.263	4,675.899

Table 4-8
Numbers and Income Distributions for Families and Singles Aged 65 and over: Option 1
(percentage within real 1980 income classes)

	Families of Two or More			*Singles*		
	1980	*1990*	*2005*	*1980*	*1990*	*2005*
Income Distribution						
$0 to $2,500	0.126	0	0	7.505	1.248	0.036
$2,500 to $5,000	7.254	2.509	0.031	43.774	42.666	27.394
$5,000 to $7,500	15.725	12.992	7.008	21.847	24.330	30.353
$7,500 to $10,000	15.312	15.167	14.061	10.679	12.134	15.588
$10,000 to $20,000	36.580	39.515	42.977	12.334	14.622	19.634
$20,000 and over	25.003	29.818	35.923	3.861	4.999	6.995
Difference from Baseline						
$0 to $2,500	0	0	0	0	-1.077	-0.052
$2,500 to $5,000	0	-0.423	-0.228	0	-0.443	-4.716
$5,000 to $7,500	0	-0.322	-1.490	0	0.990	1.814
$7,500 to $10,000	0	-0.033	-0.180	0	0.599	1.034
$10,000 to $20,000	0	0.232	0.680	0	0.674	1.276
$20,000 and over	0	0.546	1.217	0	0.257	0.643
Number (thousands)	8,632.528	10,036.230	10,656.407	7,912.373	9,901.898	11,016.897

Notes

1. This occurs because declines in participation by women since 1970 have been less rapid than for men, so returning women to 1970 levels of participation adds fewer workers (see table 4-3 and figures 4-7 and 4-9). Given the very low participation rates for elderly women, however, and the rapid employment gains that have recently occurred among younger women, this assumption may be overly conservative. In any event, the large gains that accrue to those who do continue to work underscore the importance of improved employment opportunities for elderly and near-elderly women. With such improved opportunities, actual employment gains could be considerably larger than those shown here.

2. Additional distribution tables, corresponding to the other tables in chapter 3, are presented in appendix B. In chapters 5 through 7, only the equivalent of table 4-8 is presented in the text, with the equivalent of table 4-7 joining the others in appendix B. The difference in treatment reflects the direct impact of option 1 on the income of the near elderly.

5 Option 2: An Income Guarantee for the Elderly

This simulation analyzes the results of guaranteeing the elderly a minimum level of real income beginning in 1981. The principal effects of this option are to lift the income of all elderly families and singles to the guaranteed level at the cost of a moderate increase in income-tax rates.

The BLS Intermediate Budget Level for a Retired Couple was $8,562 in 1979. An analogously defined budget for single people was $4,941. The establishment of an income floor for the elderly has often been advocated, and the BLS Intermediate Budget Level has been suggested as an adequacy standard (for example, see Borzilleri 1980). The policy analyzed in this simulation involves establishing new federal transfers to guarantee all elderly families the BLS Intermediate Budget for a Retired Couple, indexed for inflation using the NIA implicit deflator for personal-consumption expenditures. For singles, an indexed $4,941 individual equivalent budget is similarly used as a guarantee.

The new transfers are to be financed by increased personal-income taxes. The baseline simulation assumes a discrete personal-tax cut every other year to retard inflation-induced "bracket creep," so the increased transfers are actually financed by reducing the size of these tax cuts.

Compared with the baseline, the key results of option 2 are the following:

Real growth, inflation, and other major economic variables are only slightly affected. The only major difference is in personal taxes, which initially rise by about $70 (1980 dollars) per capita, and in aggregate transfers.

The elderly receive higher real income.

The relative income of the elderly increases.

All elderly achieve adequate income.

Macroeconomic Effects

The macroeconomic effects of this option are trivially small. Real GNP, potential GNP, inflation, and consumption differ only marginally from the baseline. The effective personal-tax rate does rise, however, to pay for the increased transfers.

The difference in GNP from the baseline is always less than 0.1 percent, as is the loss in potential output caused by slightly lower labor-force participation by the elderly.[1] The policy does have a systematic inflationary effect, but its magnitude is trivial. The CPI is only 0.2 percent higher than in the baseline by 2005.

Consumption also tends to be raised systematically because income is redistributed toward low-income earners, who tend to spend a higher proportion of their income. However, the total increase in real consumption for the entire twenty-five-year period is less than $7 billion (1972 dollars)—equal to only about two days' consumption spending in 1980.

The reason for the relative lack of macroeconomic effects is that, from an economywide point of view, the dimensions of the policy being implemented are trivially small. Transfers are increased by $18.6 billion in 1981 (0.6 percent of GNP). The proportionate increase in transfers shrinks over time because the income floor is expressed in absolute terms. In 2005, nominal federal government transfers are $65 billion higher (0.3 percent) of GNP than in the baseline (this figure takes account of all indirect effects, most importantly the slightly higher price level).

The simulation shows that the share of transfers in personal income is raised from an average 14.8 percent in the baseline to 15.2 percent (see figure 5-1). Correspondingly, personal-income taxes are raised from an average of 17.2 percent of personal income to 17.6 percent (see figure 5-2). These new taxes average about $160 (1980 dollars) per person in the labor force in 1981, or $70 per person in the total population. After 1981, these taxes decrease steadily in real terms because the BLS Intermediate Budget Level (adjusted for inflation but not for real-income growth) is an absolute standard, and growth continues to elevate some of the low-income elderly above that standard. These taxes support total net new transfers to the elderly of $17 billion (1980 dollars) in 1981 (plus $1.6 billion to cover the reductions in wage and salary earnings). New transfers are $15.4 billion (1980 dollars) in 1990, $9.9 billion in 2005.

In brief, the simulation shows no macroeconomic effects of option 2 (see table 5-1). It should be judged solely on the basis of its impact on the elderly and its tax-burden effects on the nonelderly.

Effects on Income and Its Distribution

Option 2 ensures that all the elderly achieve income levels defined as adequate. It thus distributes substantial new income to precisely those elderly families and singles with the greatest need.

Figure 5-3 shows the total new transfers needed to guarantee adequate

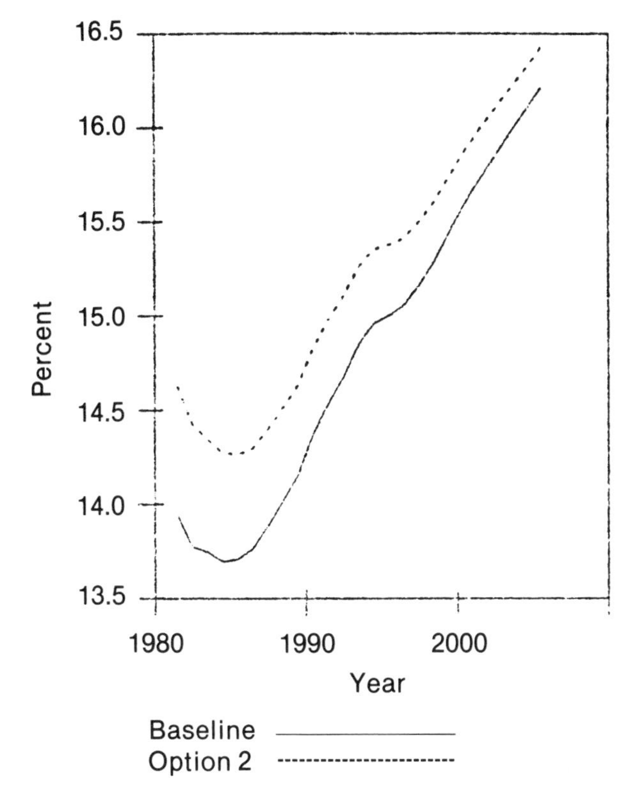

Figure 5-1. Transfers as a Percentage of Personal Income: Option 2 Compared with Baseline

income for all the elderly.[2] These transfers decrease year by year in real terms. The number of transfer recipients is shown to rise through 1992 as increases in the elderly population, especially in the oldest and poorest groups, exceed the adequacy improvements resulting from economic growth. Nonetheless, growth in average income of those elderly below the standard is sufficiently rapid to lead to a steady real diminution in total new transfers.[3] The relatively trivial size of the transfer offset for wage and salary earnings is evident in this figure.

Table 5-2 shows the number of elderly new-transfer recipients and their net new transfers. The $16.9 billion (1980 dollars) in transfers in 1981 provide an average of about $2,300 to each of the approximately 7.5 million (44 percent of the total) elderly families and singles who receive them. By 2005, economic growth reduces this total to $9.9 billion, or about $1,500 for each of the 6.7 million (31 percent) recipients. The program, therefore, provides substantial benefits to large numbers of poor elderly.

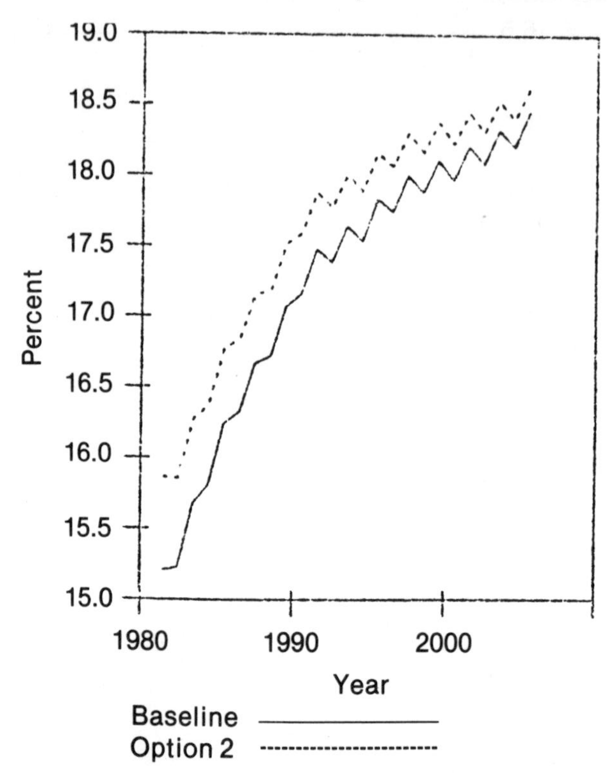

Figure 5-2. Income Taxes as a Percentage of Personal Income: Option 2 Compared with Baseline

By far the largest group to benefit from the transfers is single women aged 72 and over. These women comprise 30 percent of those who are helped in 1981 (receiving 24 percent of the net new transfers), compared with 32 percent in 2005 (receiving 25 percent of the transfers).[4] This brings up to adequacy the approximately 57 percent of this age/sex group who would have been below the standard in 1981, as compared with about 39 percent in 2005. Many fewer single men are in the oldest age group because women live longer, but by 2005 the percentage of single men aged 72 and over receiving these new transfers is about the same as that for single women in the same age group.

Real and Relative Income

Average income gains for the elderly and nonelderly are shown in figure 5-4. The immediate impact of this option is an increase of about $950 in the

Table 5-1
Capsule Summary of Option 2

	Option 2					*Difference from Baseline*				
Parameters	*1980-1985*	*1985-1990*	*1990-1995*	*1995-2000*	*2000-2005*	*1980-1985*	*1985-1990*	*1990-1995*	*1995-2000*	*2000-2005*
Composition of real GNP (average annual rates of change)										
GNP	3.3	2.7	2.2	2.2	2.3	0	0	0	0	0
Final sales	3.1	2.7	2.2	2.3	2.3	0	0	0	0	0
Total consumption	2.9	2.7	2.4	2.1	2.2	0	0	0	0	0
Nonresidential fixed investment	3.2	3.5	2.6	3.4	2.9	0	0	0	0	0
Equipment	4.3	3.7	3.2	3.9	3.4	0	0	0	0	0
Nonresidential construction	0.8	3	1.1	2	1.3	0	0	0	0	0
Residential fixed investment	8.9	1.3	−2.3	0.4	2.5	0	0	0	0	0
Exports	3.7	4.2	3.6	4.3	4.2	0	0	0	0	0
Imports	3.4	3.3	3.7	3.7	3.8	0	0	0	0	0
Federal government	3.6	2.5	1.8	1.8	1.7	0	0	0	0	0
State and local government	1.7	2.2	1.9	1.8	2	0	0	0	0	0
Shares of nominal GNP (percentage)										
Consumption	64.2	62.8	62.7	62.7	62.2	0	0	0	0	0
Business investment	10.3	10.8	11	11.4	11.7	0	0	0	0	0
Residential construction	4.9	5.2	4.7	4.3	4.6	0	0	0	0	0
Government purchases	20.5	20.6	21	21	20.9	0	0	0	0	0

Table 5-1 *(continued)*

Prices and wages (average annual rates of change)										
Implicit price deflator	8.5	7.8	6.7	5.9	5.8	0	0	0	0	0
CPI all urban consumers	8.6	8.1	7.4	6.8	6.7	0	0	0	0	0
Wholesale price index	10.3	9.3	7.4	6.7	6.8	0	0	0	0	0
Compensation per hour	10.1	9.4	8.4	7.7	7.4	0	0	0	0	0
Production and other key measures										
Industrial production (average percentage change)	4.8	3.4	2.8	3.4	3.6	0	0	0	0	0
Housing starts (million units)	2	2.2	1.9	1.8	1.9	0	0	0	0	0
Retail car sales (million units)	10.9	11.4	11.4	11.8	12	0	0	0	0	0
Unemployment rate (percentage)	7.4	6	6.3	5.9	5.8	0	0	0	0	0
Federal budget surplus (National Income Accounts	−42.2	−14.5	−40.9	−69.4	−121	0.7	0.8	−0.2	0.4	−0.1
Money and interest rates										
Money supply (M1-B) (average percentage change)	8.3	8.3	7.3	6.3	5.8	0	0	0	0	0
New AA corporate utility rate (percentage)	11.8	11.2	10.2	9.1	8.8	0	0	0	0	0
New high-grade corporate bond rate (percentage)	11.3	10.7	9.8	8.8	8.5	0	0	0	0	0
Federal funds rate (percentage)	10.2	9.2	7.9	7.1	7.2	0	0	0	0	0
Prime rate (percentage)	11.1	10.6	9.3	8.6	8.6	0	0	0	0	0

Note: Demand deposits + currency + other checking accounts (including NOW accounts) = new corporate utility bonds with a rating of AA.

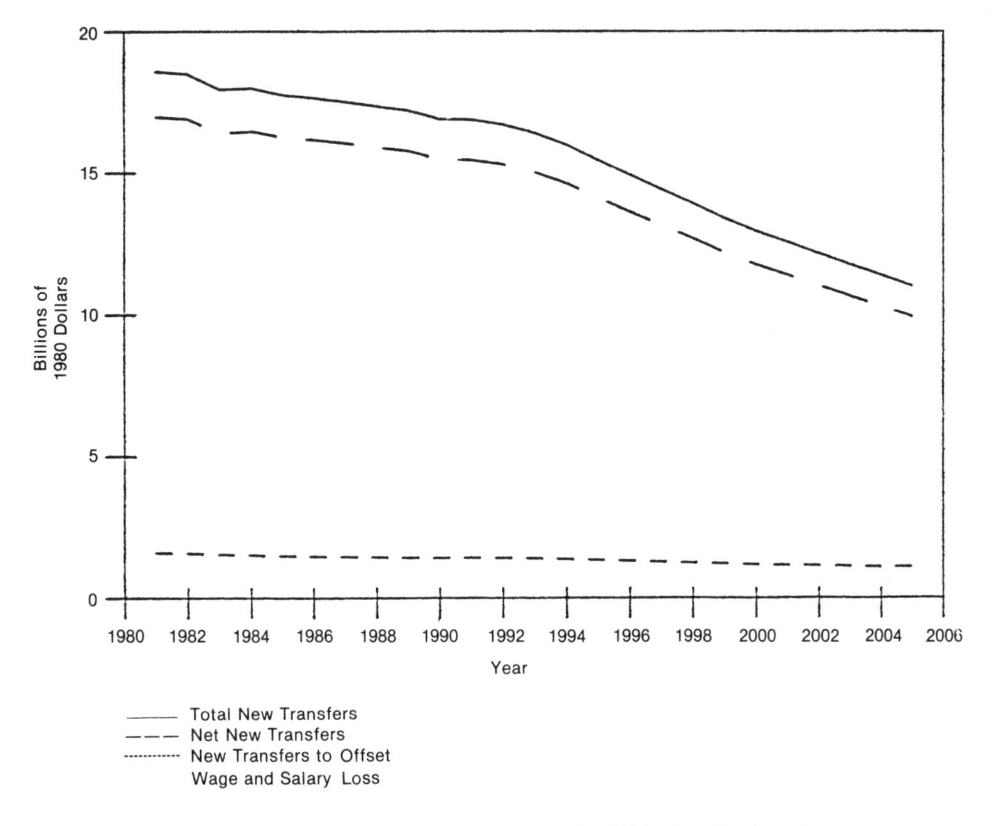

Figure 5-3. Total New Transfers to the Elderly: Option 2

mean income of all elderly. This income gain accrues entirely to those with inadequate income. The DECO Models are not structured in these simulations to estimate taxes or disposable income. However, disposable income for certain of those elderly with adequate income clearly falls somewhat in this option because of the additional taxes necessary to pay for the new transfers. The new taxes are disproportionately borne by the young and by those among the elderly with higher-than-average income. In particular, those elderly only fractionally above the adequacy standard would have either none or only minor additional tax obligations resulting from option 2.

The mean total money income of the young is essentially unaffected by this option, although their disposable income falls. Thus, figure 5-4 shows little difference in younger families' and persons' mean income, while figure 5-5 and table 5-3 show a relative, although declining, improvement in the position of the elderly. Couched in terms of disposable income, the relative improvement would be larger. Table 5-4 shows how the gains are

Table 5-2
Number of Recipients and Average Level of Net New Transfers for Families and Singles: Option 2
(thousands, 1980 dollars)

Recipients	*1985*	*1990*	*1995*	*2000*	*2005*
Age 65-71					
Single men					
Number	350.9	363.6	360.4	341.3	333.8
Average transfer	1,749	1,668	1,583	1,472	1,372
Single women					
Number	1,313	1,398.3	1,412.5	1,353.9	1,316.8
Average transfer	1,738	1,651	1,554	1,426	1,312
Families					
Number	1,354.4	1,339.4	1,316.5	1,187.1	1,101.4
Average transfer	2,626	2,404	2,226	2,024	1,833
Age 72 and over					
Single men					
Number	493.3	499	486.1	454.4	436.9
Average transfer	1,757	1,702	1,635	1,540	1,459
Single women					
Number	2,466.7	2,624.3	2,575	2,377	2,181.2
Average transfer	1,820	1,702	1,524	1,316	1,144
Families					
Number	1,654.7	1,631.2	1,602.3	1,456.9	1,372.2
Average transfer	2,686	2,474	2,305	2,101	1,921
Total elderly					
Number	7,632.9	7,855.7	7,752.8	7,179.5	6,742.3
Average transfer	2,129	1,971	1,820	1,635	1,469

distributed across age/status groups of the elderly. Average gains are shown to be similar across these groups (although somewhat larger for singles) as the larger percentage of singles who receive new transfers is partially balanced by the larger average new transfers to families.

Income Adequacy and Distribution

By definition, all the elderly achieve adequate income in this option. Table 5-5 shows this for all groups, together with the change from the baseline. The dramatic adequacy improvements shown in this table underscore the benefits of this focused option for the poorest and oldest of the elderly.

Table 5-6 shows the income distributions of elderly families and singles. All the singles who would have fallen in the lowest two income classes without the new transfers receive $5,465 (1980 dollars, or $4,941 in 1979

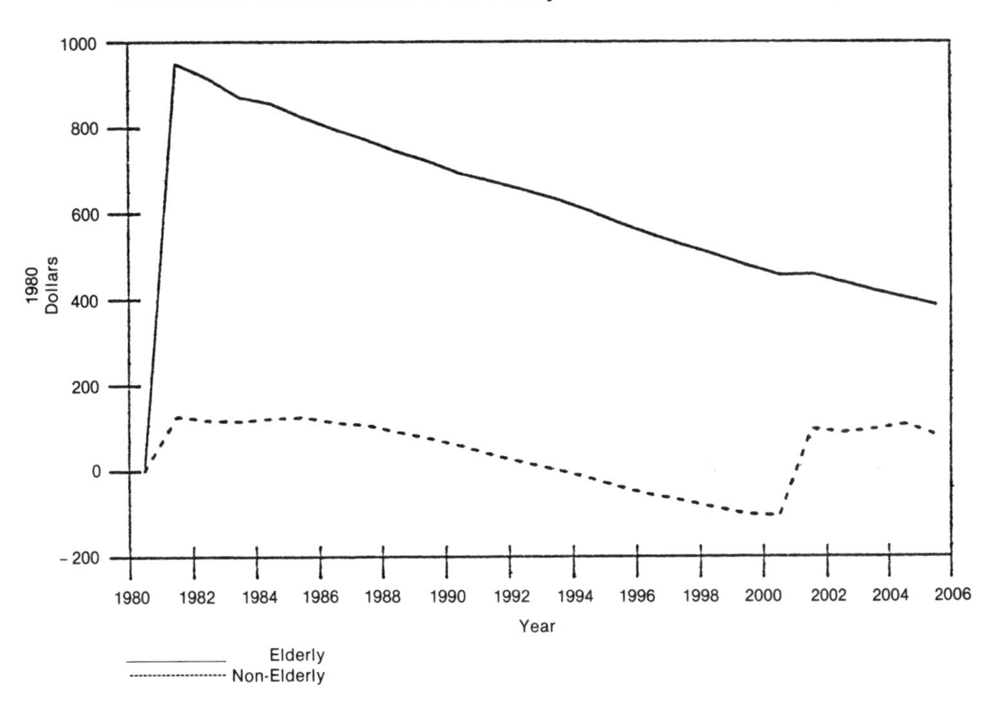

Figure 5-4. Increase in Average Elderly and Nonelderly Income: Option 2 minus Baseline

dollars increased by the 10.6 percent inflation in the personal-consumption deflator between 1979 and 1980) and are, therefore, raised to the $5,000-$7,500 income class. All elderly families who would have fallen in the lowest three income classes receive $9,470 (1980 dollars, or $8,562 adjusted for inflation) and are elevated to the $7,500-$10,000 class.

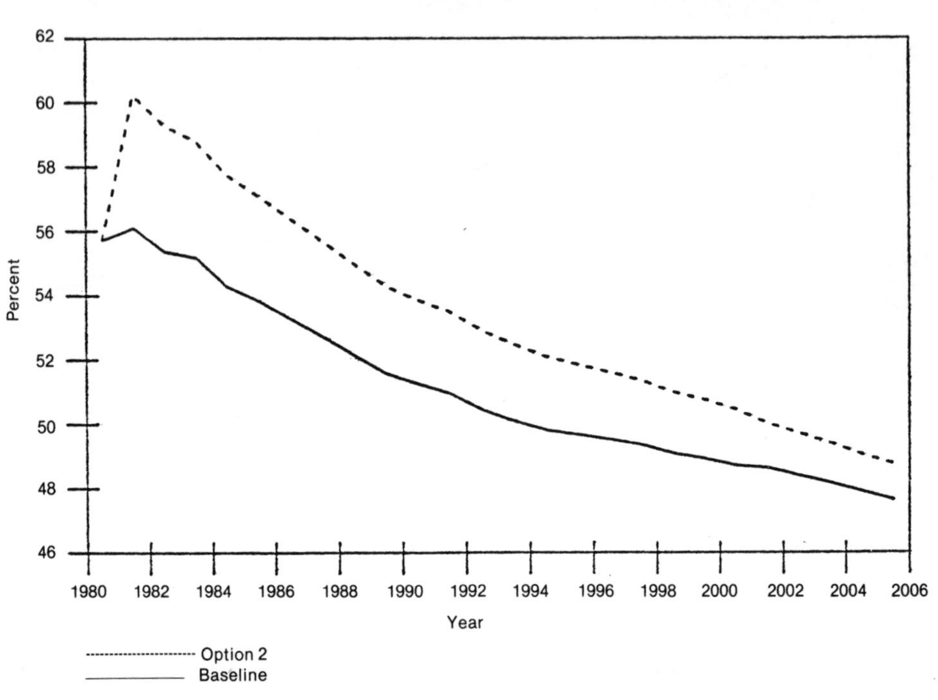

Figure 5-5. Average Elderly Income as a Percentage of Nonelderly Income: Option 2 Compared with Baseline

Table 5-3
Total Income Received by Elderly Families and Singles and Percentage of All Income: Option 2
(billions of 1980 dollars)

	1980	*1985*	*1990*	*1995*	*2000*	*2005*
Income	198.1	243	273.7	297.8	311.5	327
Percentage Share of Total income	11.6	11.7	11.3	11	10.4	9.8
Difference from baseline	0	15	13.8	12.1	9.7	8.4

Table 5-4
Average Income of Elderly Families and Singles, by Age Group: Option 2
(real 1980 dollars)

Age Group	*1980*	*1985*	*1990*	*1995*	*2000*	*2005*
Men						
65 to 71	8,369	9,414	9,717	9,939	10,271	10,545
72 and over	7,454	8,560	8,837	9,041	9,330	9,570
All elderly	7,850	8,936	9,230	9,445	9,754	10,010
Women						
65 to 71	7,297	8,437	8,696	8,903	9,208	9,465
72 and over	6,255	7,406	7,700	8,043	8,468	8,898
All elderly	6,658	7,800	8,077	8,366	8,744	9,109
Families						
65 to 71	18,019	19,669	20,409	21,016	21,830	22,515
72 and over	14,984	16,847	17,473	17,990	18,731	19,349
All elderly	16,608	18,374	19,078	19,656	20,437	21,094
		Difference from Baseline				
Men						
65 to 71	0	717	639	570	491	451
72 and over	0	805	736	667	580	528
All elderly	0	767	693	623	540	493
Women						
65 to 71	0	791	708	628	532	467
72 and over	0	942	815	652	487	370
All elderly	0	884	774	643	504	406
Families						
65 to 71	0	636	484	378	281	245
72 and over	0	969	797	676	546	475
All elderly	0	789	626	512	400	348

Table 5-5
Elderly with Inadequate Income and Change from Baseline, by Family Status and Age: Option 2
(percentage)

Age/Status Groups	*Elderly with Inadequate Income* 1979	1990	2005	*Change from Baseline* 1990	2005
Individuals					
Men, 65-71	46.6	0	0	−42.1	−36.4
Women, 65-71	49.6	0	0	−45.8	−38.8
Men, 72 and over	49.8	0	0	−46.6	−39.3
Women, 72 and over	59	0	0	−52.1	−38.1
All elderly individuals	53.7	0	0	−48.7	−38.3
Families					
Head, 65-71	29.1	0	0	−24.1	−18.6
Head, 72 and over	41.4	0	0	−35.5	−28.5
All elderly families	34.8	0	0	−29.3	−23

Table 5-6
Numbers and Income Distributions for Families and Singles Aged 65 and over: Option 2
(percentage within real 1980 income classes)

	Families of Two or More 1980	1990	2005	*Singles* 1980	1990	2005
Income Distribution						
$0 to $2,500	0.126	0	0	7.505	0	0
$2,500 to $5,000	7.254	0	0	43.774	0	0
$5,000 to $7,500	15.725	0	0	21.847	70.147	61.069
$7,500 to $10,000	15.312	31.825	23.284	10.679	11.443	14.453
$10,000 to $20,000	36.580	39.132	42.222	12.334	13.775	18.209
$20,000 and over	25.003	29.043	34.494	3.861	4.635	6.269
Difference from baseline						
$0 to $2,500	0	0	0	0	−2.325	−0.088
$2,500 to $5,000	0	−2.931	−0.260	0	−44.109	−32.110
$5,000 to $7,500	0	−13.313	−8.498	0	46.807	32.530
$7,500 to $10,000	0	16.624	9.044	0	−0.093	0.101
$10,000 to $20,000	0	−0.151	−0.075	0	−0.172	−0.148
$20,000 and over	0	−0.228	−0.212	0	−0.107	−0.083
Number (thousands)	8,632.528	10,036.230	10,656.407	7,912.373	9,901.898	11,016.897

Notes

1. A very small reduction occurs in aggregate wage and salary earnings and employment in this option because we assume that the elderly below the income floor cease to have wage and salary earnings. This assumption is somewhat arbitrary, as is the assumption that those above the floor do not change their wage and salary earnings. The policy imposes a 100 percent tax on earnings below the floor (transfers are reduced by $1 for every $1 of new income below the floor). However, those below the floor have very little wage and salary earnings anyway—the roughly 45 percent of the elderly below this standard in 1978 received about 20 percent of the elderly's total income but only about 3 percent of its wage and salary earnings. The results of the option would not be materially modified if either a smaller or a larger labor-force effect were assumed. For example, an assumption of no labor-force effect would have added to aggregate earnings and subtracted from transfers a sum only about 10 percent as large as the total new transfers.

2. The net new transfer total is calculated by subtracting (1) the aggregate income of all the elderly families and singles with less-than-adequate income from (2) the sum of their numbers multiplied by their appropriate adequacy standards. This represents the aggregate direct increase in the income of the poor elderly. Transfers to offset wage loss equal the total wage and salary earnings of those below the standard since we assume that they cease to have such earnings. Total transfers are the sum of (1) net new transfers and (2) transfers to offset wage loss.

3. Economic growth benefits the poor elderly to the extent that they have any asset, pension, or wage and salary income. Also, with growth, the new members of each age group experience higher income and earnings in their younger years, allowing them to save larger amounts, increasing the chance that they may qualify for a pension, and raising their social-security entitlements. Growth thus serves to lift above the adequacy standard some of those elderly who would otherwise have had inadequate income. At the same time, it tends to improve the average income position of those remaining below the standard.

4. Average transfers to families exceed those to individuals because the family standard is higher. The average income of those families below the standard is a somewhat larger fraction of the standard than is the case for singles, notwithstanding the larger mean absolute shortfall for families.

6 Option 3: An Increase in Personal Saving

This simulation examines the effect of an increase in the rate of personal saving by the nonelderly beginning in 1981. This change first diminishes and later accelerates economic growth. The economic fate of the elderly tracks that of the economy but without the diminished consumption of the younger groups.

Personal saving averages 4.5-5.5 percent of disposable personal income in DRI's baseline projection, compared with an average of over 6 percent in the 1960s and 1970s. For this simulation, it is assumed that the propensity to save increases by about 2 percentage points above the baseline value, with the increase phased in gradually over the three-year period of 1981-1983. The increased saving is assumed to be distributed among assets (such as savings-and-loans deposits, trading-bank deposits, and money) in approximately the same proportion that total saving is distributed.

Since we are addressing methods to increase the money available for consumption by the elderly, it did not seem reasonable to assume a drop in their current consumption to finance additional saving. Therefore, it is assumed that all new saving is done by those under age 65.

The interest income from the new saving is assumed to be treated as ordinary income by its recipients, and the new assets are assumed not to be subsequently liquidated. These assumptions ensure that the increase in the propensity to save is permanent and relatively stable.

The simulation does not specify why this additional saving occurs. It could result from an exogenous change in the overall propensity to save or from any of a range of policies designed to induce additional saving—for example, mandatory pensions or saving or a partial or total shift from an income to a value-added tax. Different policies would have somewhat different implications for the economy, but it was felt that the simulation would have the greatest generality if it abstracted from these differences.

The degree to which the increased personal saving is eventually transformed into increased domestic fixed investment has not yet been empirically determined with a high level of certainty, nor can the issue be resolved theoretically. On the one hand, one could argue that the increased saving drives down the demand for loans by consumers, since consumer spending is lowered. This reduced demand, together with the increased flows from saving, tend to drive down interest rates, thus decreasing the cost of borrowing for both business investors and those in the housing market. Therefore, all other things equal, this would lead to a higher level of both business fixed investment and residential construction. On the other hand, a signficant potential offset exists to this financing effect—that is, the increase in saving and consequent reduction in consumption reduce the rate of growth of the end markets of business. This effect, ceteris paribus, thus tends to *reduce* investment—a typical Keynesian result.

The model simulation described here reflects a belief that domestic investment is constrained mainly by a shortage of funds rather than by output expectations and projected profitability. Thus, the simulation assumes that three-quarters of the increased personal saving is translated into domestic fixed investment, distributed two-thirds to business fixed investment and one-third to housing.[1] DRI believes that this assumption is a reasonable depiction of future reality, although the true effect on investment could conceivably be somewhat less.

The key results of the increased personal saving are the following:

Real consumption is diminished and does not exceed baseline values for twenty-one years.

By 2005, real GNP is up by 2.5 percent, with consumption up only 0.5 percent.

Inflation is reduced by 0.4 percentage points per year.

There is a small fiscal dividend.

New saving creates a stock of additional wealth and income.

The real income of the elderly first decreases and then increases.

The relative income of the elderly is essentially unchanged, but relative consumption probably increases.

Little appreciable effect on adequacy and income distribution is evident.

Macroeconomic Effects

The simulation shows that the initial effect of the increased saving is to cause the rate of activity in the economy to fall relative to the baseline. Eventually, however, the increased investment consistent with the higher saving leads to an expansion in the economy's capacity to produce, and real GNP begins to exceed its baseline values. This effect is present from 1986 on so that by 2005, real GNP is 2.5 percent above its baseline reading. The increase in productivity and the lower level of resource utilization in this option lead to some improvement in the rate of inflation—that is, about 0.4 percentage points per year.

Any policy that increases personal saving clearly has an initial downward impact on consumer spending (see figure 6-1), which depresses growth in real GNP. Thus, in 1983, real GNP is 0.8 percent less than in the baseline. Eventually, however, much of the saving translates into increased investment, which augments the economy's capital stock and, therefore, its capacity to produce. By 1986, real GNP returns to its baseline value and exceeds it thereafter. Over the whole twenty-five-year-projection period, annual growth in both real and potential output average 0.1 percent greater than in the baseline (see table 6-1).

As one might expect, business fixed investment is shown to be the fastest growing category of final demand. Between 1985 and 1990, business fixed investment's share of GNP averages 11.8 percent, compared with 10.9 percent in the baseline. In 2000-2005, business fixed investment's share rises to 12.5 percent, 0.8 percentage points higher than in the baseline. By com-

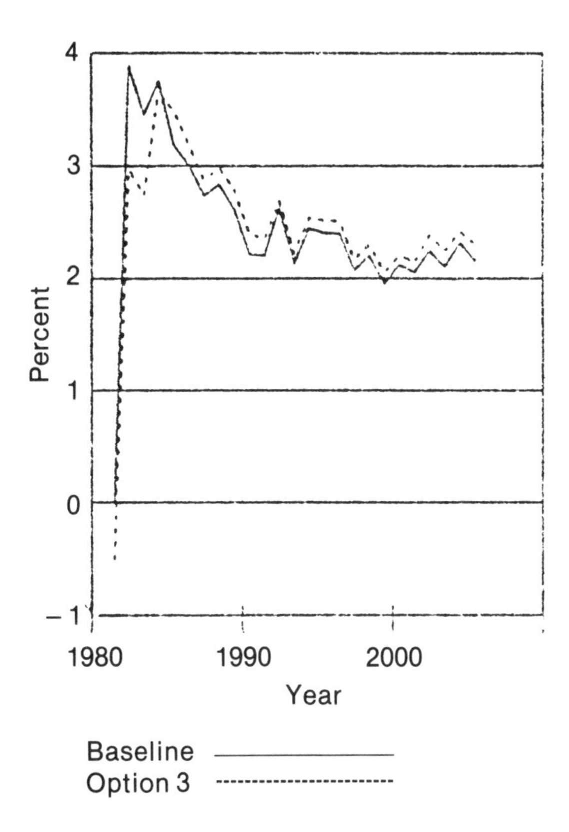

Figure 6-1. Percentage Rate of Growth in Consumption: Option 3 Compared with Baseline

Table 6-1
Macroeconomic Effects of Option 3
(averages over entire simulation period)

Effects	*Baseline 1981-2005*	*Option 3 1981-2005*
Average annual growth rates		
GNP	2.5	2.6
Consumption	2.4	2.5
Investment	3.1	3.5
Government spending	2.1	2.1
Disposable income	2.4	2.5
Industrial production	3.6	3.8
Shares of output (precentage)		
Consumption	62.9	61.3
Investment	16.5	17.7
Government	20.8	20.5
Other economic aggregates		
CPI inflation (percentage)	7.5	7.1
Unemployment (percentage)	6.3	6.6
Share of interest income in personal income (percentage)	8	8.7
Share of personal income in GNP (percentage)	81.9	81.6

parison, from 1980 to 1985, consumption's share of GNP averages 61.5 percent, compared with 62.8 percent in the baseline. From 1980 to 1985, average annual growth in real consumption is 0.4 percentage points lower than in the baseline. Over the subsequent twenty years, however, because the whole economy grows more rapidly, so does total consumption, even though its share of GNP shrinks relative to the baseline. Over the whole twenty-five-year-projection period, annual consumption growth averages 2.46 percent, compared with 2.44 percent in the baseline. This extra growth is fairly uniformly distributed over categories of consumption (durables, nondurables, and services).

The spurt in investment and the short-run decline in consumption both ameliorate inflation. The extra increment to investment, by enhancing productivity, increases the supply of goods and services produced by the economy. The short-run downturn in consumption depresses aggregate demand, which leads to subsequent improvements in inflation by reducing inflationary expectations. As a result of these developments, by 2005 the average annual rate of inflation is 0.4 percentage points lower than in the baseline (see figure 6-2).

The price of this improvement, however, is higher unemployment. The lower level of resource utilization pushes the unemployment rate up by an average of 0.3 percentage points relative to the baseline. However, employ-

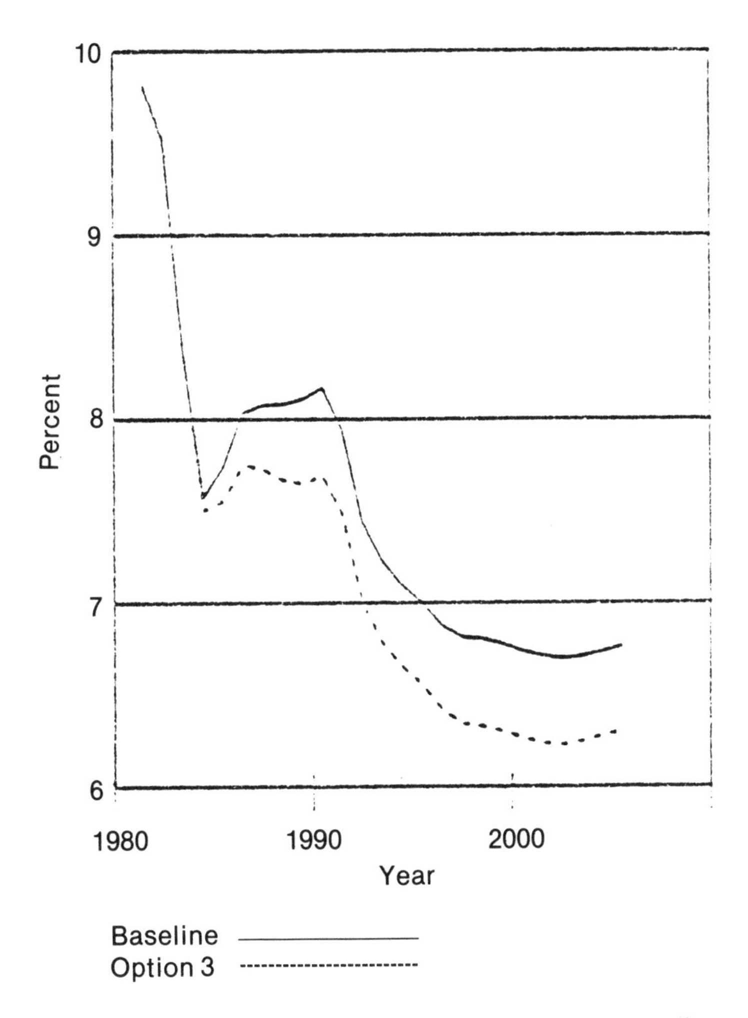

Figure 6-2. CPI Inflation: Option 3 Compared with Baseline

ment in some industries benefits from the shift in the composition of output away from consumption and toward investment. On one end of the scale, big gainers include employment in the lumber industry (10.6 percent above the baseline by 2005); in stone, clay, and glass (up 8.2 percent by 2005); and in fabricated-metal products (up 7.3 percent by 2005). At the other end of the scale, the initially weaker performance of consumption causes a loss of employment in trade of 2.8 percent by 2005.

While the deflection of consumption into saving lowers the rate of factor utilization and therefore increases unemployment, it permits households to accumulate significantly more assets. The DRI Macroeconomic Model keeps track of this accumulation in two ways. (1) It monitors the flow of deposits into savings-and-loan institutions, savings banks, and trading banks, and (2) it monitors the effect of these saving flows on household wealth. In doing this, it keeps track not only of the direct extra saving but also of the "second-round" effects of this saving on total income, interest rates, inflation, and so on.

The greater wealth of consumers tends, ceteris paribus, to increase consumption out of a given income, partially offsetting the direct effect of the change in saving habits. Thus, even though the propensity to save is increased by 2 percent in this option, the saving rate, after allowances for this wealth effect, peaks at only 1.8 percent above the base case in 1984. By 2005, it is 1.3 percent above its baseline value.

With respect to the public sector, the simulation shows that federal government spending on final goods and services is eventually increased (see figure 6-3). The lower level of utilization of the economy tends to increase the federal deficit (that is, to increase government dissaving), and this keeps federal tax receipts low for a number of years. This effect could be overcome by tax increases or expenditure reductions but only at the cost of even lower levels of utilization. By contrast, state and local government receipts are less affected by lower levels of utilization (which depresses income). Property-tax receipts are eventually boosted by the larger stock of housing (see figure 6-4), and sales-tax receipts are raised by the larger volume of goods and services flowing through the economy. Consequently, from 1990 onward, state and local government spending is significantly raised—in effect, a fiscal dividend. From 2001 to 2005, it averages 1.5 percent above its baseline levels. This fiscal dividend could alternatively be used to finance some tax relief.

Income shares are shown to be affected only marginally, with the share of personal income in GNP being reduced from an average of 81.9 percent in the baseline to 81.6 percent. Relative to the baseline, the shares of both dividends and transfer payments are eventually marginally reduced, mainly because they respond more sluggishly to the increase in activity than does personal income (see figure 6-5). The increase in saving, however, causes a significant rise in the share of interest income in personal income. This share averages 11 percent, compared with 10.3 percent in the baseline. The sum of transfers, dividends, and interest income, in real terms, is increased by 2.6 percent relative to the baseline in 1990 and by 3.6 percent in 2005.

The greater productivity growth and lower inflation permit considerable improvement in the U.S. external position (see table 6-2). Even though the faster growth of the economy requires a significant increase in oil imports, our performance vis-à-vis non-OPEC-trading partners is enhanced sufficiently to drive the value of the dollar up by 9.6 percent, relative to the baseline, by 2005.

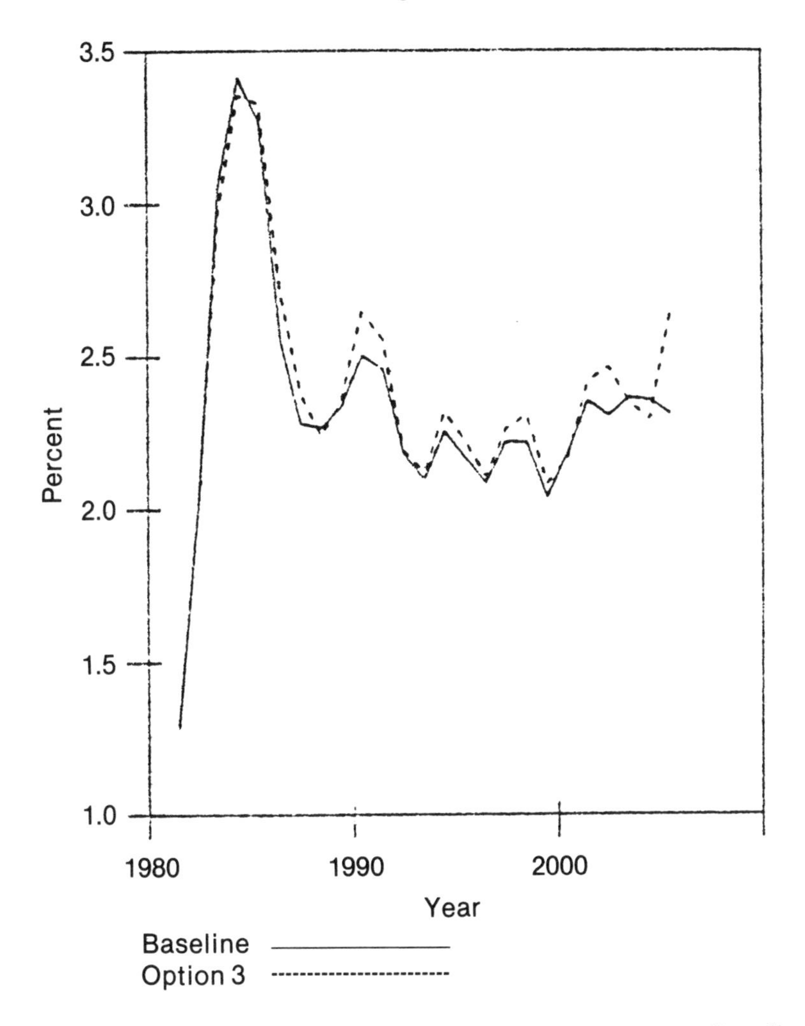

Figure 6-3. Percentage Rate of Growth in Real Government Spending: Option 3 Compared with Baseline

Effects on Income and Its Distribution

Benefits to the elderly are a long time in coming in this option. The simulation indicates that it takes almost twenty years before average real income of the elderly rises significantly above its baseline value. However, consumption by the elderly probably increases relative to that of younger groups in all periods, and the new saving by the preelderly creates a stock of wealth that will contribute to their future retirement income.

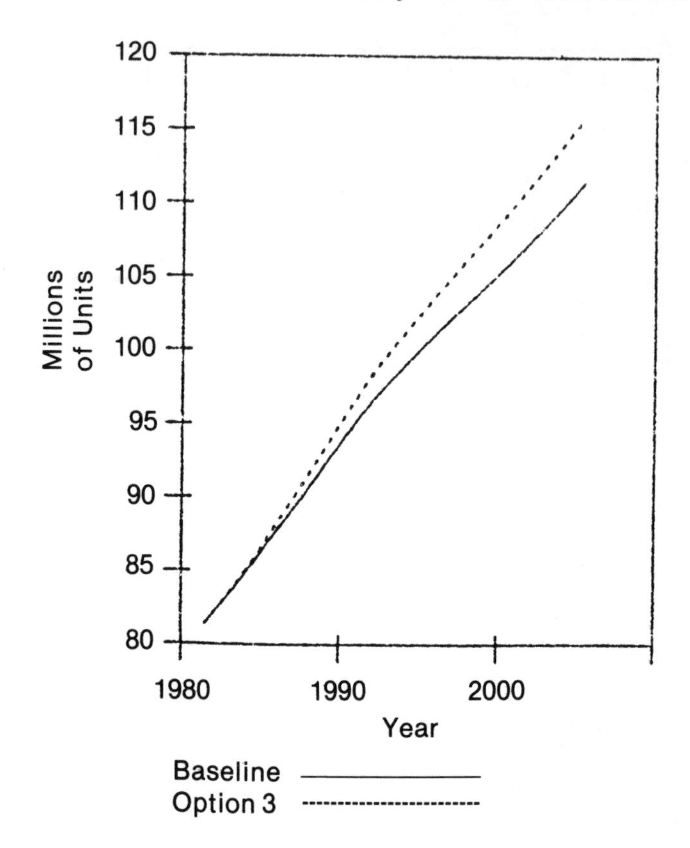

Figure 6-4. Growth in Stock of Houses: Option 3 Compared with Baseline

Figure 6-6 shows the growing stock of new wealth engendered by the additional saving.[2] Considering only the direct effects of the new saving, an additional stock of wealth is created that grows from $5.9 billion (1980 dollars) in 1981 to about $550 billion in 2005. By this time, the new wealth is owned by both the elderly and nonelderly. This $550 billion amounts to about 14 percent of aggregate personal income in 2005 (approximately the total wealth of private and public pension funds in 1980). The income from the newly created wealth, however, is only about $39 billion by 2005, or about 1 percent of all income. This represents a gain of about 10 percent in interest income by 2005 so the direct impact on income over the twenty-five-year period is relatively small. Even though the option specification rules out dissaving the new wealth, this new wealth (as the old) is clearly available to cover day-to-day needs or emergencies, and, if it is never dissaved, it eventually raises bequests.

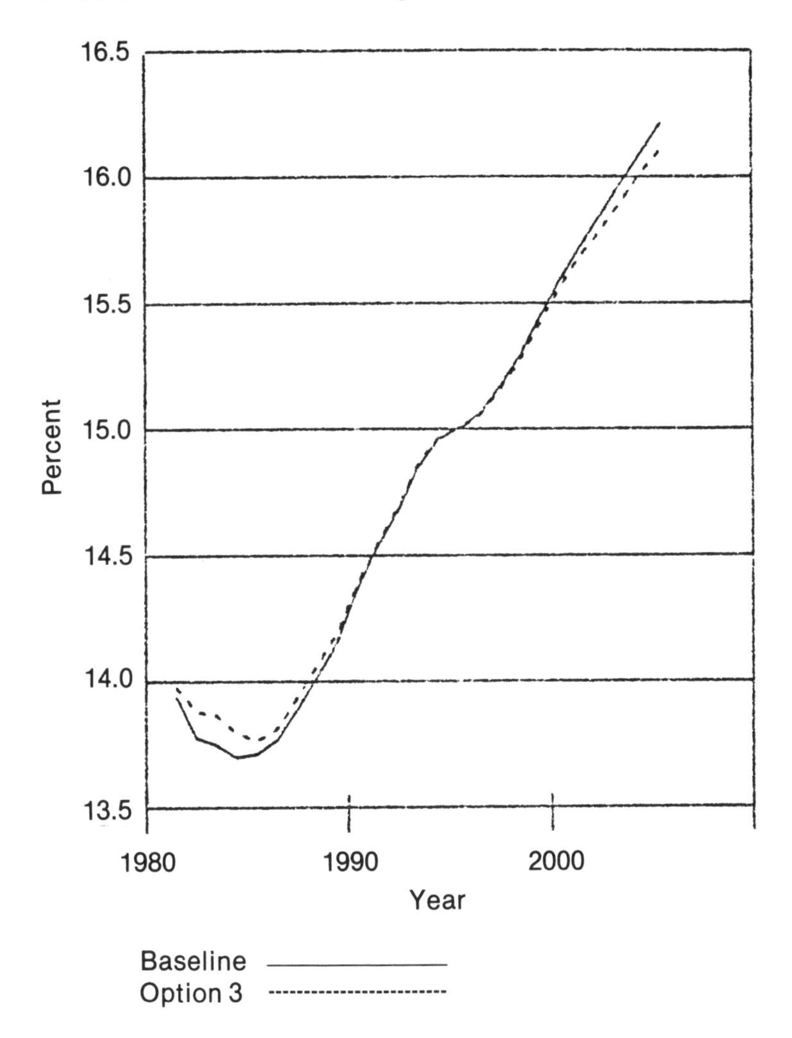

Figure 6-5. Transfers as a Percentage of Personal Income: Option 3 Compared with Baseline

Since the new saving is assumed to be done by only those under 65, benefits to the elderly are slow in arriving. For example, not until 1989 do savers who were age 64 in 1981 reach our oldest category: age 72 and over. Thus, it is some time before the elderly, particularly those in the oldest group, end up owning an appreciable share of the new assets. Even by 2005, many of the elderly will have spent much of their working lives before the initiation of the higher saving rate. Thus, it is beyond our projection hori-

Table 6-2
Capsule Summary of Option 3

	Option 3					*Difference from Baseline*				
Parameters	*1980-1985*	*1985-1990*	*1990-1995*	*1995-2000*	*2000-2005*	*1980-1985*	*1985-1990*	*1990-1995*	*1995-2000*	*2000-2005*
Composition of real GNP (average annual rates of change)										
GNP	3.2	2.9	2.3	2.3	2.5	0	0.2	0.1	0.1	0.2
Final sales	3	2.9	2.3	2.4	2.5	0	0.2	0.1	0.1	0.2
Total consumption	2.5	2.8	2.5	2.2	2.3	−0.4	0.2	0.1	0.1	0.1
Nonresidential fixed investment	4.8	3.5	2.6	3.4	3.2	1.7	0	0	0	0.4
Equipment	6	3.7	3.3	3.9	3.8	1.7	0	0	0	0.4
Nonresidential construction	2.5	3.1	1.1	2	1.7	1.7	0	0	0	0.4
Residential fixed investment	10.8	1.5	−2.1	0.5	2.3	1.9	0.2	0.2	0.1	−0.1
Exports	3.5	4.5	4	4.5	4.5	−0.2	0.3	0.3	0.2	0.3
Imports	3.5	3.2	3.8	4	4.2	0.1	−0.2	0.1	0.2	0.3
Federal government	3.6	2.5	1.8	1.8	1.7	0	0	0	0	0
State and local government	1.7	2.4	2	1.8	2.2	−0.1	0.2	0.1	0	0.2
Shares of nominal GNP (percentage)										
Consumption	63.3	61.5	61.5	61.6	61.2	−0.8	−1.3	−1.2	−1.1	−0.9
Business investment	10.8	11.8	11.9	12.2	12.5	0.5	0.9	0.9	0.8	0.8
Residential construction	5.2	5.7	5.1	4.7	4.9	0.2	0.5	0.4	0.4	0.4
Government purchases	20.5	20.4	20.7	20.6	20.5	0	−0.2	−0.3	−0.4	−0.4

Prices and wages (average annual rates of change)										
Implicit price deflator	8.5	7.4	6.1	5.3	5.2	0	−0.4	−0.5	−0.6	−0.6
CPI all urban consumers	8.5	7.7	6.9	6.3	6.3	−0.1	−0.4	−0.4	−0.5	−0.5
Wholesale price index	10.3	9	6.9	6.1	6.2	0	−0.4	−0.5	−0.6	−0.6
Compensation per hour	10	9	7.8	7.1	6.8	−0.1	−0.4	−0.6	−0.6	−0.5
Production and other key measures										
Industrial production (average percentage change)	5.2	3.6	2.9	3.5	3.7	0.4	0.1	0.1	0.1	0.3
Housing starts (million units)	2.1	2.4	2.1	2	2.2	0.1	0.2	0.2	0.2	0.2
Retail car sales (million units)	10.7	11.3	11.4	11.9	12.1	−0.2	0	0	0.1	0.1
Unemployment rate (percentage)	7.6	6.4	6.7	6.2	6.1	0.2	0.3	0.4	0.3	0.2
Federal budget surplus (National Income Accounts	−48.5	−22.1	−50.9	−90.2	−153.5	−5.6	−6.8	−10.3	−20.3	−32.6
Money and interest rates										
Money supply (M1-B) (average percentage change)	7.9	8.2	7.2	6.2	5.6	−0.3	−0.1	0	−0.1	−0.1
New AA corporate utility rate (percentage)	11.7	10.7	9.5	8.5	8.2	−0.1	−0.4	−0.6	−0.6	−0.6
New high-grade corporate bond rate (percentage)	11.2	10.3	9.2	8.2	7.9	−0.1	−0.4	−0.6	−0.6	−0.6
Federal funds rate (percentage)	10.2	8.9	7.5	6.7	6.7	−0.1	−0.4	−0.5	−0.5	−0.5
Prime rate (percentage)	11.2	10.3	8.8	8	8.1	0	−0.3	−0.5	−0.6	−0.5

Note: Demand deposits + currency + other checking accounts (including NOW accounts) = new corporate utility bonds with a rating of AA.

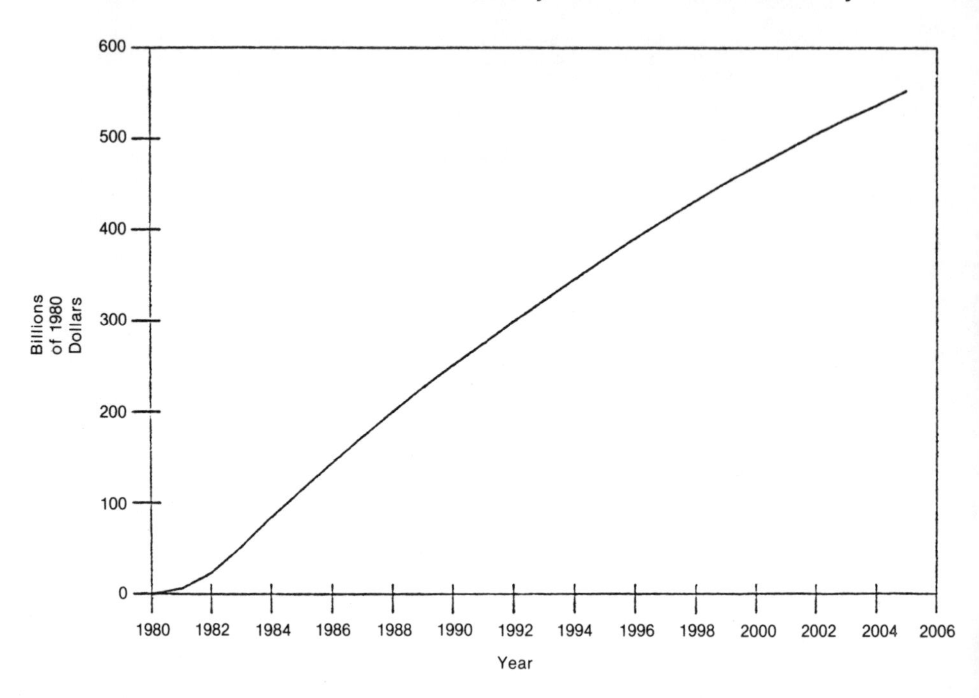

Figure 6-6. New Wealth from Added Saving: Option 3

zon, when the then new elderly will have shared in saving at the new rate for most of their working lives, that the policy has its greatest personal impact (and its greatest macroeconomic implications depending on the disposition of these baby-boom elderly on the use of their extra accumulations).

The projected distribution of the new-asset income is shown to favor the preelderly for many years. This is in contrast to the existing distribution of assets in which the elderly have a disproportionate share. These gains to the preelderly follow from the assumption of no new saving by the elderly. A rise in personal saving contributes only slowly to wealth. As was acknowledged by the late economist Frank Knight, great wealth arises as the result of inheritance, luck, and skill (or thrift), in that order. Therefore, a rise in the personal-saving rate by 2 percent increases the stock of wealth and, hence, income from assets only slowly and by a relatively small amount.

Real and Relative Income

This option first decreases the income of the elderly and then, after a long lag, increases it. Relative income is shown to be essentially unaffected for the elderly, but relative consumption is probably raised. Figure 6-7 shows how the real income of those aged 65 and over differs from the baseline. The income of the elderly is depressed for almost twenty years in this option, reflecting the interplay between the new saving and the very gradual aging of the younger savers into the 65-and-over age group.

The income of younger age groups also declines at first, but their initially greater share of the new saving leads to a more-rapid recovery. This, in turn, ensures that, in comparison with the baseline, the relative-income position of the elderly is in some periods (although probably not significantly) diminished in this option (see figure 6-8). Still, the assumption that all new saving in option 3 is performed by those under 65 makes it quite likely that the relative consumption expenditures of the elderly are raised in this option.[3]

Table 6-3 shows the total income of the elderly in option 3 and its relation to the baseline. Total income decreases relative to the baseline, both absolutely and as a share of aggregate income, until about the start of the twenty-first century. For the reasons listed before, however, the elderly's share of aggregate consumption is probably somewhat higher in option 3 than in the baseline.

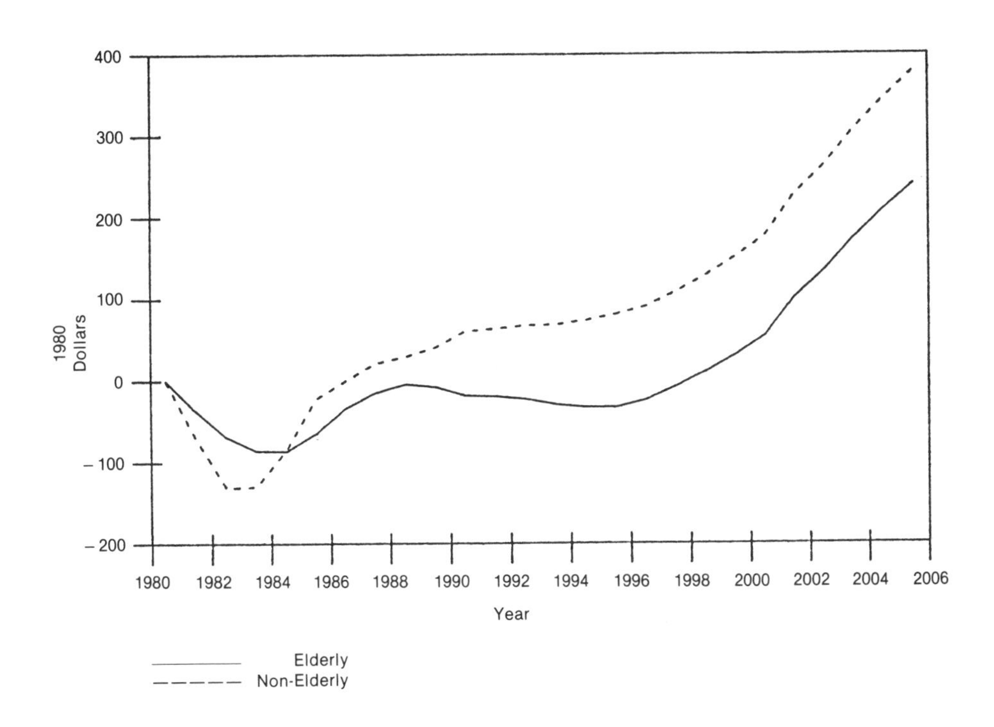

Figure 6-7. Increase in Average Elderly and Nonelderly Income: Option 3 minus Baseline

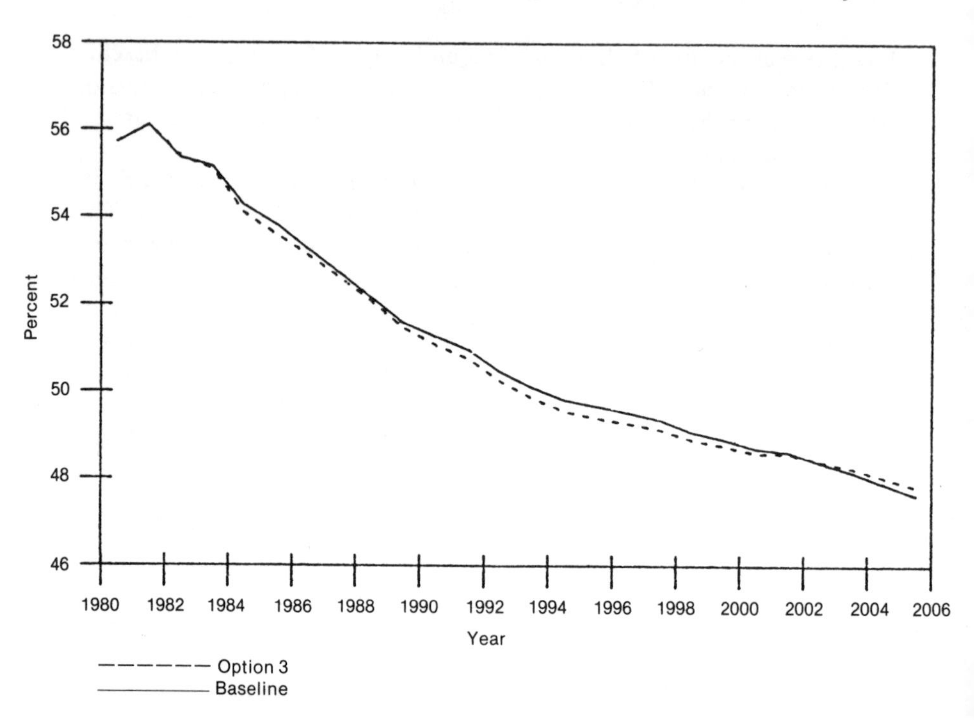

Figure 6-8. Average Elderly Income as a Percentage of Nonelderly Income: Option 3 Compared with Baseline

Table 6-4 shows gains in mean income by age/status groups. Gains are slow in coming to all groups. Reflecting the assumption that all new saving is done by those under 65, ultimate gains are somewhat smaller for the 72-and-over age groups.

Income Adequacy and Distribution

Gains in income adequacy are small and inconclusive in this option.

Table 6-3
Total Income Received by Elderly Families and Singles, and Percentage of All Income: Option 3
(billions of 1980 dollars)

	1980	*1985*	*1990*	*1995*	*2000*	*2005*
Income	198.1	226.8	259.5	284.9	303	323.8
Percentage share of total income	11.6	11.1	10.8	10.5	10.1	9.6
Difference from baseline	0	−1.2	−0.4	−0.7	1.2	5.2

Income-distribution changes are very small. Table 6-5 shows the percent of each age/status group with inadequate income in option 3 and the baseline. This table shows changes in both directions in 1990. By 2005, adequacy percentages are smaller than in the baseline for all groups but one. The size of these changes, however, is too small to be significant, so no conclusive evidence exists of any substantial effect on adequacy. In other words, the poorest elderly do not appear to share fully in the eventual income gains shown in figure 6-7 and table 6-4.

Table 6-6 presents percentage income distributions in option 3 and their relation to the baseline. Differences are again very small, although the table does show an eventual tendency for the distributions to slide upward from the lower-income classes to the higher-income classes, reflecting the income growth that occurs in the later years of the simulation.

Table 6-4
Average Income of Elderly Families and Singles, by Age Group: Option 3
(real 1980 dollars)

Age Group	*1980*	*1985*	*1990*	*1995*	*2000*	*2005*
Men						
65 to 71	8,369	8,646	9,066	9,365	9,846	10,302
72 and over	7,454	7,698	8,065	8,339	8,776	9,192
All elderly	7,850	8,116	8,512	8,800	9,258	9,693
Women						
65 to 71	7,297	7,601	7,981	8,271	8,735	9,178
72 and over	6,255	6,460	6,897	7.402	8,031	8,652
All elderly	6,658	6,897	7,307	7,728	8,293	8,849
Families						
65 to 71	18,019	18,933	18,923	20,621	21,676	22,720
72 and over	14,984	15,776	16,600	17,189	18,158	19,065
All elderly	16,608	17,484	18,417	19,079	20,094	21,079
		Difference from Baseline				
Men						
65 to 71	0	−51	−12	−4	65	208
72 and over	0	−56	−36	−35	26	150
All elderly	0	−54	−25	−21	44	176
Women						
65 to 71	0	−45	−8	−4	59	180
72 and over	0	−3	12	10	50	125
All elderly	0	−19	5	4	53	145
Families						
65 to 71	0	−100	−3	−17	127	449
72 and over	0	−102	−75	−125	−27	191
All elderly	0	−101	−36	−65	58	333

Table 6-5
Elderly with Inadequate Income and Change from Baseline, by Family Status and Age: Option 3
(percentage)

Age/Status Groups	Elderly with Inadequate Income 1979	Elderly with Inadequate Income 1990	Elderly with Inadequate Income 2005	Change from Baseline 1990	Change from Baseline 2005
Individuals					
Men, 65-71	46.6	42.1	35.7	0	−0.7
Women, 65-71	49.6	45.8	38.1	0	−0.7
Men, 72 and over	49.8	46.7	38.6	0.1	−0.7
Women, 72 and over	59	51.9	37.5	−0.2	−0.6
All elderly individuals	53.7	48.6	37.6	−0.1	−0.7
Families					
Head, 65-71	29.1	24.3	18.3	0.2	−0.3
Head, 72 and over	41.4	35.9	28.5	0.4	0
All elderly families	34.8	29.6	22.9	0.3	−0.1

Table 6-6
Numbers and Income Distributions for Families and Singles Aged 65 and over: Option 3
(percentage within real 1980 income classes)

	Families of Two or More 1980	Families of Two or More 1990	Families of Two or More 2005	Singles 1980	Singles 1990	Singles 2005
Income Distribution						
$0 to $2,500	0.13	0	0	7.51	2.36	0.07
$2,500 to $5,000	7.25	3.03	0.20	43.77	43.92	31.13
$5,000 to $7,500	15.72	13.45	8.30	21.85	23.41	28.75
$7,500 to $10,000	15.31	15.22	14.14	10.68	11.59	14.76
$10,000 to $20,000	36.58	39.13	42.05	12.33	14	18.69
$20,000 and over	25	29.17	35.32	3.86	4.72	6.60
Difference from baseline						
$0 to $2,500	0	0	0	0	0.03	−0.02
$2,500 to $5,000	0	0.10	−0.06	0	−0.19	−0.98
$5,000 to $7,500	0	0.14	−0.20	0	0.07	0.21
$7,500 to $10,000	0	0.02	−0.10	0	0.05	0.21
$10,000 to $20,000	0	−0.15	−0.25	0	0.06	0.33
$20,000 and over	0	−0.10	0.61	0	−0.02	0.25
Number (thousands)	8,632.53	10,036.23	10,656.41	7,912.37	9,901.90	11,016.90

Notes

1. This assumption does not contradict the economic axiom that *total* saving equals *total* investment. Personal saving is only one of many forms of saving (for example, corporate saving and government saving, or dissaving). Similarly, total investment includes foreign investment and investment in nonfixed assets as well as domestic fixed investment. The increased personal saving leads to an increase in government dissaving and in investment other than domestic fixed investment. The identity between total saving and total investment still holds.

2. The values in figure 6-6 are the cumulative total of the direct new additions to wealth. In other words, each year's value is (1) the previous year's new wealth, plus (2) that year's additional saving, plus (3) the amount assumed saved out of the interest from the previous year's wealth (that is, the new-saving rate times the new-interest income). The interest rate used for this calculation is a simple average of three rates that DRI projects: (1) the average rate paid by mutual savings banks, (2) the effective rate paid by insured savings and loans, and (3) the commercial-bank rate on savings and consumer-type time deposits.

3. In other words, the approximate 2 percent increase in the rate of personal saving will decrease the consumption of those under 65 relative to those over 65. This should not be thought of as making the young worse off than they were in the baseline, since the new saving is presumably done voluntarily, but it does shift the pattern of consumption more toward those goods and services consumed relatively intensively by the elderly.

7 Option 4: Investment-Oriented Tax Cuts

This simulation examines the effect of corporate-tax cuts, beginning in 1981, aimed at increasing investment and growth. Economic growth is increased and inflation is reduced after a lag of one to two years. In the absence of new transfer initiatives, the elderly gain less from the economic improvements that flow from this investment than do younger age groups, and this is especially true for the poorest and oldest among the elderly.

The corporate-tax cuts include an increased investment-tax credit and liberalized depreciation rules. The investment-tax credit is raised to a statutory rate of 18 percent from 10 percent. The average allowable depreciation-tax lifetimes for equipment and structures are reduced to 5.6 years and 17.3 years respectively, from 8.1 and 19.8 in the baseline.[1]

The effective tax rate on corporate income is eventually reduced by close to 40 percent in this simulation. Because the effect of liberalized depreciation schedules tends to build over time, the full effects of the cut are not experienced until 1986. Reductions in corporate-tax liabilities, inclusive of all indirect effects, build from $12 billion in 1981 to $20 billion in 1983 to $46 billion in 1986 (1980 dollars).

Corporate-tax cuts have been proposed by some policymakers as a means of promoting investment and consequently raising productivity and economic growth. The elderly tend to suffer from slow growth because it both reduces the value of their retirement assets and the younger population is more willing to address the needs of the elderly when the economic "pie" is growing rapidly. Also, evidence exists to show that the elderly bear a disproportionate burden of inflation. This simulation helps to illustrate whether one policy that has been suggested for increasing economic growth and reducing inflation appears to help the economy and its elderly.

Corporate-tax cuts of the type considered here have a double-barreled effect. They directly affect the incentive to invest, and they also increase the corporate cash flow—the major source of finance for business investment. Economists sometimes dispute the amount by which investment can be expected to be increased. The DRI macroeconomic model projects that corporate-tax cuts of this magnitude would lift the share of GNP devoted to business fixed investment by about 1 percentage point.

This tax cut would need to be financed, of course. The cut is assumed to be one-half offset by reduced government spending in the form of lower grants-in-aid to state and local units and by lower federal final purchases of goods and services. The other half of the tax cut is assumed to be translated, at least initially, into a larger federal deficit.

This simulation's corporate-tax cuts lead to the following changes from the baseline:

Cuts in corporate-tax liabilities grow steadily to one-third by 1986.

Real GNP rises 4.2 percent above the baseline by 2005, with consumption up 2.6 percent and business fixed investment up 15.7 percent, with no appreciable fiscal dividend.

Inflation is reduced by an average 0.3 percentage points per year.

The absolute income of the elderly increases.

The relative income of the elderly declines despite this increase as younger groups gain even more.

The percentage of the elderly with inadequate income is essentially unchanged.

Income distributions among the elderly are affected only slightly.

Macroeconomic Effects

Option 4 significantly enlarges the total size of the economic pie. The difference between real GNP and its baseline value grows steadily throughout the simulation period. Additional growth in investment accounts for most of the difference, although housing is depressed slightly in the short run. The federal government's fiscal dividend never materializes because the magnitude of the tax cuts is so large.

The short-run costs of this option are small. From 1980 to 1985, the wholesale price index is 0.2 of a percentage point higher than in the baseline, but the CPI and the implicit GNP price deflator are virtually unchanged. This short-run inflationary impact is so small mainly because during the period 1980-1985, unemployment averages 7.1 percent. If the investment boom were imposed on an overheated economy, the inflationary consequences would be severe.

The simulation indicates that short-run costs are borne by the housing sector due to the "crowding-out" effect caused by the increased capital demands of the business sector. However, housing also benefits from the increased income of the economy as a whole. Even in the worst year, this simulation shows only 40,000 fewer housing starts than the baseline (a 2 percent decline).

Beyond 1985, as the long-run benefits of the tax cut become dominant, the economy's growth prospects become noticeably improved. The difference between potential GNP and its baseline value grows steadily so that by 2005 it is increased by 4.3 percent. Thus, close to 0.2 percent per year is added to the economy's potential growth rate. Note that this increase in potential is about half as great again as the increase that results from option 3, in part because option 4 provides positive, targeted incentives to increase investment, whereas option 3 merely loosens some financial constraints.

This increased potential is shown to lead to greater growth in productivity, which reduces costs per unit of output and therefore inflation. Thus, from 1986 onward the rate of inflation is lower than in the baseline, with the average annual decrease for the entire 1980-2005 period being 0.3 percentage points per year. Some price is paid for this improvement, however. From 1985 to 1997, the supply-side effects of increases in the capital stock exceed the demand-side effects of increases in investment. As a consequence, the rate of unemployment is marginally increased by about 0.1 percentage points on average.

Like potential GNP, the simulation indicates that actual real GNP grows faster than in the baseline throughout the simulation period so that by 2005 it stands 4.2 percent above its baseline value (see figure 7-1). The increase in demand components is far from even. In 2005, total investment is higher by 13.2 percent, accounting for almost half of the increase in real GNP. Business fixed investment is 15.7 percent higher, growing at an average annual rate of 3.7 percent, compared with 3.1 percent in the baseline. After experiencing some crowding out in the short run, housing eventually responds to the higher real income of this option. From 1990 to 2005, total housing starts are about 2 million units above their baseline value.

Private consumption is shown to grow by an average of 2.5 percent in option 4, compared with 2.4 percent in the baseline (see table 7-1). Consequently, by 2005 consumption is 2.6 percent higher. This growth is fairly uniform across categories, although ultimately durables, which have a greater discretionary element, fare somewhat better than other components. By 2005, durable consumption is 3.3 percent above the baseline, while consumption of services is raised by only 2.2 percent. From the point of view of total spending, on the one hand, consumers do noticeably better under this option than under option 3—not surprising since no direct cutback in consumption is involved. In terms of asset accumulation, on the other hand, consumers fare less well than under option 3. Real household net worth by 2005 is raised by only 2.9 percent, compared with 8.9 percent in option 3.

Despite the higher growth of the economy, no net federal fiscal dividend emerges (see figure 7-2). At no stage is the flow of increased tax receipts from the extra growth sufficient to permit the federal government to increase its spending without causing the deficit to increase beyond its baseline values. The principal reason for this result is the corporate-tax cut

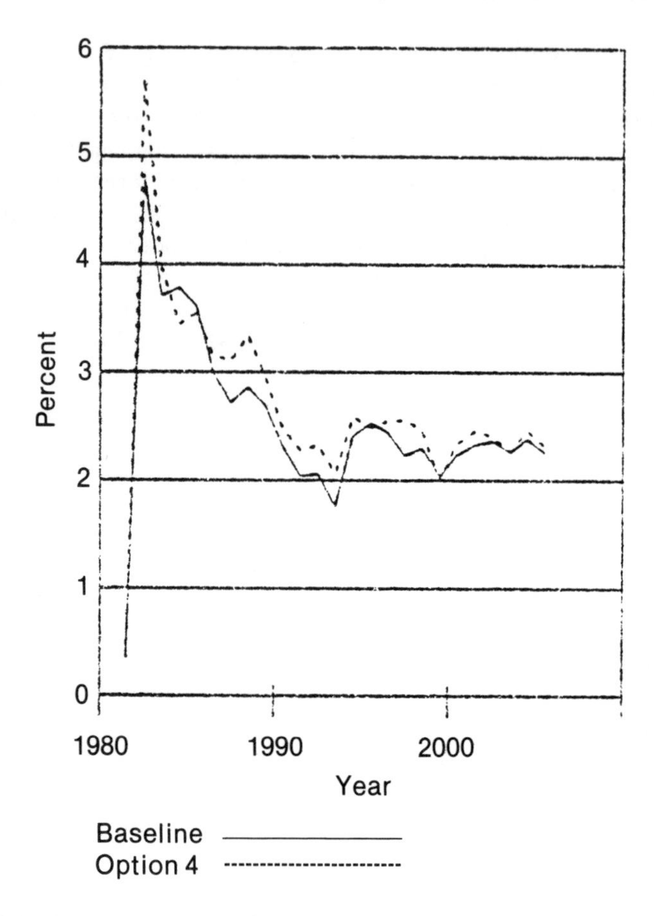

Figure 7-1. Percentage Rate of Increase in Real GNP: Option 4 Compared with Baseline

itself. The ever-increasing flow of investment qualifying for the greater tax credit and liberalized depreciation allowances means that the corporate-tax cut increases steadily to about 40 percent by 2005 (see figure 7-3). Of course, this increase could be offset by some reversal of the original measures but only at the cost of losing some of the increased growth.

The absence of any fiscal dividend means that those components of federal spending that were held down initially to finance the tax cut remain permanently below their baseline paths. Nonmilitary federal government final purchases and grants-in-aid to state and local governmental units are reduced by 1 percent in 1981, 2.7 percent in 1983, and 3.3 percent in 1985 and thereafter. Transfers are maintained close to their baseline values. The

Table 7-1
Macroeconomic Effects of Option 4
(averages over entire simulation period)

Effects	*Baseline 1981-2005*	*Option 4 1981-2005*
Average annual growth rates		
GNP	2.5	2.7
Consumption	2.4	2.5
Investment	3.1	3.6
Government spending	2.1	2.1
Disposable income	2.4	2.5
Industrial production	3.6	3.9
Shares of output (percentage)		
Consumption	62.9	62.4
Investment	16.5	17.6
Government	20.8	20.2
Other economic aggregates		
CPI inflation	7.5	7.2
Unemployment	6.3	6.3
Share of personal Income in GNP (percentage)	81.9	81.7

tax burden (defined as the share of total taxes in GNP) is reduced from an average of 34.1 percent in the baseline to 33 percent, though almost all of this reduction is accounted for by the corporate-tax cut itself. Corporate taxes are reduced from 3 percent of GNP to 2.1 percent.

State and local government units are initially hurt by the cut in federal grants-in-aid to them, though this reduction is quickly offset by the increased flow of tax receipts accruing from the larger economy. By 1990, real state and local spending is 0.8 percent above its baseline level. This difference expands to 1.6 percent by 2000 and 1.8 percent by 2005.

The simulation shows that neither employment nor unemployment is altered significantly from the baseline. The shift in output composition produces some changes in employment at the industry level. The stronger investment picture pushes employment in durable manufacturing up by 910,000 workers (6.8 percent in 2005). Total manufacturing employment is up by 1,060,000 workers (5.1 percent) in the same year. Employment in wholesale and retail trade, however, is down by 490,000 workers (1.7 percent).

Income shares in this option are affected only marginally, with the share of personal income in GNP being reduced from an average of 81.9 percent in the baseline to 81.7 percent. Because transfer payments are assumed not to benefit directly from the stronger economy, the share of transfers in per-

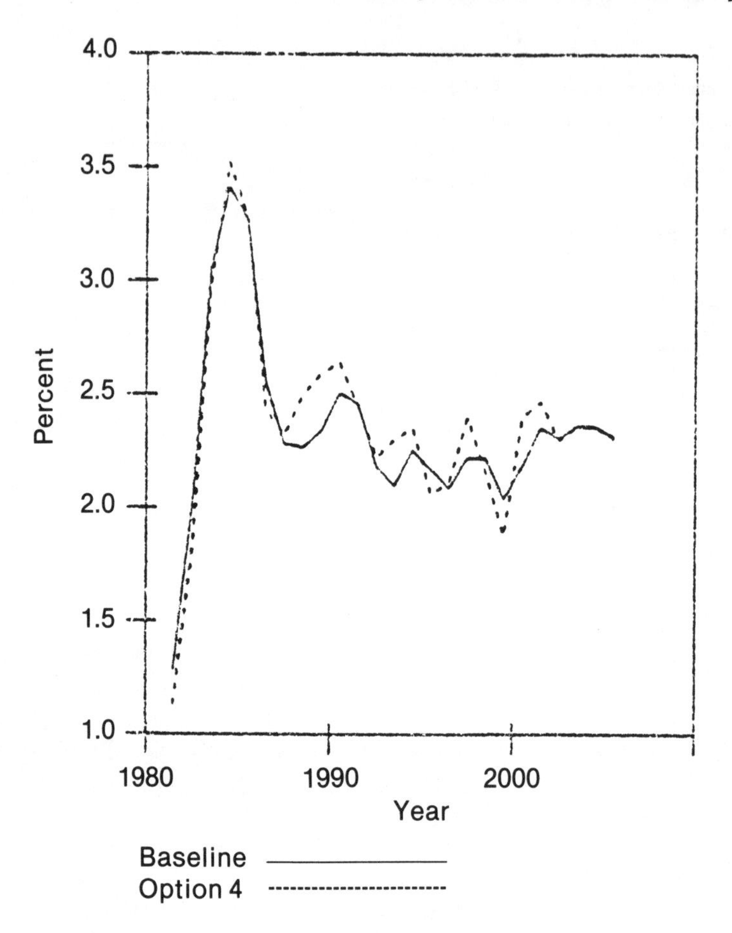

Figure 7-2. Percentage Rate of Increase in Real Government Spending: Option 4 Compared with Baseline

sonal income falls somewhat from its baseline level, from an average of 14.8 percent to 14.5 percent. Dividend recipients benefit marginally from the better corporate cash-flow position in this option, while interest income as a proportion of personal income increases initially in response to higher rates, and then returns to its former share. In real terms, the sum of transfers, interest income, and dividends, highly important income categories for the elderly, is eventually raised by 1.9 percent by 2005, compared with a 4.2 percent total increase in GNP.

The balance-of-payments outcome is close to neutral (see table 7-2). The

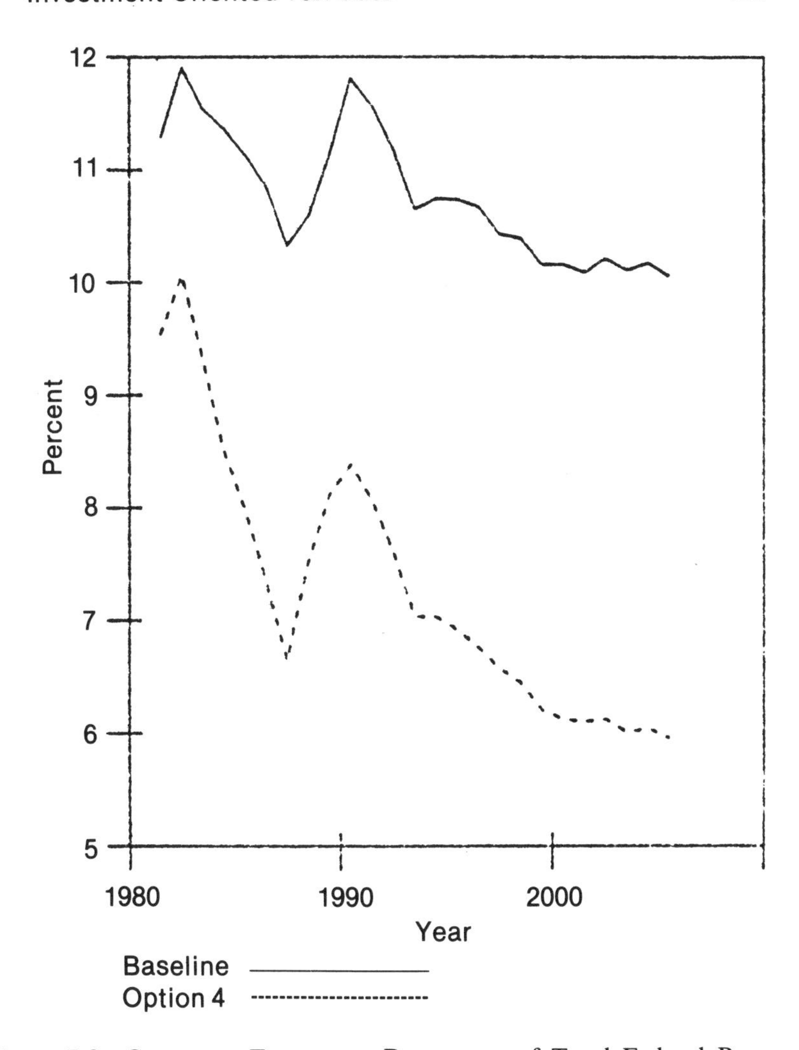

Figure 7-3. Corporate Taxes as a Percentage of Total Federal Revenue: Option 4 Compared with Baseline

improvement in inflation enhances the U.S. competitive position, but this is largely offset by the extra import demands of the larger economy. Oil imports in particular are increased substantially. The higher investment path also significantly raises imports of capital equipment, already one of the fastest growing import categories. Overall, the exchange rate is improved by 2.6 percent in 2005.

Table 7-2
Capsule Summary of Option 4

	Option 4					*Difference from Baseline*				
Parameters	*1980-1985*	*1985-1990*	*1990-1995*	*1995-2000*	*2000-2005*	*1980-1985*	*1985-1990*	*1990-1995*	*1995-2000*	*2000-2005*
Composition of real GNP (average annual rates of change)										
GNP	3.4	3	2.4	2.4	2.4	0.2	0.3	0.2	0.1	0.1
Final sales	3.2	3	2.4	2.4	2.4	0.2	0.3	0.2	0.1	0.1
Total consumption	2.9	2.9	2.5	2.2	2.2	0	0.2	0.2	0.1	0
Nonresidential fixed investment	5.3	3.9	2.5	3.7	3.2	2.2	0.4	−0.1	0.3	0.3
Equipment	6.8	4.3	3.1	4.2	3.6	2.6	0.6	−0.2	0.3	0.2
Nonresidential construction	2	2.8	0.9	2	1.8	1.2	−0.3	−0.2	0	0.5
Residential fixed investment	8.5	2.2	−1.4	0.3	1.9	−0.4	0.8	0.8	−0.1	−0.5
Exports	3.4	4.8	4.2	4.5	4.4	−0.3	0.6	0.5	0.3	0.2
Imports	3.7	3.3	3.8	4	4	0.3	0	0.1	0.3	0.2
Federal government	3.2	2.6	1.8	1.8	1.7	−0.4	0	0	0	0
State and local government	1.8	2.3	2	1.8	2	0	0.1	0.1	0.1	0
Shares of nominal GNP (percentage)										
Consumption	63.8	62.2	62.1	62.2	61.9	−0.3	−0.5	−0.6	−0.4	−0.3
Business investment	11.1	12	12.1	12.4	12.9	0.8	1.2	1.1	1	1.2
Residential construction	4.9	5.2	4.8	4.5	4.5	0	0	0.1	0.1	0
Government purchases	20.2	20	20.2	20.2	20.1	−0.3	−0.6	−0.8	−0.8	−0.8
Prices and wages (average annual rates of change)										
Implicit price deflator	8.5	7.5	6.1	5.4	5.4	0	−0.3	−0.5	−0.5	−0.4
CPI all urban consumers	8.6	7.8	6.9	6.4	6.4	0	−0.3	−0.4	−0.4	−0.3
Wholesale price index	10.5	9.1	6.9	6.1	6.4	0.2	−0.2	−0.5	−0.5	−0.4
Compensation per hour	10.1	9.2	8	7.3	7.1	0.1	−0.2	−0.4	−0.4	−0.3

Production and other key measures										
Industrial production (average percentage change)	5.2	3.9	3	3.6	3.6	0.5	0.4	0.2	0.3	0.2
Housing starts (million units)	2	2.2	2.1	2	2	0	0	0.1	0.2	0.1
Retail car sales (million units)	11	11.6	11.8	12.3	12.5	0.1	0.2	0.4	0.5	0.5
Unemployment rate (percentage)	7.3	6.2	6.4	5.9	5.9	−0.1	0.2	0.1	0	0
Federal budget surplus (National Income Accounts	−51	−27.2	−41.5	−65	−122	−8.1	11.9	−0.8	4.9	−1.1
Money and interest rates										
Money supply (M1-B) (average percentage change)	8.3	8.3	7.2	6.2	5.6	0	0	−0.1	−0.1	−0.1
New AA corporate utility rate (percentage)	12	10.9	9.8	8.8	8.6	0.2	−0.2	−0.4	−0.3	−0.2
New high-grade corporate bond rate (percentage)	11.5	10.5	9.4	8.5	8.3	0.2	−0.2	−0.4	−0.3	−0.2
Federal funds rate (percentage)	10.2	9	7.4	6.7	7	−0.1	−0.3	−0.6	−0.5	−0.3
Prime rate (percentage)	11.1	10.2	8.5	7.9	8.3	−0.1	−0.4	−0.8	−0.7	−0.3

Effects on Income and Its Distribution

Following a short lull, the elderly appear to enjoy increased income in this option as compared with the baseline. This difference grows throughout the simulation horizon. Gains are less rapid for the elderly than the nonelderly, however, and those elderly with the lowest income gain little from the increased economic growth.

Real and Relative Income

Figure 7-4 shows the real-income gains in option 4, as compared with the baseline, for both the elderly and nonelderly populations. The mean income of the elderly is moderately less than in the baseline from 1981-1983 because the simulation shows that macroeconomic effect of the newly induced in-

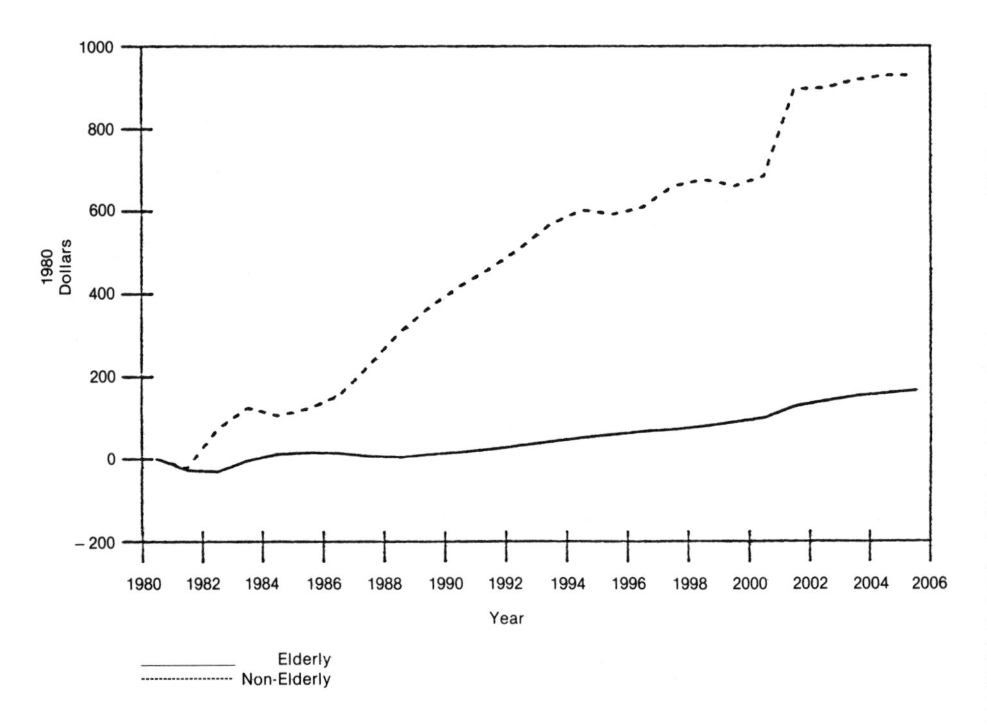

Figure 7-4. Increase in Average Elderly and Nonelderly Income: Option 4 minus Baseline

vestment is initially somewhat negative. Starting in 1984, however, the elderly do somewhat better in this option because the increased growth and improved functioning of the economy elevate real yields on assets and real wage and salary earnings.

Over the entire projection period, the average income of those over 65 grows at about a 0.87 percent annual rate, up .05 percentage points from the baseline. By 2005, this improvement raises this group's average income by about $170 (1980 dollars) higher than in the baseline (an increase of about 1.1 percent).

Younger age groups achieve larger increases than the elderly in this simulation. Real-income growth for those under age 65 averages 1.6 percent annually in option 4 (up 0.12 percentage points from the baseline). By 2005, the averge income for all those under 65 is increased by about $930 (1980 dollars) over the baseline (a rise of about 2.9 percent). This higher growth for the nonelderly shows up both as the steeper increases shown in figure 7-4 and as a decline in the relative-income position of the elderly shown in figure 7-5. Basically, this difference reflects the different rates at which the increased growth benefits older and younger groups. In the absence of any new transfers, economic growth has its greatest impact on those who most fully share in the functioning of the economy—asset holders and (especially) wage earners. The large transfer share of the elderly's income is relatively unaffected by growth. Also, the full CPI indexing of social security tends to insulate the income of the elderly from real gains attained by higher growth and lower inflation.

The latter point may be overstated in the results shown here since we have, of necessity, employed the same price deflator (the NIA implicit deflator for personal-consumption expenditures) to convert each group's income from nominal to real. The elderly consume somewhat different bundles of goods and services than the young (with heavier concentration in food, fuel, and health care), so the true difference in their relative income depends in part on how inflation in the bundle they consume differs from inflation in the bundle consumed by younger age groups. Such an analysis would, however, be very unlikely to change the qualitative result that the relative-income gains to younger groups exceed those to the elderly in this option.

Table 7-3 shows the total income received by the elderly and their share of aggregate income. This total reaches $322 billion (1980 dollars) by 2005 in option 4, an increase of nearly $4 billion over the baseline. Because younger groups experience more-rapid growth, the elder-income share declines more rapidly in this simulation than in the baseline.

Table 7-4 shows the average income levels in option 4 compared with

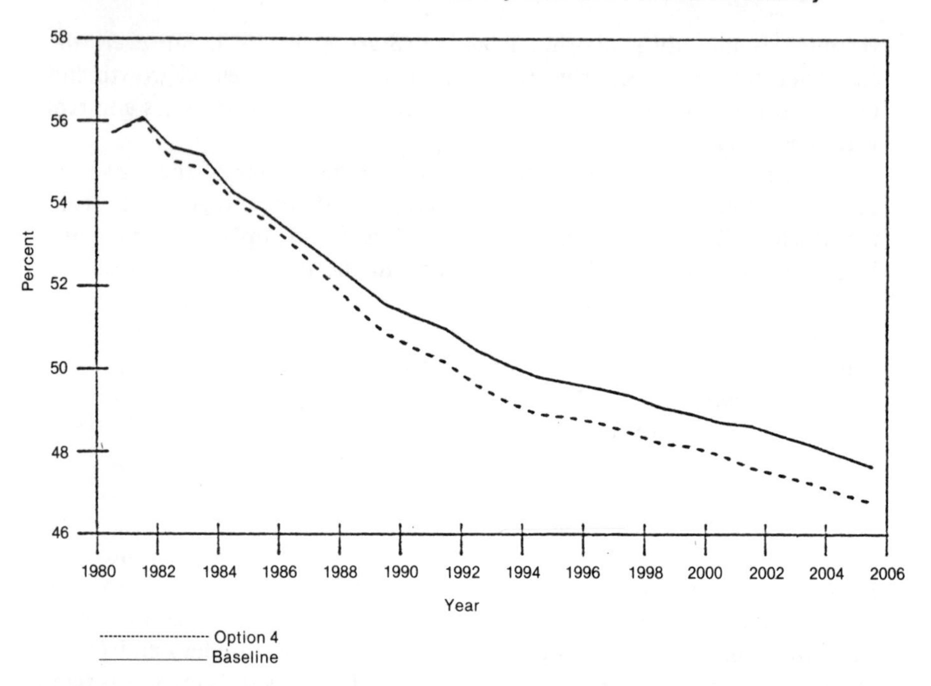

Figure 7-5. Average Elderly Income as a Percentage of Nonelderly Income: Option 4 Compared with Baseline

the baseline. Nearly all groups experience eventually higher average income, but real and percentage gains by 2005 are slightly larger among those groups that already have higher income. As an example, the oldest group of elderly women starts at the lowest level and gains the smallest amount ($30 by 2005, or about 0.4 percent more than in the baseline).

Table 7-3
Total Income Received by Elderly Families and Singles, and Percentage of All Income: Option 4
(billions of 1980 dollars)

	1980	*1985*	*1990*	*1995*	*2000*	*2005*
Income	198.1	228.3	260.2	286.9	303.9	322.2
Percentage share of total income	11.6	11.1	10.6	10.4	9.9	9.4
Difference from baseline	0	0.3	0.3	1.3	2.1	3.6

Income Adequacy and Distribution

The option 4 simulation leads to only minor changes in income distribution within groups of the elderly, but within each group, those at the lowest income levels appear to gain less than those at higher levels.

Table 7-5 shows the percentage with inadequate income in 1979, 1990, and 2005 in option 4 and relative to the baseline. Adequacy percentages are sometimes slightly larger than in the baseline, sometimes slightly smaller, without any clear pattern. Since the average income across all the elderly is increased, these data imply that those elderly below adequacy, on average,

Table 7-4
Average Income of Elderly Families and Singles, by Age Group: Option 4
(real 1980 dollars)

Age Group	*1980*	*1985*	*1990*	*1995*	*2000*	*2005*
Men						
65 to 71	8,369	8,697	9,061	9,371	9,820	10,209
72 and over	7,454	7,749	8,077	8,365	8,774	9,130
All elderly	7,850	8,166	8,516	8,817	9,245	9,618
Women						
65 to 71	7,297	7,645	7,978	8,280	8,704	9,076
72 and over	6,255	6,462	6,881	7,395	7,999	8,558
All elderly	6,658	6,915	7,296	7,727	8,262	8,751
Families						
65 to 71	18,019	19,092	20,004	20,795	21,781	22,640
72 and over	14,984	15,877	16,673	17,381	18,296	19,040
All elderly	16,608	17,617	18,495	19,261	20,214	21,024
			Difference from Baseline			
Men						
65 to 71	0	0	−17	2	39	116
72 and over	0	−5	−24	−10	23	88
All elderly	0	−3	−21	−4	31	101
Women						
65 to 71	0	−1	−11	4	28	78
72 and over	0	−1	−4	3	18	30
All elderly	0	−1	−7	4	22	48
Families						
65 to 71	0	60	79	158	232	369
72 and over	0	0	−2	67	111	166
All elderly	0	32	42	117	177	278

Table 7-5
Elderly with Inadequate Income and Change from Baseline, by Family Status and Age: Option 4
(percentage)

Age/Status Groups	*Elderly with Inadequate Income*			*Change from Baseline*	
	1979	*1990*	*2005*	*1990*	*2005*
Individuals					
Men, 65-71	44.6	42.1	36.2	0	−0.2
Women, 65-71	49.6	45.9	38.7	0.1	−0.1
Men, 72 and over	49.8	46.6	39.2	0	−0.1
Women, 72 and over	59	52.1	38.5	0	0.4
All elderly individuals	53.7	48.7	38.4	0	0.1
Families					
Head, 65-71	29.1	24.3	18.5	0.2	−0.1
Head, 72 and over	41.4	35.8	28.6	0.3	0.1
All elderly families	34.8	29.5	23	0.2	0

enjoy relatively little of the added growth that the new investment generates.

Table 7-6 reinforces the evidence from the income-adequacy table. As the simulation ages toward 2005, the essential movement is upward, lifting families and singles toward higher-than-baseline income levels. In general, however, the percentage of the elderly in the bottom two income classes

Table 7-6
Numbers and Income Distributions for Families and Singles Aged 65 and over: Option 4
(percentage within real 1980 income classes)

	Families of Two or More			*Singles*		
	1980	*1990*	*2005*	*1980*	*1990*	*2005*
Income Distribution						
$0 to $2,500	0.13	0	0	7.51	2.66	0.09
$2,500 to $5,000	7.25	3.20	0.34	43.77	43.65	32.40
$5,000 to $7,500	15.72	13.41	8.67	21.85	23.34	28.07
$7,500 to $10,000	15.31	15.07	14	10.68	11.60	14.48
$10,000 to $20,000	36.58	38.92	41.63	12.33	14.03	18.44
$20,000 and over	25	29.40	35.36	3.86	4.71	6.52
Difference from baseline						
$0 to $2,500	0	0	0	0	0.34	0
$2,500 to $5,000	0	0.27	0.08	0	−0.46	0.29
$5,000 to $7,500	0	0.09	0.17	0	0	−0.47
$7,500 to $10,000	0	−0.13	−0.24	0	0.06	−0.08
$10,000 to $20,000	0	−0.36	−0.67	0	0.09	0.08
$20,000 and over	0	0.13	0.66	0	−0.03	0.17
Number (thousands)	8,632.53	10,036.23	10,656.41	7,912.37	9,901.90	11,016.90

does not shrink. Thus, here again, the poorest groups are shown not to have fully shared in the additional growth.

Note

1. By comparison, the Reagan administration's economic program calls for average tax lifetimes of 4.7 years for equipment and 12.4 years for structures. The Senate Finance Committee seeks lifetimes of 6.2 years and 16.4 years, respectively. The administration program also envisions a small liberalization in the investment-tax credit, while the Senate Finance Committee program proposes no such liberalization.

Editor's Note

By comparison, the Reagan proposals presented in the March 10, 1981, June 10, 1981, budget revisions call for reducing average effective investment lifetimes for structures and equipment to 14.3 and 4.3 years respectively.

Although the Reagan proposals would leave unchanged the statutory rate for the investment tax credit, the new equipment lifetime categories that the depreciation reform would create would also increase the average effective tax credit for equipment. As of July 10, 1981, these proposals are still under consideration by Congress.

8 Conclusions and Policy Implications

This chapter compares the simulated options with one another and with the baseline, reviews possible combinations of the options, and discusses their implications for the period beyond 2005.

All the options eventually provide some additional real income to the elderly, although the greatest gains occur in options 1 and 2, which are explicitly directed toward the elderly. Only option 2 among those simulated provides a really effective method of addressing the problem of income adequacy for the elderly. Without additional transfers to the elderly, any of the other options ignores the current problems of many of the poorest and oldest among this group. Various combinations of the options are possible, however, and combining them may yield the best mix of benefits for both the economy and the elderly.

Comparison of the Baseline and the Four Policy Options

The four policy options we have examined involve the following factors:

A gradual increase in the labor-force-participation rates of elderly and near-elderly men and women to the rates prevailing in 1970; the baseline simulation projects continued declines in participation by these groups.

An income guarantee for the elderly at the BLS Intermediate Budget Level; the baseline assumes no new transfer initiatives.

An approximately 2 percent rise in the rate of personal saving, with all the additional saving assumed done by those under age 65; the baseline projects a continuation of recent, historically low rates.

Corporate-tax cuts aimed at increasing investment and growth and reducing inflation; the baseline assumes personal-tax cuts every other year to reduce inflation bracket creep, but it assumes only a small $7 billion corporate-tax reduction in 1981.

The options differ in their structure, their macroeconomic effects, and their effects on younger and older Americans. Options 1 and 2 focus on the elderly—option 1 by increasing their ability to provide for themselves and option 2 by guaranteeing all elderly an adequate income. Options 3 and 4 respond to often-voiced suggestions for improving the overall functioning of the economy—option 3 by changing consumer behavior to provide money for investment and retirement financing and option 4 by fostering growth and productivity.

Figures 8-1 through 8-3 summarize the macroeconomic effects of the four options by showing their effects on GNP, inflation, and government expenditures on goods and services. Option 2 is shown to have no signifi-

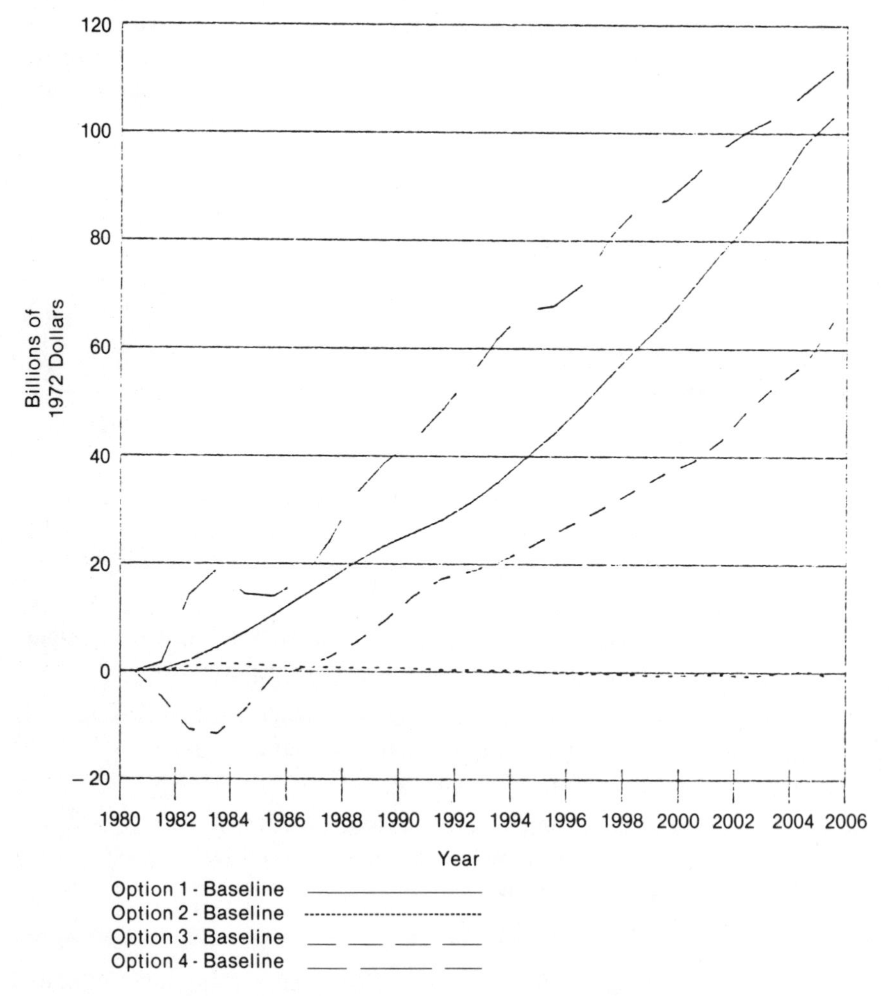

Figure 8-1. Real GNP: Options minus Baseline

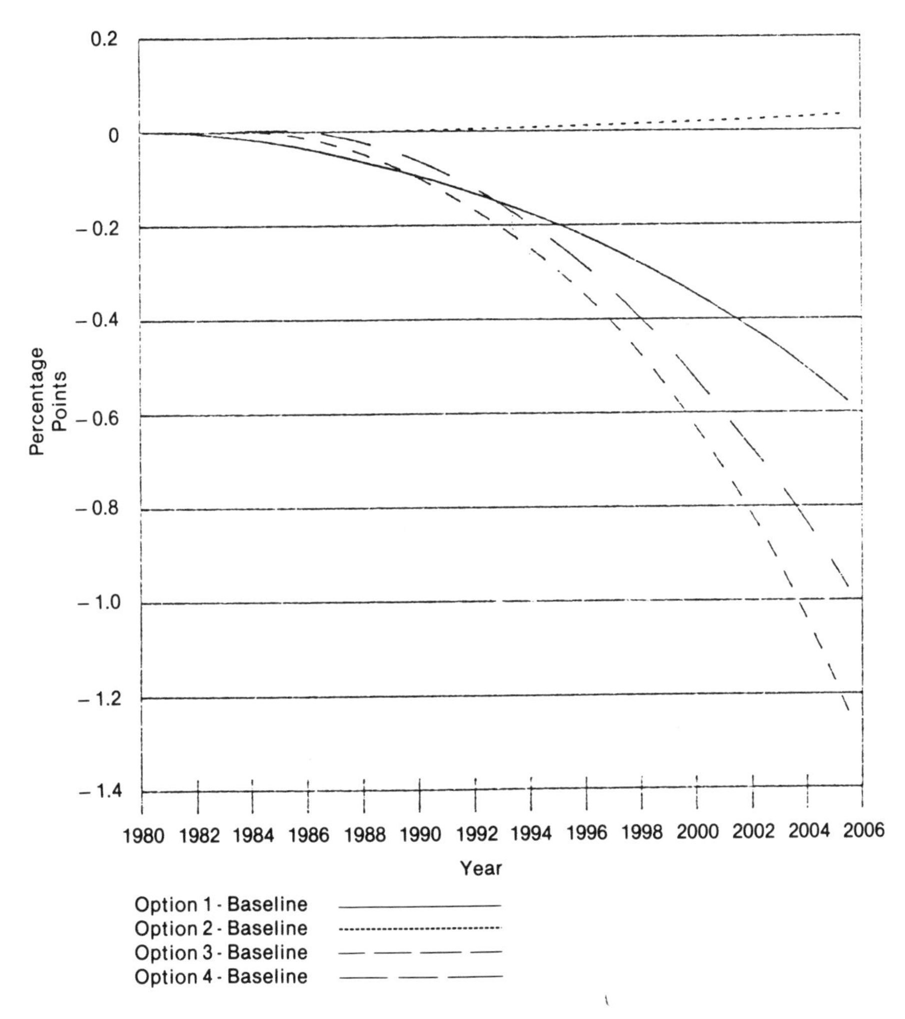

Figure 8-2. CPI: Options minus Baseline

cant effects on economic growth, inflation, or federal government expenditures because it is essentially a redistributive program. It does have an impact on the personal-tax burden, however, by increasing taxes by about $70 per capita. This impact falls over time, however, because the BLS Intermediate Budget Level is an absolute standard, and continued growth in real income raises more of the elderly above the standard.

Options 1 and 4 are shown to have the largest long-run impacts on economic growth because they increase the availability of productive factors quickly and directly, without creating disincentives to factor utilization. By

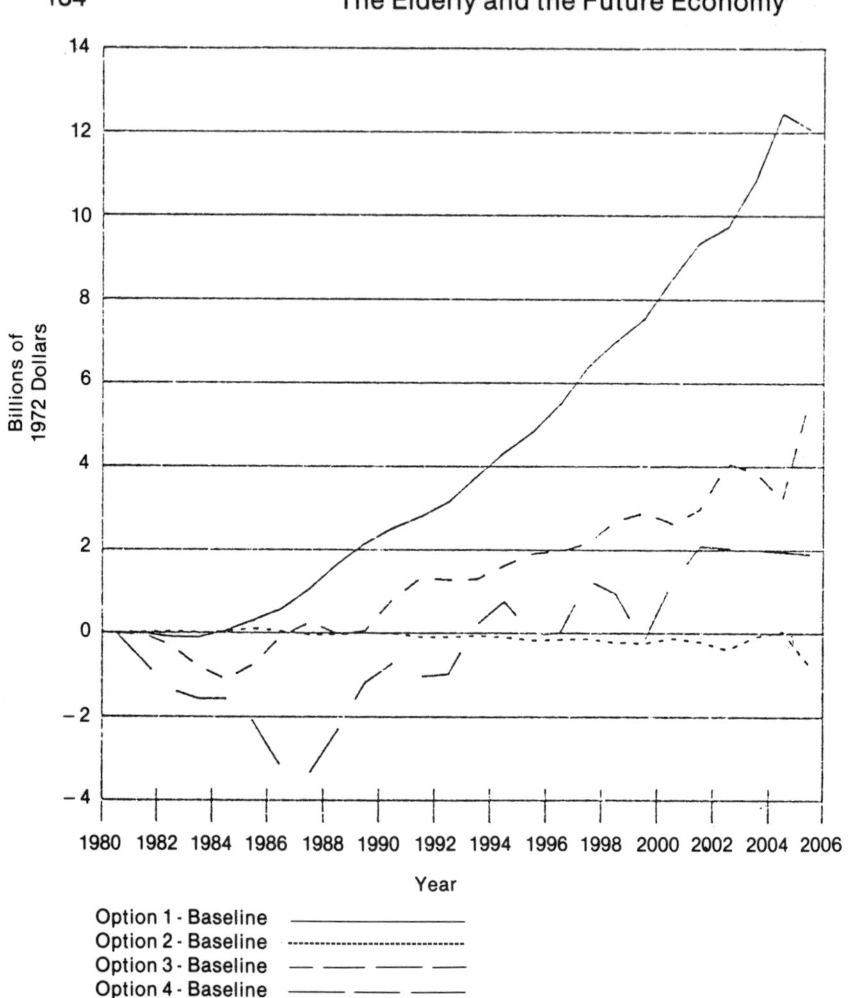

Figure 8-3. Real Government Spending: Options minus Baseline

contrast, option 3 enhances factor availability slowly and indirectly, in the process reducing incentives to employ fully those increases in productive capacity that do occur. Only 75 percent of the additional saving in option 3 is channeled into fixed investment. Furthermore, since the additional saving takes place at the expense of consumption, aggregate demand is reduced in the short run. Producers therefore have less incentive to press into service newly available labor and capital. Finally, because it takes time for the increased saving to translate into investment, the aggregate demand effect dominates the positive effects of this investment in the short turn, thus lowering the rate of economic growth below its baseline value. If federal tax incentives induced more of the increased saving, this short-run effect would be somewhat ameliorated.

Inflation is shown to improve in options 1, 3, and 4 because all three options enhance aggregate supply. The decrease in inflation is relatively large in option 3 because of its initially lower levels of resource utilization. Higher productivity from a larger capital/labor ratio accounts for the relatively large long-run improvement in inflation in option 4.

Figure 8-3 shows that government expenditures on goods and services are higher in the long run in options 1 and 3 because the greater growth in the economy generates additional tax receipts that in turn lead to increased spending. The option 3 change is much less than that in option 1, however. These fiscal dividends of automatically increased government expenditures on goods and services could alternatively be used to finance some tax relief. In option 4, the corporate-tax cuts are financed in part out of decreased government expenditures. Thus, only because state and local governments eventually enjoy higher receipts do total real government expenditures on goods and services eventually exceed those in the baseline, and this difference is too small to be significant.

Figures 8-4 and 8-5 show the comparative effects of the options on real and relative income. Although the elderly enjoy some eventual benefit from all the options, their average real income is helped most by those options that serve them most directly (options 1 and 2). Options 1, 3, and 4, all provide long-term benefits to the nonelderly, while option 2 does little to the total money income of younger groups and moderately diminishes their disposable income (disposable income by age is not shown in our simulations), particularly in its early years. The benefits to the elderly of option 1 are larger on average than benefits that accrue to younger groups. Thus, the elderly gain relatively in options 1 and 2. Gains to the young exceed those to the elderly in options 3 and 4 although eventual relative gains are similar for the elderly and nonelderly in option 3.

Table 8-1 shows a similar pattern for the total income of the elderly. The absolute and relative share of total income accruing to the elderly is higher in options 1 and 2, but significant absolute gains also accrue eventually in options 3 and 4.

Percentages of the elderly receiving less than the adequacy standard are shown in table 8-2. Improvements are shown to occur in the baseline and all the options. The differences between the baseline and options 3 and 4 are so small that they contain only limited information. Therefore, the poor elderly do not appear to benefit significantly more than in the baseline from the real, average gains in options 3 and 4. Substantial adequacy gains accrue from option 1, but they benefit mainly the relatively few low-income elderly who are net accruals to the labor force. The rest of the low-income elderly

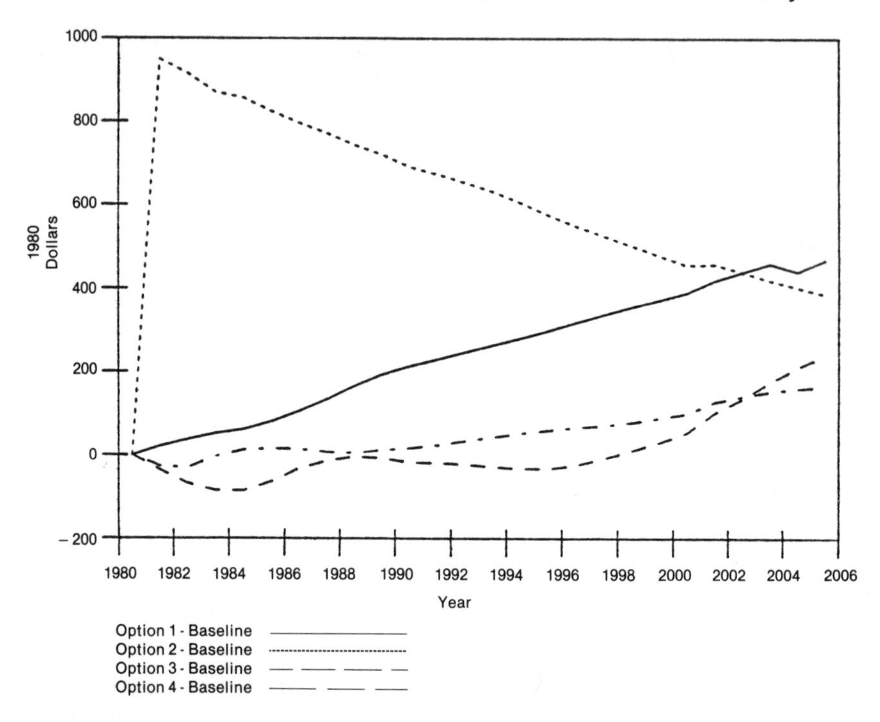

Note: Values shown are the difference between (1) average income of family/single units aged 65 and over in each option and (2) the identical concept in the baseline.

Figure 8-4. Average Elderly Income: Options minus Baseline

are helped little by this option, although the fiscal capacity for transfers to the recipient elderly is enhanced. In option 1, the net new labor-force members are concentrated among the younger and more-vigorous of the elderly. Therefore, although it is not obvious from table 7-2, adequacy gains are significantly larger for singles aged 65-71, for example, than for singles age 72 and over.

Thus, to the extent that new policy for the elderly aims to improve the income position of the poorest and oldest, a direct approach similar to that in option 2 is desirable. This result is not surprising. Transfer payments comprise the preponderant majority of the income of the lowest income elderly. In fact, it is precisely because they have little income from wages, assets, or pensions that many of the elderly find themselves in unenviable straits. Improvements in the economy, unaccompanied by new transfer initiatives, help these elderly relatively little. Greater enhancement of labor-force opportunities serves only those who can work. Thus, only focused transfers enable many of the poor elderly to share fully in economic growth.

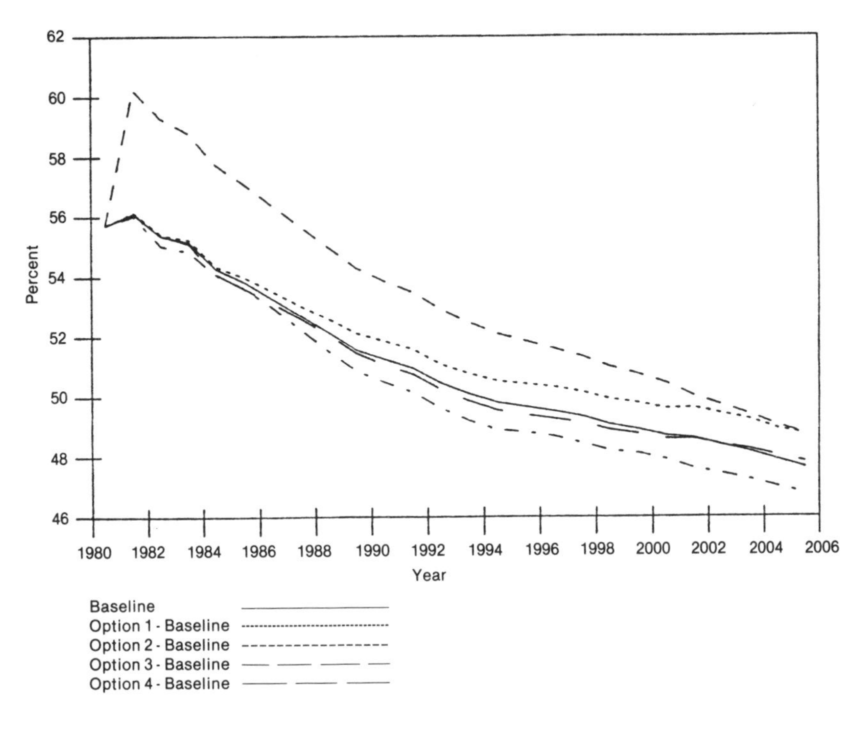

Figure 8-5. Average Elderly Income as a Percentage of Nonelderly Income: Baseline and All Options

Table 8-1
Total Income Received by Elderly Families and Singles, and Percentage of all Income: Baseline and All Options
(billions of 1980 dollars)

	1980	*1985*	*1990*	*1995*	*200*	*2005*
Income						
Baseline	198.06	227.97	259.87	285.64	301.79	318.59
Option 1	198.06	229.44	264.12	291.92	310.10	328.74
Option 2	198.06	243.01	273.66	297.75	311.49	326.95
Option 3	198.06	226.79	259.50	284.95	302.96	323.80
Option 4	198.06	228.06	260.20	286.90	303.92	322.19
Percentage Share of Total Income						
Baseline	11.63	11.13	10.79	10.55	10.07	9.56
Option 1	11.63	11.16	10.90	10.70	10.24	9.77
Option 2	11.63	11.73	11.27	10.97	10.39	9.77
Option 3	11.63	11.09	10.75	10.52	10.10	9.60
Option 4	11.63	11.09	10.64	10.39	9.92	9.41

Table 8-2
Elderly with Inadequate Income, by Family Status: Baseline and All Options
(percentage)

Status	*1979*	*1990*	*2005*
Individuals			
Baseline	53.7	48.7	38.3
Option 1	53.7	46.8	35.3
Option 2	53.7	0	0
Option 3	53.7	48.6	37.6
Option 4	53.7	48.7	38.4
Families			
Baseline	34.8	29.3	23
Option 1	34.8	28.7	22
Option 2	34.8	0	0
Option 3	34.8	29.6	22.9
Option 4	34.8	29.5	23

Note: Adequate income is defined for elderly families by the BLS Intermediate Budget Level for a Retired Couple ($8,562 in 1979) adjusted for inflation; for elderly single individuals, by an analogously defined budget for retired individuals ($4,941 in 1979).

Speculation on the Outlook beyond 2005

Speculation beyond 2005 must center on the most easily foreseeable changes in that period—changes in the population's age structure—and on the long-term effects of the options. The postwar-baby-boom "babies," currently ranging in age from about 21 to 34, will be aged about 45 to 53 in 2005 and will begin reaching age 65 around 2012. In just over thirty years, the United States will begin to experience a much increased elderly population, both in absolute numbers and relative to the total population and working-age groups. Such an increase can lead to difficulties between generations.

Faster economic growth will eventually provide a larger economic pie, one which, more easily divisible between the young and the old, could support transfer initiatives to aid the elderly. Of course, the faster economic growth resulting from increased participation by the elderly has particular appeal in this regard. Increased labor-force participation delays the transition from the working to the retired populations, creating salutary effects on both the potential costs of supporting the elderly and the ability of the economy to finance higher transfers.

With an extended horizon, the effects of the aging baby boom on the future economy and its retirees are more apparent. Option 1 has its largest positive effects in the period 2012 and beyond. Under its conditions, more elderly are working, and they are better off. In turn, the retirees and their transfers are fewer. Also, the better-functioning economy contributes to improved retirement and human capital as more skills are acquired over a longer average work life.

Under option 2, costs beyond 2005 will be further diminished by the salutary effects of continued growth on real income. Relatively fewer elderly will fall below the fixed adequacy standard. In absolute terms, however, the aging of the baby boom will greatly swell the total numbers of the elderly and increase the potential for transfers correspondingly.

In a sense, option 3 matures only beyond the 2005 horizon. Option 3's assumption that all additional saving is done by the young ensures that well over twenty-five years must elapse before the future elderly will have saved at the higher rate for most of their working years. When this transition is complete, however, the income accruing from the additional wealth that this new saving generates will become increasingly important for the elderly. (This new wealth totals about $550 billion (1980 dollars) by 2005 and continues to grow in subsequent years.) The new wealth is a resource for a higher standard of living for the elderly and for other purposes such as additional bequests. Large-scale dissaving by the baby-boom elderly could have major implications in the future for capital markets, but such dissaving may not occur unless other macroeconomic changes force this outcome.

The macroeconomic effects of option 3 also come to full flower only after a long period, and the near-term effects are decidedly negative. The highest additions to growth from this option occur in the last decade of the twenty-five-year period. Beyond 2005, the higher saving rate should lead to even more-substantial growth (unless the new wealth is dissaved in a major way). The growth-depressing Keynesian effect of the initially reduced consumption, so dramatic in the 1980s, ceases to be important in the twenty-first century. Beyond 2005, the rate of growth, level of consumption, and real household wealth will all be permanently higher than in the baseline.

Option 4 has both earlier and larger benefits than option 3, but these gains are less viable beyond the twenty-five-year horizon. The effect of option 4 on growth should eventually diminish because an increased capital stock requires a higher investment share just to replace the depreciating stock. This equilibrating effect, however, takes decades to complete, and when it does so the economy is permanently larger than in the baseline. This larger economy then provides greater potential for subsequent transfer initiatives in the twenty-first century. Perhaps new initiatives will be less pressing since more of the then elderly will have lived through periods with a better-functioning economy. Through these times, they will have had greater opportunities to save, to gain entitlement to pensions, and to improve their job skills—all positive factors that can augment their ability to finance more of their own retirement.

Combinations of the Options

None of the options has uniformly good effects, but each provides some improvement for some groups in some periods. Therefore, a combination of the options may provide a better mix of results for the elderly, the nonelderly, and the economy.

The effect of the options is neither strictly proportional (in the sense that a policy half as large would have half as big an effect) or strictly additive (in the sense that the effects of two options performed simultaneously would approximate the sum of their separate effects). Nonetheless, it is judicious to start with these simplifications and discuss where they might be inappropriate.

Consider a combination of options 1 and 2. Option 1 generates a substantial fiscal dividend that, in principle, could be used to pay part of the costs of the new transfers in option 2. Yet, a certain conflict exists between gains in labor supply by the elderly implied in option 1 and the likely disincentives toward market work caused by a guaranteed income (option 2).

It is not clear how important this work disincentive is because the low-income elderly, the main beneficiaries of option 2, now have very little wage and salary earnings. Clearly, the current retirees would receive an unanticipated benefit, while current workers, both young and old, would pay the lion's share for the poor retirees' gain. The adequacy guarantee seems to have only limited static repercussions, but its imposition may lead to greater dynamic losses as more and more young people plan for their retirement years in a world that guarantees them an adequate retirement income. The combination of options seeking to increase both the preelderly and elderly work effort and the retirees' income adequacy would have to be artfully integrated. For example, if the disincentive effect is shown to be important, it might be appropriate to increase work incentives over and above those that would otherwise accomplish the changes assumed in option 1. Alternatively, the policy in option 2 could be restructured to reduce its work disincentives—for example, by changing its implicit tax rate (below the guarantee) from 100 percent to some lower percentage, by reducing the level of the guarantee, or by raising the age at which the guarantee becomes effective. If the latter course were chosen, age 70 has some appeal both because there seems to be agreement that work disincentives for those over 70 are less worrisome than for younger ages and because the social-security-earnings test (which may act as a work disincentive) will apply to workers only up to age 69 starting in 1982. (The test currently applies up to age 71; see Gordon and Schoeplein 1979.)

It is interesting to compare the new transfers needed to raise all the elderly to adequacy in option 2 with the overall fiscal dividend (the increase in total government expenditures, all components at all levels, that results from the increased income) that occurs in option 1. Figure 8-6 presents this comparison. Real new transfers in option 2 decline, and the real fiscal dividend in option 1 grows so that, by 1997, the option 1 dividend exceeds the option 2 transfer cost. Continued rapid growth in the option 1 dividend raises it to over three times the size of the option 2 new transfers by 2005 about twice the option 2 transfers in their highest year).

Care must be taken in interpreting this comparison. In particular, it does not necessarily mean that if options 1 and 2 were combined, the fiscal dividend from the net new older workers would be sufficient to pay for the transfers required to guarantee an income floor at the BLS Intermediate Budget Level.[1] It does imply, however, that additional elderly and near-elderly workers could greatly improve the economy's ability to assist its low-income elderly, especially if the income guarantee were carefully coordinated with new work incentives and opportunities for older Americans. Also, the comparison shown in figure 8-6 may have particular force in the period beyond our simulation horizon, if greater numbers of the baby-boom generation continue to work longer than now anticipated and thereby increase the tax base and decrease the need for transfers.

It may be politically difficult, however, to initiate new transfer programs, even as small as those simulated in option 2, if the future outlook is no more favorable than that depicted in the baseline simulation. Thus, it may not be all that important whether the improved economy generates a large total fiscal dividend, as in option 1, or larger total income and wealth that can more easily bear the burden of new transfers. Growth as depicted in options 1, 3, and 4 provides relatively little relief for the poorest and oldest elderly unless new transfer initiatives are launched. Therefore, it may be appropriate to consider this increased growth (shown in figure 8-1) as a "GNP dividend," part of which could be used to finance new transfers for the poor elderly. This added growth exceeds the direct cost of the option 2 new transfers by the mid-1980s in options 1 and 4 and by the early 1990s in option 3.

Considering a combination of options 3 and 4, these options probably display positive synergy at low levels and yet are probably competitive at high levels. Small increases in the incentive to invest through corporate-tax cuts may work better if, in addition to an increase in corporate retained earnings (option 4), there is a rise in personal saving as well (option 3). Conversely, small amounts of increased personal saving clearly have greater benefits if the incentives for business fixed investment are simultaneously raised, improving the real return on that saving. Thus, at low levels the policies are probably complementary. At high levels, however, both policies are pursuing essentially similar ends, and the gain from ever-larger incentives to divert money from consumption becomes less. Thus, it is probably inadvisable to combine options 3 and 4 at the scale simulated in this study.

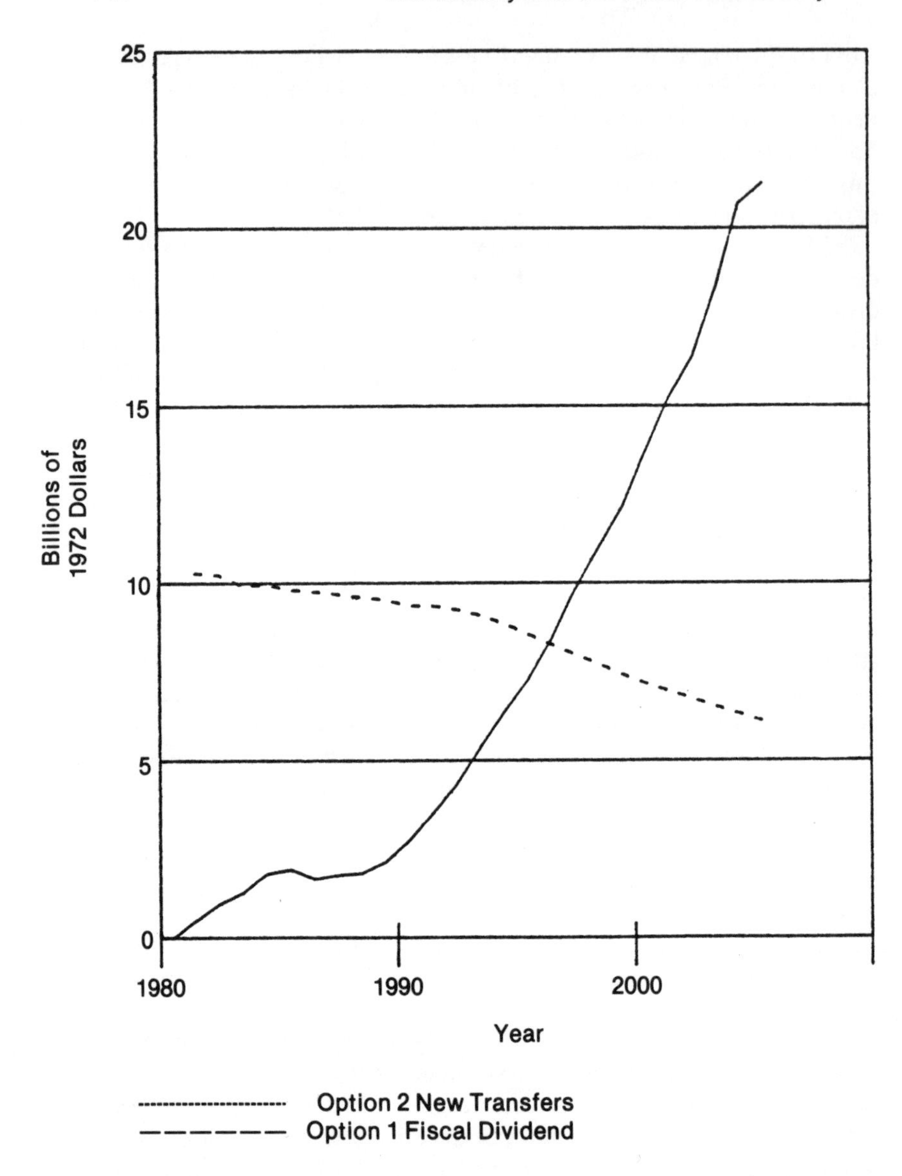

Note: The option 2 new transfers are the total direct cost of the income guarantee, including net added income to the poor elderly plus transfers to offset reductions in wage and salary earnings. The option 1 fiscal dividend is the net increase in total, real government expenditures at the federal, state, and local levels. These expenditures include the purchases of goods and services, transfers, interest payments, net subsidies of government-owned enterprises, and net interest payments.

Figure 8-6. Comparison between the Option 1 Fiscal Dividend and the New Transfer Cost of Option 2

The four options, addressing the issues of early retirement, elderly poverty, low saving rates, and the poor performance of investment and productivity, are as a group, quite comprehensive. It may, therefore, make the most sense to pursue an approach including elements of all four options. The choices ultimately made must consider the problems of declining labor-force participation, the low rate of personal saving, lagging investment, and poverty among the elderly with an aim of improving living standards for all Americans. The simulation results reported in this volume may help clarify some of the available choices as well as their effects on the elderly, the nonelderly, and the economy.

Note

1. On the one hand, the work disincentives implied by option 2 might reduce the fiscal dividend. On the other hand, the adequacy gains in option 1 could decrease the total transfers needed to bring the elderly up to the BLS budget. Options 3 and 4 also generate fiscal dividends, but these are neither as large nor as certain as those that flow from increased availability of labor, the principal productive input (and the one in most restricted supply in the baseline).

Appendix A: Technical Appendix for DRI's TRENDLONG2005 Twenty-Five-Year Macroeconomic Simulation

The material from the TRENDLONG2005 macroeconomic simulation presented in the text represents only a small fraction of the wealth of detail available from any DRI long-term simulation. This appendix presents additional material on the TRENDLONG2005 simulation, the assumptions it embodies, and its results. This technical appendix is a modified version of the DRI model note for the TRENDLONG2005 simulation (Data Resources, Inc. 1980).

Demographic Underpinnings

Demographic considerations are of paramount importance in a twenty-five-year projection. The rate of growth of the population and changes in its composition have considerable impact on the likely rate of growth of the labor force, the full-employment-unemployment rate, and the demand for housing and several other spending categories—notably, consumption of motor vehicles and state and local government spending.

The trend outlook is consistent with the Bureau of the Census Series II population projection. In this projection, the fertility rate is assumed to return gradually to 2.1. Some small improvement in mortality is assumed. Combined with a net immigration of 400,000 persons per year, these assumptions lead to a total population of 244 million in 1990, 261 million in 2000, and 268 million in 2005.

The Outlook

Real GNP was expected to fall by 1.5 percent in 1980 and to show only a weak growth of 0.4 percent in 1981 as the economy begins to recover. In the following three years, the economy is expected to continue on a recovery path, though in the context of uncomfortably high inflation that will keep real-growth rates below those of previous cyclical upswings. In 1985, real GNP will be 3.1 percent below potential, and the unemployment rate will improve to 6.4 percent from 8.6 percent in 1981. Between 1985 and 1990, growth in real output will slow though some further closing of the output gap will take place. Real GNP will be 1.8 percent below potential by 1990.

In the early 1990s, demographic influences will lead to a prolonged period of weakness for housing, a reflection of the end of the postwar baby boom in the early 1960s. Due mainly to this weakness, the economy is expected to experience relatively low growth in the first half of the 1990s, and thereafter it will converge gradually toward potential.

The Labor Force and Potential Output

A significant slowing in labor-force growth is envisaged for the simulation period, primarily reflecting slower growth in the prime-age population (aged 16 and over) and in participation rates. The population aged 16 and over has averaged 1.6 percent annual increases in the decade to 1980. Average annual increases of 1.1 percent are expected from 1980 to 1990, with the slowing due mainly to the pattern of postwar births. A further slowing to 0.8 percent is projected for the period 1990 to 2005.

The civilian labor-force-participation rate, defined here as the ratio between the civilian labor force and the population aged 16 and over, has risen from 57.8 percent in 1970 to 62.2 percent in 1980, with increasing female participation being the most important factor. Further rises to 65.3 percent by 1990 and to 66.6 percent by 2005 are projected. Labor-force growth slows from an annual average of 2.5 percent in the last decade to 1.5 percent from 1980 to 1990 and then to only 0.9 percent a year from 1990 to 2005.

Such dramatic slowing in the rate of growth of the labor force is the prime reason for a projected slowing in the annual rate of growth of potential output—from 2.6 percent in the first half of the 1980s to 2.4 percent by 1990 and to 2.2 percent in 2001 and thereafter.

Employment and Unemployment

Employment growth in the long run tends to follow labor-force growth. Thus, the average increase in employment (household-survey basis) between 1980 and 1990 is projected at 1.6 percent, with 0.9 percent average annual growth expected between 1990 and 2005. The unemployment rate is expected to peak at 8.7 percent in early 1981 and then to fall only slowly. From 1986 on, it stabilizes close to 6 percent. The full employment rate of unemployment (the rate of unemployment that would exist if the economy were operating at peak efficiency) falls by about 0.2 percentage points by 1996 as the composition of the labor force shifts toward older workers.

Energy and Energy Policy

In the near term, energy prices can be expected to rise strongly, due both to the likelihood of further large OPEC increases and to the effects of domestic decontrol. The average acquisition price of imported oil is expected to increase at an annual rate of 12.4 percent through 1985 and then to average 11.8 percent annual increases through to 1990 and 10.8 percent thereafter. These increases put the average acquisition price per barrel at $500 by 2005.

Domestic-energy prices grow at an even more-rapid rate in the near term, owing to decontrol. The wholesale price index for fuels, related products, and power in 1985 is expected to be more than triple its 1979 value. The annual rate of increase of this index slows to 13.8 percent by 1985 but is pushed up to 14.8 percent by 1990, reflecting the assumed phasing in of natural-gas deregulation over a five-year period. In the next decade, some deceleration takes place, but this index is still increasing at a 9 percent rate in 2000.

In response to these continued high price increases, the rate of growth of energy consumption is low by historical standards. Energy usage falls by 3.5 percent in 1980 and by 2.5 percent in 1981. Average annual growth of 1.3 percent between 1981 and 1990 brings energy usage in this latter year to 87 quads. Expected usage in 2000 is 101 quads.

A progressive reduction is expected in the proportion of energy requirements provided by petroleum and natural gas from 71 percent in 1979 to 49 percent by 2000. In addition, some expansion in the domestic supply of petroleum can be expected, primarily due to enhanced recovery techniques. The domestic-petroleum supply is projected at 8.6 million barrels per day (mmbd) in 1985, 9.1 mmbd in 1990, and 9.7 mmbd in 2000.

As a result, the projected rate of growth of fuel imports in real terms is relatively modest. Fuel imports (which include natural gas in barrel equivalents) are projected at 8.3 mmbd in 1982, 7.1 mmbd in 1990, and 6.7 mmbd in 2000. These quantities, combined with the price trajectory outlined previously, imply that the imported-oil bill will rise from $82 billion in 1980 to $254 billion by 1990 to nearly $1.2 trillion by 2005. This last figure represents 4.7 percent of GNP in that year, up from an estimated 2.6 percent in 1979.

Fiscal Policy

The forecast incorporates a tax cut of $32 billion in mid-1981. This cut includes a personal-income-tax reduction of $25 billion and $7 billion in corporate investment incentives from a higher investment tax credit and from increased depreciation allowances. The corporate-tax cuts are assumed to be retroactive to January. The revenue effect of the increased allowances will grow significantly beyond 1982 as the cumulative flow of eligible investment increases. This projected effect thus rises from $2 billion in 1981 to an average of more than $18 billion per year by the latter half of the 1980s.

Discrete personal tax cuts are enacted every second year, beginning in 1984. Despite the cuts, the effective personal-tax rate is projected to rise from 14.2 percent in 1980 to 15.9 percent in 1990 to 17.6 percent in 2005.

The windfall-oil-profits tax is assumed to yield $12.6 billion in 1980, $29.6 billion in 1981, and $40.5 billion in 1982. Revenues peak in 1987 at $63.6 billion and thereafter decline toward zero by 1991. Total revenue raised is projected at $450 billion.

On the expenditure side, pressures to hold down the proportion of GNP that passes through the federal budget are assumed to be at least partially successful. This proportion is projected to fall from 23.6 percent in 1981 to 22.4 percent in 1990. The government's portion of output then slowly returns to the 23 percent level. Real expenditures on final goods and services are projected to average about 2.3 percent annual growth throughout the forecast period, with the military component growing significantly faster than other purchases.

Transfers to persons are assumed to average 3.8 percent annual real growth from 1980 to 1990, with their share of the budget thus increasing from 41 percent to 45 percent over that period. Further increases of this order are not sustainable given political constraints on the share of federal spending in GNP. Thus, a slowing to 3.2 percent real annual growth is projected for the period 1990 to 2005.

One consideration that makes this slowing possible is a marked change in the age structure of the population in the 1990s. The proportion of the elderly population has risen steadily in the past from 8.1 percent in 1950 to 11.1 percent in 1978. Further increases to 12.3 percent in 1990 and 12.4 percent by 1995 are projected. Subsequent to 1995, however, the low birth rates of the depression years lead to a diminution in the proportion of the elderly to 12.1 percent by 2005. Even with this assumed slackening of growth, transfers to persons as a share of the budget continue to climb to 50 percent by 2005.

Personal-Consumption Expenditures

Real personal-consumption expenditures are projected to average 2.8 percent growth between 1980 and 1985, 2.7 percent between 1985 and 1990, and 2.2 percent between 1990 and 2005. The share of consumption in GNP is projected to average 64.3 percent from 1980 to 1985, 62.9 percent from 1986 to 1990, and 62.5 percent after 1990.

Conservation efforts are assumed to be moderately successful. The share of energy-intensive consumption (gasoline, fuel oil and coal, gas and electricity) rises from 9.7 percent in 1980 to 12.2 percent in 1990 to 14.2 percent in 2005.

Housing

The fundamental determinants of the long-run outlook for housing are demographic factors and real-income growth. Total potential housing demand is derived from an analysis of trends in age-specific headship rates. In the near term, cyclical variations in housing are relatively large, stemming mainly from variations in financial conditions. Thus, starts recover from 1.23 million units in 1980 to 1.96 million in 1982. Starts average 2.1 million units from 1981 to 1990 and 1.87 million units from 1991 to 2000.

From 1990 onward, demographic considerations lead to a long, slow decline in housing activity, with starts bottoming out at 1.76 million units in 1998. The most important demographic determinant of this decline is the exit of the postwar baby boom from the prime house-buying age groups. Thus, for example, the population aged 21 through 28 is projected to peak at 33.1 million in 1984 and then to fall to as low as 26 million by 2000.

Business Fixed Investment

Real business fixed investment is projected to average 3.1 percent annual growth between 1980 and 1985, 3.5 percent between 1985 and 1990, and 3 percent between 1990 and 2005. The share of business fixed investment in GNP averages 10.3 percent from 1980 to 1985, 10.8 percent from 1986 to 1990, and 11.4 percent thereafter. These figures are consistent with annual growth in the business fixed-capital stock of 2.7 percent between 1980 and 1985, 3.2 percent between 1985 and 1990, and 2.9 percent thereafter.

Inventory investment in 1972 dollars is projected to average $6.9 billion from 1980 to 1985, $11.9 billion from 1986 to 1990, and $12.6 billion thereafter. These figures are consistent with an almost constant inventory-to-sales ratio.

This relatively high business fixed-investment share occurs despite the assumption that the personal-saving rate continues at close to its recent low levels. Low personal saving is offset by significant changes in the contribution to total-saving flows of the government and external sectors. Part of the increase in the business-fixed-investment share is offset by an eventual decrease in the share of GNP devoted to residential construction.

State and Local Government

Real state and local government spending on final goods and services is forecast to grow at an average 1.7 percent between 1980 and 1985, 2.2 percent between 1985 and 1990, and 1.9 percent thereafter. The ratio of the school-age population to the total, which has been in decline since the late 1960s, is projected to stabilize in the 1990s, thus limiting the decline in the rate of growth of spending.

Foreign Trade

The rate of growth of foreign trade is expected to continue to exceed that of the domestic economy, with exports reaching 18.5 percent of GNP in 2005, compared with 12.2 percent in 1980 and 6 percent as recently as 1971.

Industrial production in Canada is projected to average 3.1 percent from 1980 to 1985, 4.2 percent from 1985 to 1990, and 3.7 percent thereafter. In Europe, the projected growth rate is 3.2 percent from 1980 to 1985, 3 percent between 1985 and 1990, and 3.4 percent thereafter, while in Japan, 5.5 percent growth is expected from 1980 to 1985, followed by a further 5.9 percent from 1985 to 1990, and 5.1 percent thereafter.

It is assumed that approximate balance in the external account will be achievable through the 1980s and 1990s with the exchange rate held constant. The proportion of cars imported is projected to stabilize at close to 24 percent after 1990.

Prices, Wages, and Productivity

The assumption that the economy remains significantly below its potential path throughout the 1980s permits only gradual improvement, with the projected rate of increase of the implicit GNP deflator falling from the 9.6 percent expected in 1981 to 7.7 percent by 1990. By this measure, inflation stabilizes at close to 6 percent from 1995 on.

Table A-1 gives the projected annual rates of increase of several price indexes, together with figures for average earnings and productivity per man-hour in the nonfarm business sector. Both the CPI and the wholesale price index are fixed-weight indexes for which no explicit rebasing is assumed in the next twenty-five years. As a consequence, these indexes tend significantly to overstate the rate of inflation toward the end to the projection period.

Table A-1
Average Inflation in TRENDLONG2005
(percentage)

Factors	*1980-1985*	*1985-1990*	*1990-2005*
Implicit GNP deflator	8.5	7.8	6.1
Implicit consumption deflator	8.5	7.4	6.1
CPI	8.6	8.1	7
Wholesale price index	10.3	9.3	7
Processed foods and feeds	9.6	7.6	5.5
Energy	16.8	14.4	9.5
Average hourly earnings	9.5	9.2	7.6
Productivity	1.7	1.6	1.7

Contributing factors to the projected improvement of productivity from its recent abysmal performance include the maturation of the work force, capital deepening, and use of more-efficient labor-management techniques made possible by the relatively smooth growth in output.

Production and Capacity Utilization

The generated outputs implied by projections of final demands were monitored for individual industries, and, where necessary, production indexes were add factored to preserve long-run relationships between the growth rates of production and the generated output series. The overall industrial-production index is projected to average 7.8 percent growth from 1980 to 1985, 3.5 percent from 1985 to 1990, and 3.2 percent thereafter. This pattern is, of course, consistent with the slowing in the rate of growth of potential. No radical changes in production technologies are assumed.

Some imbalance between capacity utilization and unemployment will be evident at least through the first half of the projection period, a reflection of the impact of the recession on the path of investment spending. In 1985, for example, capacity utilization is at a tight 85.2 percent, while the unemployment rate records 6.4 percent. The continual risk of capacity bottlenecks implied by the high level of overall utilization contributes both to the stubbornness of inflation and to the likelihood of an increase in the business fixed-investment share.

Profits

The effect of the 1981 liberalization of depreciation allowances will exert downward pressure on the before-tax profit share, as will the windfall-profits tax (actually an excise tax). Corporate cash flow, defined as retained earnings plus the book value of capital-consumption allowances minus inventory profits, will be relatively healthy, in part due to the 1981 tax measures. The cash flow is projected to average 8.3 percent of GNP, above its 1955-1978 average of 7.8 percent.

Financial Conditions

The projection incorporates many of the elements of the Depository Institutions Deregulation and Monetary Control Act of 1980, as well as the approach to monetary policy embodied in the new Fed policy of October 1979. The annual rate of growth of nonborrowed reserves is assumed to average 6.6 percent between 1980 and 1985 before stabilizing at 7.4 percent between 1985 and 1990. The slowing in inflation in the 1990s leads to slower rates of growth in most nominal magnitudes including deposit flows. Nonborrowed-reserves growth thus slows to 6.2 percent.

The prime rate is expected to fall only as far as 10 percent in early 1981 before renewed economic growth increases loan demand sufficiently to push the rate upward again. A subsequent peak of 11.9 percent is recorded in late 1983, and only in early 1992 does the prime rate finally fall below the double-digit range. Late in the projection period this rate stabilizes near 8.6 percent.

Fluctuations in the high-grade corporate-bond rate are less marked, although this rate also is expected to remain above 10 percent for much of the next decade. The rate drops to 9.8 percent in 1993 and 8.6 percent in 2000 as the real-bond rate stabilizes at about 2.7 percent.

Maximum effective rates payable on deposits at savings and loans, commercial banks, and mutual savings banks are assumed to be phased out by mid-1986 in accordance with the Depository Institutions Deregulation and Monetary Control Act of 1980.

Appendix B: Additional Tables and Figures Relating to Income and Its Distribution

Table B-1
Total Income of Elderly Families and Singles, by Age Group: Baseline
(billions of real 1980 dollars)

Age Group	*1980*	*1985*	*1990*	*1995*	*2000*	*2005*
Men						
65 to 71	6.10	6.91	7.77	8.25	8.64	9.17
72 and over	7.12	7.83	8.60	9.03	9.43	9.96
All elderly	13.22	14.74	16.36	17.29	18.08	19.13
Women						
65 to 71	17.60	20.82	24.15	26.40	28.30	30.24
72 and over	23.87	28.42	34.16	39.27	43.77	48.15
All elderly	41.47	49.24	58.32	65.67	72.08	78.39
Families						
65 to 71	83.22	96.06	109.35	120.31	125.29	130.77
72 and over	60.15	67.92	75.84	82.38	86.36	90.30
All elderly	143.37	163.98	185.19	202.69	211.64	221.07

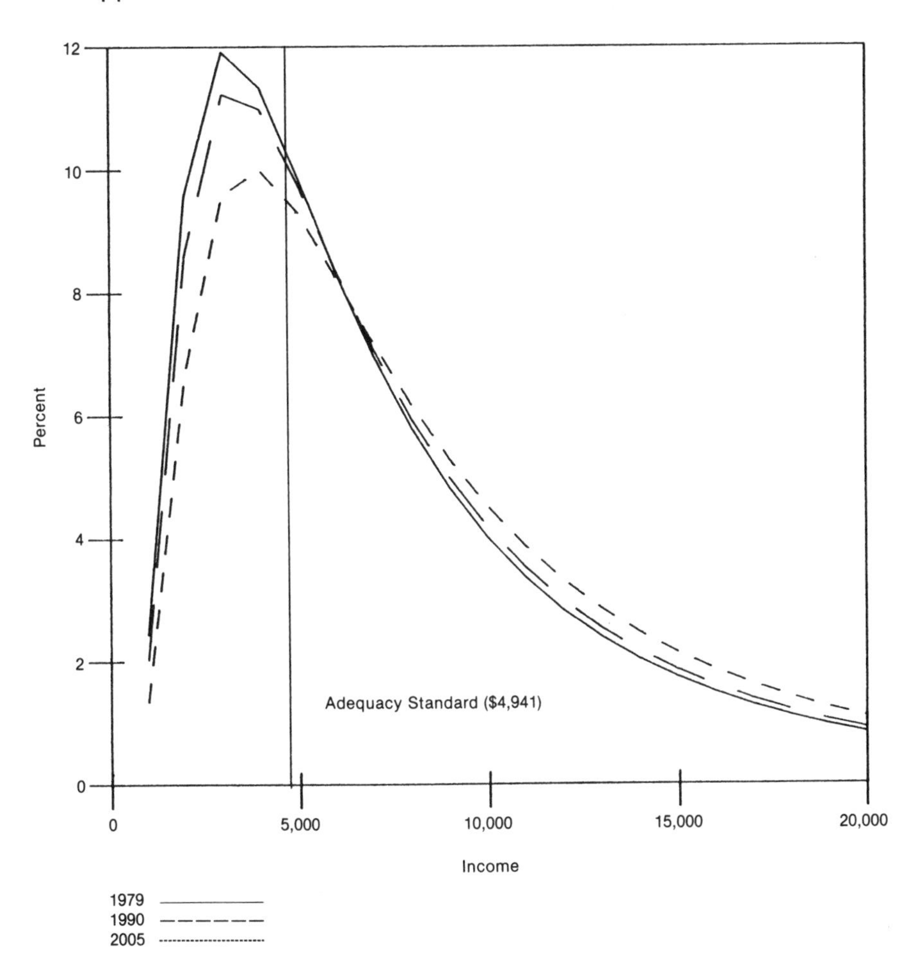

Figure B-1. Percentages of Income Distribution (1979 Dollars) for Male Individuals Aged 65-71: Baseline

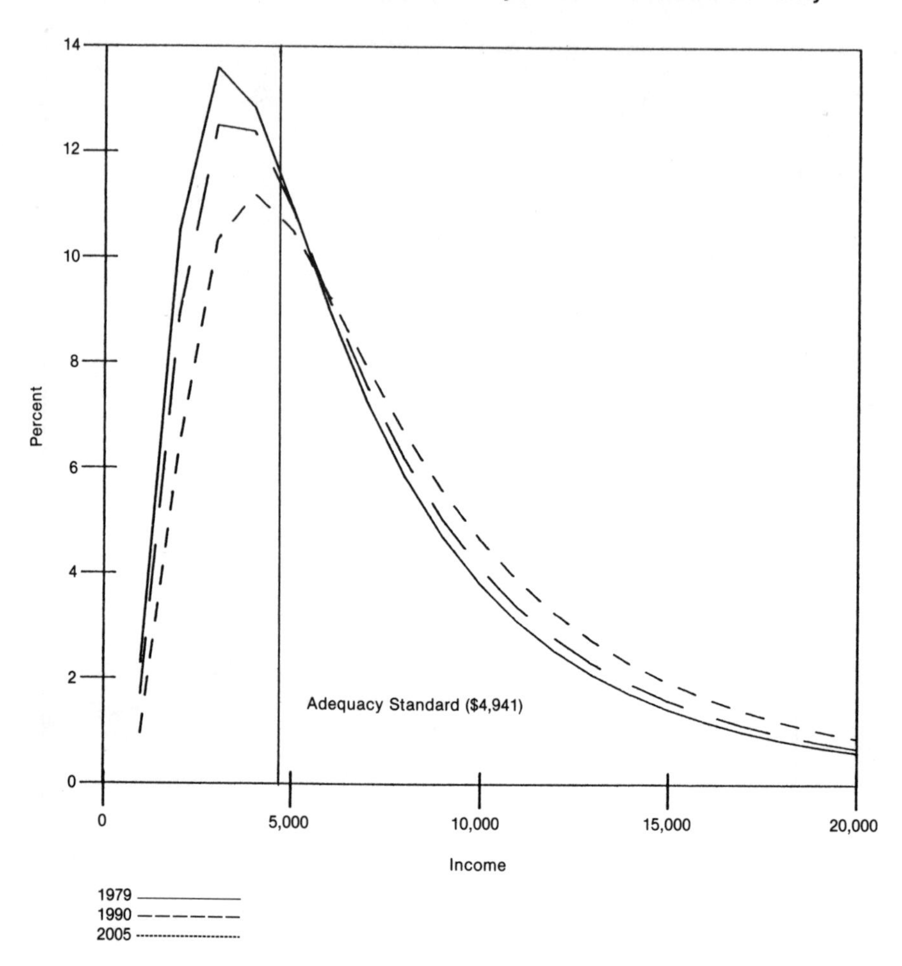

Figure B-2. Percentages of Income Distribution (1979 Dollars) for Female Individuals Aged 65-71: Baseline

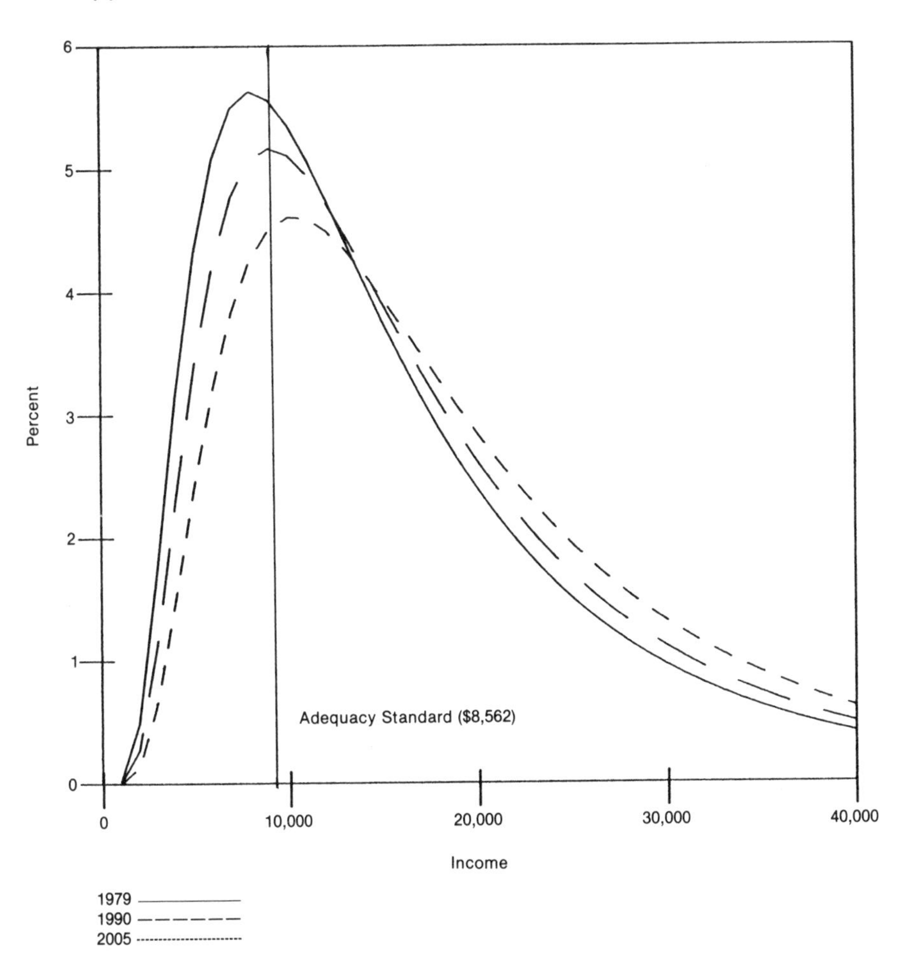

Figure B-3. Percentages of Income Distribution (1979 Dollars) for Families with Head Aged 65-71: Baseline

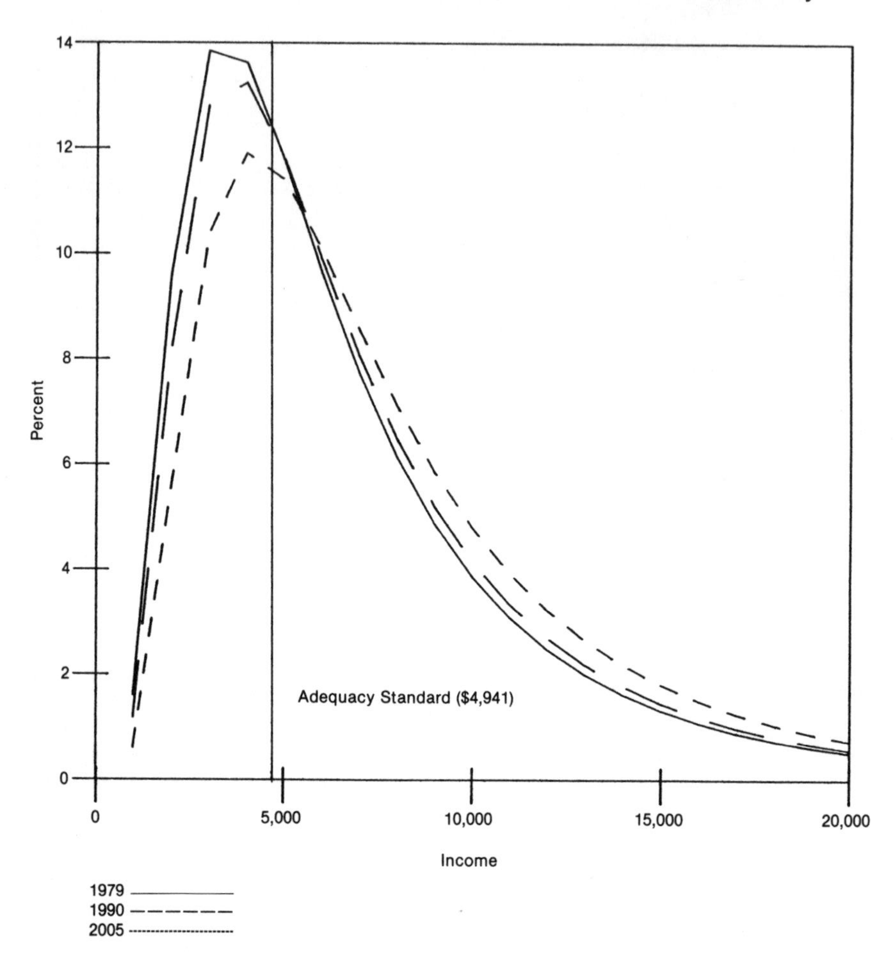

Figure B-4. Percentages of Income Distribution (1979 Dollars) for Male Individuals Aged 72 and over: Baseline

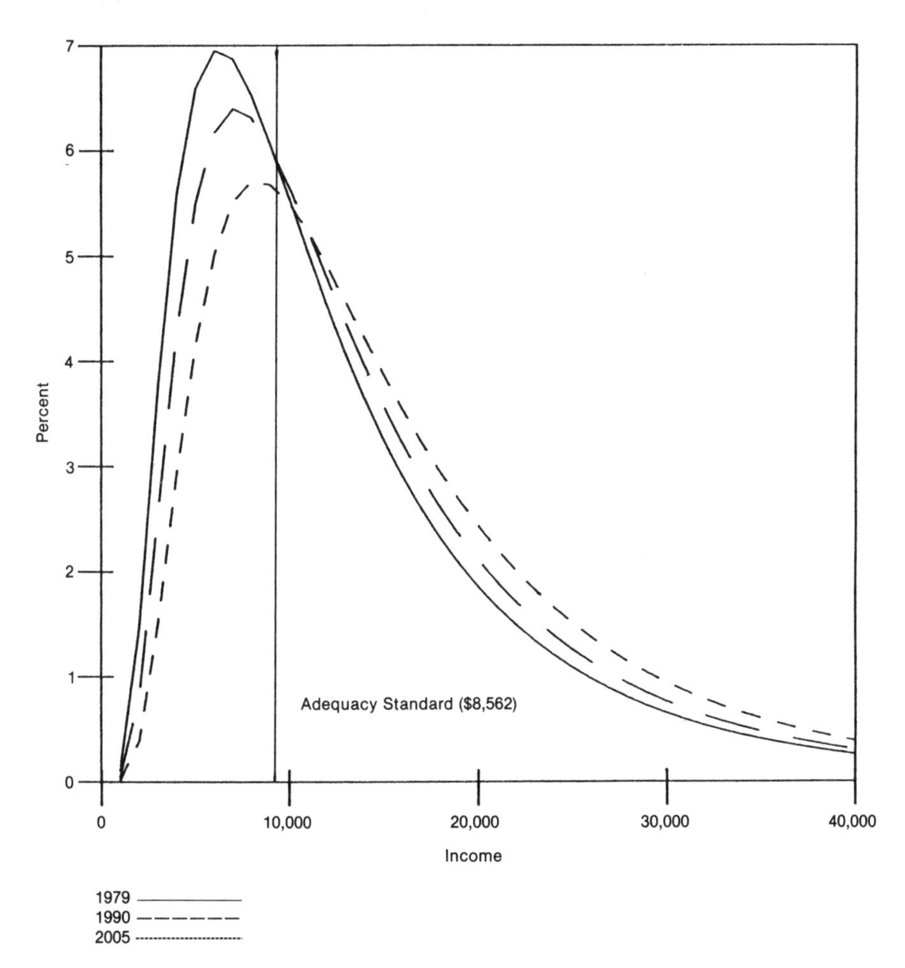

Figure B-5. Percentages of Income Distribution (1979 Dollars) and Adequacy Standard for Families with Head Aged 72 and over: Baseline

Table B-2
Total Income of Elderly Families and Singles, by Age Group: Option 1
(billions of real 1980 dollars)

Age Group	*1980*	*1985*	*1990*	*1995*	*2000*	*2005*
Men						
65 to 71	6.10	7.02	8.22	8.84	9.37	10.11
72 and over	7.12	7.91	8.86	9.36	9.82	10.44
All elderly	13.22	14.93	17.08	18.21	19.19	20.56
Women						
65 to 71	17.60	21.05	24.97	27.54	29.83	32.26
72 and over	23.87	28.49	34.87	40.20	44.96	49.73
All elderly	41.47	49.54	59.83	67.74	74.79	82
Families						
65 to 71	83.22	96.68	110.72	122.62	128.50	134.63
72 and over	60.15	68.29	76.49	83.36	87.61	91.56
All elderly	143.37	164.97	187.21	205.98	216.11	226.19
			Difference from Baseline			
Men						
65 to 71	0	0.11	0.45	0.59	0.73	0.95
72 and over	0	0.07	0.26	0.33	0.39	0.48
All elderly	0	0.18	0.71	0.92	1.12	1.43
Women						
65 to 71	0	0.23	0.81	1.14	1.53	2.02
72 and over	0	0.07	0.71	0.93	1.19	1.59
All elderly	0	0.29	1.52	2.07	2.72	3.61
Families						
65 to 71	0	0.62	1.37	2.31	3.21	3.85
72 and over	0	0.37	0.64	0.98	1.26	1.26
All elderly	0	0.99	2.02	3.29	4.47	5.12

Table B-3
Numbers and Income Distributions for Families and Singles under Age 55: Option 1
(percentage in real 1980 income classes)

	Families of Two or More			Singles		
	1980	1990	2005	1980	1990	2005
Income Distribution						
$0 to $2,500	3.511	2.688	2.015	11.166	7.973	5.639
$2,500 to $5,000	2.697	1.828	1.219	11.064	8.352	5.841
$5,000 to $7,500	3.852	2.597	1.719	13.029	10.489	7.954
$7,500 to $10,000	5.036	3.441	2.292	13.028	11.330	9.363
$10,000 to $20,000	28.226	21.243	15.059	36.306	38.091	36.829
$20,000 and over	56.678	68.203	77.697	15.406	23.764	34.375
Difference from Baseline						
$0 to $2,500	0	0.062	-0.031	0	0.036	-0.256
$2,500 to $5,000	0	0.009	-0.025	0	0.065	0.032
$5,000 to $7,500	0	0.001	-0.028	0	-0.032	0.043
$7,500 to $10,000	0	-0.010	-0.027	0	-0.104	0.016
$10,000 to $20,000	0	-0.139	-0.074	0	-0.104	0.021
$20,000 and over	0	0.076	0.185	0	0.139	0.144
Number (thousands)	41,708.857	49,971.838	54,093.006	15,419.634	21,978.559	26,113.182

Table B-4
Numbers and Income Distributions for Families and Singles Aged 55 to 61: Option 1
(percentage in real 1980 income classes)

	Families of Two or More			Singles		
	1980	1990	2005	1980	1990	2005
Income Distribution						
$0 to $2,500	2.400	1.285	0.556	10.119	6.837	3.712
$2,500 to $5,000	2.467	1.458	0.743	16.180	12.584	8.770
$5,000 to $7,500	3.640	2.273	1.253	16.711	14.433	11.726
$7,500 to $10,000	4.788	3.150	1.860	14.152	13.308	11.922
$10,000 to $20,000	26.167	19.663	13.518	30.068	32.925	34.485
$20,000 and over	60.538	72.170	82.070	12.770	19.914	29.385
Difference from Baseline						
$0 to $2,500	0	0.010	-0.137	0	-0.248	-0.611
$2,500 to $5,000	0	-0.022	-0.101	0	-0.164	-0.488
$5,000 to $7,500	0	-0.048	-0.124	0	-0.109	-0.253
$7,500 to $10,000	0	-0.076	-0.140	0	-0.061	-0.108
$10,000 to $20,000	0	-0.462	-0.566	0	0.057	0.153
$20,000 and over	0	0.598	1.068	0	0.525	-1.308
Number (thousands)	7,000.337	6,775.089	8,933.183	2,214.078	2,230.154	3,145.447

Table B-5
Numbers and Income Distributions for Families and Singles Aged 62 to 64: Option 1
(percentage in real 1980 income classes)

	Families of Two or More			Singles		
	1980	1990	2005	1980	1990	2005
Income Distribution						
$0 to $2,500	2.774	1.836	1.140	10.529	5.636	1.049
$2,500 to $5,000	4.191	2.844	1.796	25.596	22.678	16.888
$5,000 to $7,500	6.191	4.402	2.904	20.022	19.996	19.877
$7,500 to $10,000	7.634	5.722	3.970	13.446	14.230	15.195
$10,000 to $20,000	32.705	27.989	22.191	22.284	25.472	29.500
$20,000 and over	46.504	57.207	67.998	8.124	11.987	17.491
Difference from Baseline						
$0 to $2,500	0	−0.019	−0.134	0	−0.428	−0.702
$2,500 to $5,000	0	−0.060	−0.135	0	−0.191	−1.276
$5,000 to $7,500	0	−0.099	−0.174	0	0.026	0.173
$7,500 to $10,000	0	−0.436	−0.708	0	0.162	0.629
$10,000 to $20,000	0	−0.436	−0.708	0	0.162	0.629
$20,000 and over	0	0.740	1.347	0	0.377	0.933
Number (thousands)	2,593.945	2,454.800	3,787.943	1,141.162	1,094.109	1,530.452

Table B-6
Numbers and Income Distributions for Families and Singles Aged 65 to 71: Option 1
(percentage in real 1980 income classes)

	Families of Two or More			Singles		
	1980	1990	2005	1980	1990	2005
Income Distribution						
$0 to $2,500	0.236	0	0	6.589	0.900	0
$2,500 to $5,000	5.918	2.138	0.040	40.251	38.155	26.931
$5,000 to $7,500	12.268	9.569	4.478	21.610	23.841	27.648
$7,500 to $10,000	13.594	12.864	10.946	11.348	12.809	15.190
$10,000 to $20,000	38.099	40.112	42.269	15.268	17.681	21.294
$20,000 and over	29.885	35.317	42.268	4.935	6.615	8.936
Difference from Baseline						
$0 to $2,500	0	0	0	0	−1.108	0
$2,500 to $5,000	0	−0.382	−0.247	0	−1.803	−5.807
$5,000 to $7,500	0	−0.367	−1.500	0	0.886	1.673
$7,500 to $10,000	0	−0.115	−0.515	0	0.640	1.192
$10,000 to $20,000	0	0.176	0.590	0	0.863	1.766
$20,000 and over	0	0.689	1.673	0	0.522	1.176
Number (thousands)	4,618.359	5,487.917	5,872.101	3,140.664	3,879.170	4,269.474

Table B-7
Numbers and Income Distributions for Families and Singles Aged 72 and over: Option 1
(percentage in real 1980 income classes)

	Families of Two or More			Singles		
	1980	1990	2005	1980	1990	2005
Income Distribution						
$0 to $2,500	0	0	0	8.109	1.472	0.058
$2,500 to $5,000	8.790	2.955	0.021	46.093	45.572	27.688
$5,000 to $7,500	19.702	17.121	10.114	22.002	24.646	32.065
$7,500 to $10,000	17.289	17.947	17.884	10.238	11.700	15.839
$10,000 to $20,000	34.833	38.794	43.846	10.403	12.651	18.583
$20,000 and over	19.387	23.183	28.135	3.155	3.959	5.767
Difference from Baseline						
$0 to $2,500	0	0	0	0	-1.058	-0.085
$2,500 to $5,000	0	-0.472	-0.205	0	-1.211	-4.026
$5,000 to $7,500	0	-0.267	-1.477	0	1.057	1.904
$7,500 to $10,000	0	0.066	0.232	0	0.572	0.934
$10,000 to $20,000	0	0	0	0	0	0
$20,000 and over	0	0.374	0	0	0.086	0.306
Number (thousands)	4,014.170	4,548.314	4,784.306	4,771.709	6,022.728	6,747.424

Table B-8
Numbers and Income Distributions for Singles Aged 55 to 61: Option 1
(percentage in real 1980 income classes)

	Men			Women		
	1980	1990	2005	1980	1990	2005
Income Distribution						
$0 to $2,500	9.150	6.919	4.813	10.681	6.783	2.854
$2,500 to $5,000	11.343	8.578	6.161	18.985	15.219	10.804
$5,000 to $7,500	13.220	10.609	8.120	18.736	16.947	14.536
$7,500 to $10,000	12.905	11.109	9.108	14.875	14.754	14.114
$10,000 to $20,000	34.311	34.723	33.229	27.608	31.742	35.463
$20,000 and over	19.070	28.062	38.568	9.116	14.555	22.229
Difference from Baseline						
$0 to $2,500	0	-0.162	-0.375	0	-0.305	-0.796
$2,500 to $5,000	0	-0.107	-0.183	0	-0.201	-0.727
$5,000 to $7,500	0	-0.115	-0.162	0	-0.105	-0.324
$7,500 to $10,000	0	-0.105	-0.138	0	-0.032	-0.085
$10,000 to $20,000	0	-0.142	-0.251	0	0.188	0.468
$20,000 and over	0	0.631	1.109	0	0.455	1.463
Number (thousands)	812.650	884.720	1,377.586	1,401.428	1,345.435	1,767.861

Table B-9
Numbers and Income Distributions for Singles Aged 62 to 64: Option 1
(percentage in real 1980 income classes)

	Men			*Women*		
	1980	*1990*	*2005*	*1980*	*1990*	*2005*
Income Distribution						
$0 to $2,500	9.789	6.028	2.639	10.834	5.473	0.388
$2,500 to $5,000	18.838	15.102	10.753	28.385	25.833	19.437
$5,000 to $7,500	17.542	15.932	13.686	21.044	21.689	22.449
$7,500 to $10,000	13.674	13.521	12.910	13.352	14.526	16.145
$10,000 to $20,000	26.873	30.171	33.060	20.391	23.516	28.021
$20,000 and over	13.283	19.247	26.952	5.995	8.964	13.560
Difference from Baseline						
$0 to $2,500	0	−0.245	−0.571	0	−0.504	−0.756
$2,500 to $5,000	0	−0.075	−0.324	0	−0.239	−1.672
$5,000 to $7,500	0	−0.058	−0.074	0	0.060	0.276
$7,500 to $10,000	0	−0.017	0.058	0	0.237	0.866
$10,000 to $20,000	0	−0.017	0.058	0	0.237	0.866
$20,000 and over	0	0.447	0.934	0	0.348	0.933
Number (thousands)	333.329	321.628	449.268	807.833	772.481	1,081.184

Table B-10
Numbers and Income Distributions for Singles Aged 65 to 71: Option 1
(percentage in real 1980 income classes)

	Men			*Women*		
	1980	*1990*	*2005*	*1980*	*1990*	*2005*
Income Distribution						
$0 to $2,500	6.296	0.936	0	6.677	0.889	0
$2,500 to $5,000	36.380	33.630	23.554	41.421	39.435	27.844
$5,000 to $7,500	21.014	22.820	25.432	21.790	24.130	28.247
$7,500 to $10,000	11.800	13.191	15.137	11.212	12.700	15.205
$10,000 to $20,000	17.650	19.875	23.336	14.547	17.061	20.742
$20,000 and over	6.860	9.549	12.542	4.353	5.784	7.962
Difference from Baseline						
$0 to $2,500	0	−1.507	0	0	−0.995	0
$2,500 to $5,000	0	−2.295	−6.934	0	−1.664	−5.502
$5,000 to $7,500	0	0.769	1.329	0	0.920	1.765
$7,500 to $10,000	0	0.708	1.242	0	0.621	1.178
$10,000 to $20,000	0	1.142	2.458	0	0.784	1.579
$20,000 and over	0	1.183	1.905	0	0.335	0.979
Number (thousands)	729,170	855,523	908,478	2,411.495	3,023.647	3,360.996

Table B-11
Numbers and Income Distributions for Singles Aged 72 and over: Option 1
(percentage in real 1980 income classes)

	Men			Women		
	1980	*1990*	*2005*	*1980*	*1990*	*2005*
Income Distribution						
$0 to $2,500	7.080	3.054	0.357	8.366	1.134	0
$2,500 to $5,000	40.413	37.260	29.820	47.514	47.350	27.271
$5,000 to $7,500	23.089	24.801	26.879	21.731	24.612	33.077
$7,500 to $10,000	11.836	13.392	15.707	9.839	11.338	15.865
$10,000 to $20,000	13.013	15.866	20.280	9.750	11.964	18.252
$20,000 and over	4.570	5.627	6.957	2.801	3.602	5.535
Difference from Baseline						
$0 to $2,500	0	−1.055	−0.522	0	−1.058	0
$2,500 to $5,000	0	−1.627	−3.196	0	−1.122	−4.187
$5,000 to $7,500	0	0.842	0.754	0	1.103	2.129
$7,500 to $10,000	0	0.707	0.930	0	0.543	0.935
$10,000 to $20,000	0	0.915	1.554	0	0.475	0.852
$20,000 and over	0	0.217	0.480	0	0.058	0.272
Number (thousands)	954.688	1,061.071	1,101.657	3,817.020	4,961.656	5,645.767

Table B-12
Total Income of Elderly Families and Singles, by Age Group: Option 2
(billions of real 1980 dollars)

Age Group	*1980*	*1985*	*1990*	*1995*	*2000*	*2005*
Men						
65 to 71	6.10	7.48	8.31	8.75	9.07	9.58
72 and over	7.12	8.65	9.38	9.75	10.06	10.54
All elderly	13.22	16.13	17.69	18.51	19.13	20.12
Women						
65 to 71	17.60	22.98	26.29	28.40	30.04	31.81
72 and over	23.87	32.56	38.20	42.73	46.45	50.24
All elderly	41.47	55.54	64.50	71.13	76.48	82.05
Families						
65 to 71	83.22	99.27	112.00	122.51	126.92	132.21
72 and over	60.15	72.06	79.47	85.60	85.95	92.57
All elderly	143.37	171.34	191.47	208.11	215.87	224.78
		Difference from Baseline				
Men						
65 to 71	0	0.57	0.55	0.50	0.43	0.41
72 and over	0	0.81	0.78	0.72	0.63	0.58
All elderly	0	1.38	1.33	1.22	1.06	0.99
Women						
65 to 71	0	2.15	2.14	2	1.74	1.57
72 and over	0	4.14	4.04	3.46	2.67	2.09
All elderly	0	6.30	6.18	5.46	4.41	3.66
Families						
65 to 71	0	3.21	2.65	2.21	1.63	1.44
72 and over	0	4.15	3.63	3.22	2.59	2.27
All elderly	0	7.36	6.28	5.42	4.23	3.71

Table B-13
Numbers and Income Distributions for Families and Singles under Age 55: Option 2
(percentage in real 1980 income classes)

	Families of Two or More			Singles		
	1980	1990	2005	1980	1990	2005
Income Distribution						
$0 to $2,500	3.511	2.642	2.045	11.166	8.010	5.889
$2,500 to $5,000	2.697	1.817	1.240	11.064	8.273	5.778
$5,000 to $7,500	3.852	2.587	1.740	13.029	10.492	7.870
$7,500 to $10,000	5.036	3.434	2.309	13.028	11.406	9.305
$10,000 to $20,000	28.226	21.262	15.055	36.306	38.192	36.738
$20,000 and over	56.678	68.258	77.611	15.406	23.627	34.420
Difference from Baseline						
$0 to $2,500	0	0.017	−0.001	0	0.072	−0.007
$2,500 to $5,000	0	−0.002	−0.004	0	−0.015	−0.031
$5,000 to $7,500	0	−0.009	−0.007	0	−0.029	−0.041
$7,500 to $10,000	0	−0.016	−0.011	0	−0.028	−0.042
$10,000 to $20,000	0	−0.120	−0.077	0	−0.003	−0.069
$20,000 and over	0	0.131	0.099	0	0.002	0.190
Number (thousands)	41,708.857	49,971.838	54,093.006	15,419.634	21,978.559	26,113.182

Table B-14
Numbers and Income Distributions for Families and Singles Aged 55 to 61: Option 2
(percentage in real 1980 income classes)

	Families of Two or More			Singles		
	1980	1990	2005	1980	1990	2005
Income Distribution						
$0 to $2,500	2.400	1.306	0.695	10.119	7.097	4.322
$2,500 to $5,000	2.467	1.485	0.841	16.180	12.658	9.219
$5,000 to $7,500	3.640	2.316	1.371	16.711	14.460	11.937
$7,500 to $10,000	4.788	3.209	1.989	14.152	13.326	12.003
$10,000 to $20,000	26.167	19.975	14.016	30.068	32.908	34.332
$20,000 and over	60.538	71.709	81.088	12.770	19.551	28.187
Difference from Baseline						
$0 to $2,500	0	0.031	0.001	0	0.012	−0.002
$2,500 to $5,000	0	0.005	−0.003	0	−0.090	−0.040
$5,000 to $7,500	0	−0.005	−0.006	0	−0.082	−0.042
$7,500 to $10,000	0	−0.018	−0.010	0	−0.043	−0.028
$10,000 to $20,000	0	−0.149	−0.068	0	0.040	0.001
$20,000 and over	0	0.137	0.085	0	0.162	0.111
Number (thousands)	7,000.337	6,775.089	8,933.183	2,214.078	2,230.154	3,145.447

Table B-15
Numbers and Income Distributions for Families and Singles Aged 62 to 64: Option 2
(percentage in real 1980 income classes)

	Families of Two or More			*Singles*		
	1980	*1990*	*2005*	*1980*	*1990*	*2005*
Income Distribution						
$0 to $2,500	2.774	1.870	1.274	10.529	6.076	1.747
$2,500 to $5,000	4.191	2.895	1.923	25.596	22.706	18.082
$5,000 to $7,500	6.191	4.477	3.063	20.022	19.911	19.666
$7,500 to $10,000	7.634	5.811	4.147	13.446	14.183	14.950
$10,000 to $20,000	32.705	28.297	22.822	22.284	25.401	28.926
$20,000 and over	46.504	56.651	66.771	8.124	11.723	16.629
Difference from Baseline						
$0 to $2,500	0	0.014	−0.001	0	0.013	−0.003
$2,500 to $5,000	0	−0.009	−0.008	0	−0.163	−0.083
$5,000 to $7,500	0	−0.025	−0.015	0	−0.059	−0.038
$7,500 to $10,000	0	−0.128	−0.077	0	0.090	0.054
$10,000 to $20,000	0	−0.128	−0.077	0	0.090	0.054
$20,000 and over	0	0.185	0.120	0	0.113	0.071
Number (thousands)	2,593.945	2,454.800	3,787.943	1,141.162	1,094.109	1,530.452

Table B-16
Numbers and Income Distributions for Families and Singles Aged 65 to 71: Option 2
(percentage in real 1980 income classes)

	Families of Two or More			*Singles*		
	1980	*1990*	*2005*	*1980*	*1990*	*2005*
Income Distribution						
$0 to $2,500	0.236	0	0	6.589	0	0
$2,500 to $5,000	5.918	0	0	40.251	0	0
$5,000 to $7,500	12.268	0	0	21.610	65.194	58.979
$7,500 to $10,000	13.594	25.807	18.006	11.348	12.113	13.927
$10,000 to $20,000	38.099	39.819	41.631	15.268	16.711	19.421
$20,000 and over	29.885	34.374	40.363	4.935	5.982	7.673
Difference From Baseline						
$0 to $2,500	0	0	0	0	−2.008	0
$2,500 to $5,000	0	−2.520	−0.288	0	−39.958	−32.737
$5,000 to $7,500	0	−9.936	−5.977	0	42.239	33.003
$7,500 to $10,000	0	12.828	6.545	0	−0.055	−0.071
$10,000 to $20,000	0	−0.118	−0.048	0	−0.107	−0.108
$20,000 and over	0	−0.254	−0.232	0	−0.111	−0.087
Number (thousands)	4,618.359	5,487.917	5,872.101	3,140.664	3,879.170	4,269.474

Table B-17
Numbers and Income Distributions for Families and Singles Aged 72 and over: Option 2
(percentage in real 1980 income classes)

	Families of Two or More			Singles		
	1980	1990	2005	1980	1990	2005
Income Distribution						
$0 to $2,500	0	0	0	8.109	0	0
$2,500 to $5,000	8.790	0	0	46.093	0	0
$5,000 to $7,500	19.702	0	0	22.002	73.337	62.391
$7,500 to $10,000	17.289	39.086	29.763	10.238	11.011	14.785
$10,000 to $20,000	34.833	38.303	42.947	10.403	11.884	17.443
$20,000 and over	19.387	22.611	27.290	3.155	3.768	5.381
Difference from Baseline						
$0 to $2,500	0	0	0	0	−2.530	−0.144
$2,500 to $5,000	0	−3.428	−0.225	0	−46.783	−31.713
$5,000 to $7,500	0	−17.388	−11.591	0	49.749	32.231
$7,500 to $10,000	0	21.204	12.111	0	−0.117	−0.120
$10,000 to $20,000	0	0	0	0	0	0
$20,000 and over	0	−0.198	0	0	−0.104	−0.080
Number (thousands)	4,014.170	4,548.314	4,784.306	4,771.709	6,022.728	6,747.424

Table B-18
Numbers and Income Distributions for Singles Aged 55 to 61: Option 2
(percentage in real 1980 income classes)

	Men			Women		
	1980	1990	2005	1980	1990	2005
Income Distribution						
$0 to $2,500	9.150	7.084	5.186	10.681	7.106	3.649
$2,500 to $5,000	11.343	8.631	6.317	18.985	15.307	11.480
$5,000 to $7,500	13.220	10.658	8.249	18.736	16.959	14.811
$7,500 to $10,000	12.905	11.161	9.216	14.875	14.750	14.174
$10,000 to $20,000	34.311	34.834	33.443	27.608	31.641	35.025
$20,000 and over	19.070	27.632	37.588	9.116	14.237	20.862
Income Distribution						
$0 to $2,500	0	0.003	−0.003	0	0.018	−0.001
$2,500 to $5,000	0	−0.055	−0.026	0	−0.113	−0.051
$5,000 to $7,500	0	−0.065	−0.033	0	−0.093	−0.050
$7,500 to $10,000	0	−0.053	−0.030	0	−0.036	−0.025
$10,000 to $20,000	0	−0.030	−0.037	0	0.087	0.031
$20,000 and over	0	0.200	0.129	0	0.137	0.096
Number (thousands)	812.650	884.720	1,377.586	1,401.428	1,345.435	1,767.861

Table B-19
Numbers and Income Distributions for Singles Aged 62 to 64: Option 2
(percentage in real 1980 income classes)

	Men			Women		
	1980	*1990*	*2005*	*1980*	*1990*	*2005*
Income Distribution						
$0 to $2,500	9.789	6.273	3.205	10.834	5.995	1.142
$2,500 to $5,000	18.838	15.075	11.020	28.385	25.883	21.016
$5,000 to $7,500	17.542	15.917	13.713	21.044	21.574	22.139
$7,500 to $10,000	13.674	13.545	12.911	13.352	14.448	15.798
$10,000 to $20,000	26.873	30.247	33.030	20.391	23.383	27.220
$20,000 and over	13.283	18.943	26.120	5.995	8.717	12.685
Difference from Baseline						
$0 to $2,500	0	0	−0.005	0	0.018	−0.003
$2,500 to $5,000	0	−0.102	−0.056	0	−0.188	−0.094
$5,000 to $7,500	0	−0.073	−0.047	0	−0.054	−0.034
$7,500 to $10,000	0	0.059	0.028	0	0.104	0.065
$10,000 to $20,000	0	0.059	0.028	0	0.104	0.065
$20,000 and over	0	0.143	0.102	0	0.101	0.058
Number (thousands)	333.329	321.628	449.268	807.833	772.481	1,081.184

Table B-20
Numbers and Income Distributions for Singles Aged 65 to 71: Option 2
(percentage in real 1980 income classes)

	Men			Women		
	1980	*1990*	*2005*	*1980*	*1990*	*2005*
Income Distribution						
$0 to $2,500	6.296	0	0	6.677	0	0
$2,500 to $5,000	36.380	0	0	41.421	0	0
$5,000 to $7,500	21.014	60.712	54.854	21.790	66.462	60.094
$7,500 to $10,000	11.800	12.424	13.835	11.212	12.025	13.952
$10,000 to $20,000	17.650	18.648	20.768	14.547	16.163	19.056
$20,000 and over	6.860	8.216	10.543	4.353	5.350	6.898
Difference from Baseline						
$0 to $2,500	0	−2.443	0	0	−1.885	0
$2,500 to $5,000	0	−35.925	−30.488	0	−41.100	−33.345
$5,000 to $7,500	0	38.662	30.751	0	43.251	33.612
$7,500 to $10,000	0	−0.059	−0.060	0	−0.054	−0.074
$10,000 to $20,000	0	−0.084	−0.109	0	−0.114	−0.107
$20,000 and over	0	−0.151	−0.094	0	−0.099	−0.085
Number (thousands)	729.170	855.523	908.478	2,411.495	3,023.647	3,360.996

Table B-21
Numbers and Income Distributions for Singles Aged 72 and over: Option 2
(percentage in real 1980 income classes)

	Men			*Women*		
	1980	*1990*	*2005*	*1980*	*1990*	*2005*
Income Distribution						
$0 to $2,500	7.080	0	0	8.366	0	0
$2,500 to $5,000	40.413	0	0	47.514	0	0
$5,000 to $7,500	23.089	67.276	60.324	21.731	74.633	62.794
$7,500 to $10,000	11.836	12.621	14.701	9.839	10.667	14.801
$10,000 to $20,000	13.013	14.782	18.565	9.750	11.265	17.224
$20,000 and over	4.570	5.321	6.409	2.801	3.436	5.180
Difference from Baseline						
$0 to $2,500	0	−4.110	−0.879	0	−2.192	0
$2,500 to $5,000	0	−38.886	−33.016	0	−48.472	−31.459
$5,000 to $7,500	0	43.317	34.200	0	51.124	31.846
$7,500 to $10,000	0	−0.064	−0.076	0	−0.128	−0.129
$10,000 to $20,000	0	−0.169	−0.161	0	−0.224	−0.176
$20,000 and over	0	−0.089	−0.068	0	−0.108	−0.082
Number (thousands)	954.688	1,061.071	1,101.657	3,817.020	4,961.656	5,645.767

Table B-22
Numbers and Income Distributions for Families and Singles Aged 55 to 64: Option 2
(percentage in real 1980 income classes)

	Families of Two or More			*Singles*		
	1980	*1990*	*2005*	*1980*	*1990*	*2005*
Income Distribution						
$0 to $2,500	2.501	1.456	0.867	10.258	6.761	3.479
$2,500 to $5,000	2.933	1.860	1.163	19.383	15.965	12.120
$5,000 to $7,500	4.330	2.890	1.875	17.837	16.254	14.467
$7,500 to $10,000	5.558	3.901	2.632	13.912	13.608	12.967
$10,000 to $20,000	27.934	22.189	16.638	27.421	30.437	32.563
$20,000 and over	56.744	67.704	76.825	11.190	16.975	24.404
Difference from Baseline						
$0 to $2,500	0	0.026	0.001	0	0.012	−0.002
$2,500 to $5,000	0	0.001	−0.004	0	−0.114	−0.054
$5,000 to $7,500	0	−0.011	−0.009	0	−0.075	−0.041
$7,500 to $10,000	0	−0.023	−0.013	0	−0.027	−0.019
$10,000 to $20,000	0	−0.144	−0.071	0	0.057	0.018
$20,000 and over	0	0.150	0.096	0	0.146	0.098
Number (thousands)	9,594.282	9,229.888	12,721.125	3,355.240	3,324.263	4,675.899

Table B-23
Total Income of Elderly Families and Singles, by Age Group: Option 3
(billions of real 1980 dollars)

Age Group	*1980*	*1985*	*1990*	*1995*	*2000*	*2005*
Men						
65 to 71	6.10	6.87	7.78	8.25	8.70	9.36
72 and over	7.12	7.78	8.56	9	9.46	10.13
All elderly	13.22	14.65	16.31	17.24	18.16	19.49
Women						
65 to 71	17.60	20.70	24.13	26.39	28.49	30.85
72 and over	23.87	28.41	34.22	39.32	44.05	48.85
All elderly	41.47	49.11	58.35	65.71	72.54	79.70
Families						
65 to 71	83.22	95.56	109.33	120.21	126.02	133.41
72 and over	60.15	67.48	75.50	81.79	86.23	91.21
All elderly	143.37	163.04	184.84	202	212.25	224.62
		Difference from Baseline				
Men						
65 to 71	0	−0.04	−0.01	0	0.06	0.19
72 and over	0	−0.06	−0.04	−0.04	0.03	0.17
All elderly	0	−0.10	−0.05	−0.04	0.09	0.35
Women						
65 to 71	0	−0.12	−0.02	−0.01	0.19	0.60
72 and over	0	−0.02	0.06	0.05	0.27	0.70
All elderly	0	−0.14	0.04	0.04	0.47	1.31
Families						
65 to 71	0	−0.50	−0.01	−0.10	0.74	2.64
72 and over	0	−0.44	−0.34	−0.59	−0.13	0.91
All elderly	0	−0.94	−0.36	−0.69	0.61	3.55

Table B-24
Numbers and Income Distributions for Families and Singles under Age 55: Option 3
(percentage in real 1980 income classes)

	Families of Two or More			*Singles*		
	1980	*1990*	*2005*	*1980*	*1990*	*2005*
Income Distribution						
$0 to $2,500	3.51	2.75	2.07	11.17	8.17	5.94
$2,500 to $5,000	2.70	1.85	1.24	11.06	8.32	5.81
$5,000 to $7,500	3.85	2.62	1.73	13.03	10.49	7.87
$7,500 to $10,000	5.04	3.46	2.29	13.03	11.36	9.26
$10,000 to $20,000	28.23	21.26	14.89	36.31	38.02	36.38
$20,000 and over	56.68	68.06	77.78	15.41	23.64	34.74
Difference from Baseline						
$0 to $2,500	0	0.12	0.02	0	0.23	0.05
$2,500 to $5,000	0	0.03	-0.01	0	0.03	0
$5,000 to $7,500	0	0.02	-0.02	0	-0.03	-0.04
$7,500 to $10,000	0	0.01	-0.03	0	-0.07	-0.09
$10,000 to $20,000	0	-0.12	-0.24	0	-0.18	-0.43
$20,000 and over	0	-0.07	0.27	0	0.01	0.51
Number (thousands)	41,708.86	49,971.84	54,093.01	15,419.63	21,978.56	26,113.18

Table B-25
Numbers and Income Distributions for Families and Singles Aged 55 to 61: Option 3
(percentage in real 1980 income classes)

	Families of Two or More			*Singles*		
	1980	*1990*	*2005*	*1980*	*1990*	*2005*
Income Distribution						
$0 to $2,500	2.40	1.31	0.67	10.12	7.02	4.25
$2,500 to $5,000	2.47	1.48	0.82	16.18	12.64	9.04
$5,000 to $7,500	3.64	2.31	1.33	16.71	14.46	11.76
$7,500 to $10,000	4.79	3.19	1.94	14.15	13.33	11.88
$10,000 to $20,000	26.17	19.87	13.72	30.07	32.92	34.30
$20,000 and over	60.54	71.84	81.52	12.77	19.63	28.77
Difference from Baseline						
$0 to $2,500	0	0.03	−0.02	0	−0.06	−0.07
$2,500 to $5,000	0	0	−0.03	0	−0.11	−0.22
$5,000 to $7,500	0	−0.02	−0.04	0	−0.08	−0.22
$7,500 to $10,000	0	−0.04	−0.06	0	−0.04	−0.15
$10,000 to $20,000	0	−0.25	−0.36	0	0.05	−0.03
$20,000 and over	0	0.27	0.52	0	0.24	0.69
Number (thousands)	7,000.34	6,775.09	8,933.18	2,214.08	2,230.15	3,145.45

Table B-26
Numbers and Income Distributions for Families and Singles Aged 62 to 64: Option 3
(percentage in real 1980 income classes)

	Families of Two or More			*Singles*		
	1980	*1990*	*2005*	*1980*	*1990*	*2005*
Income Distribution						
$0 to $2,500	2.77	1.86	1.24	10.53	5.89	1.63
$2,500 to $5,000	4.19	2.86	1.87	25.60	22.61	17.57
$5,000 to $7,500	6.19	4.43	2.98	20.02	19.92	19.51
$7,500 to $10,000	7.63	5.75	4.04	13.45	14.21	14.96
$10,000 to $20,000	32.70	28.09	22.39	22.28	25.48	29.23
$20,000 and over	46.50	57.01	67.49	8.12	11.89	17.11
Difference from Baseline						
$0 to $2,500	0	0	−0.04	0	−0.18	−0.12
$2,500 to $5,000	0	−0.04	−0.06	0	−0.26	−0.60
$5,000 to $7,500	0	−0.08	−0.10	0	−0.05	−0.20
$7,500 to $10,000	0	−0.33	−0.51	0	0.17	0.36
$10,000 to $20,000	0	−0.33	−0.51	0	0.17	0.36
$20,000 and over	0	0.55	0.84	0	0.28	0.55
Number (thousands)	2,593.94	2,454.80	3,787.94	1,141.18	1,094.11	1,530.45

Table B-27
Numbers and Income Distributions for Families and Singles Aged 65 to 71: Option 3
(percentage in real 1980 income classes)

	Families of Two or More			Singles		
	1980	1990	2005	1980	1990	2005
Income Distribution						
$0 to $2,500	0.24	0	0	6.59	2.10	0
$2,500 to $5,000	5.92	2.57	0.23	40.25	39.87	31.66
$5,000 to $7,500	12.27	10.02	5.71	21.61	22.95	26.17
$7,500 to $10,000	13.59	13.01	11.28	11.35	12.18	14.21
$10,000 to $20,000	38.10	39.86	41.45	15.27	16.82	19.87
$20,000 and over	29.88	34.55	41.33	4.93	6.07	8.09
Difference from Baseline						
$0 to $2,500	0	0	0	0	0.10	0
$2,500 to $5,000	0	0.05	−0.06	0	−0.08	−1.08
$5,000 to $7,500	0	0.08	−0.26	0	0	0.20
$7,500 to $10,000	0	0.03	−0.18	0	0.01	0.21
$10,000 to $20,000	0	−0.08	−0.23	0	0	0.34
$20,000 and over	0	−0.08	0.74	0	−0.02	0.33
Number (thousands)	4,618.36	5,487.92	5,872.10	3,140.66	3,879.17	4,269.47

Table B-28
Numbers and Income Distributions for Families and Singles Aged 72 and over: Option 3
(percentage in real 1980 income classes)

	Families of Two or More			Singles		
	1980	1990	2005	1980	1990	2005
Income Distribution						
$0 to $2,500	0	0	0	8.11	2.52	0.12
$2,500 to $5,000	8.79	3.58	0.16	46.09	46.53	30.79
$5,000 to $7,500	19.70	17.60	11.46	22	23.70	30.37
$7,500 to $10,000	17.29	17.89	17.65	10.24	11.20	15.12
$10,000 to $20,000	34.83	38.25	42.79	10.40	12.19	17.94
$20,000 and over	19.39	22.68	27.94	3.15	3.85	5.66
Difference from Baseline						
$0 to $2,500	0	0	0	0	−0.01	−0.03
$2,500 to $5,000	0	0.15	−0.07	0	−0.26	−0.92
$5,000 to $7,500	0	0.22	−0.13	0	0.11	0.21
$7,500 to $10,000	0	0.01	−0.01	0	0.08	0.21
$10,000 to $20,000	0	0	0	0	0	0
$20,000 and over	0	−0.03	0	0	−0.02	0.20
Number (thousands)	4,014.17	4,548.31	4,784.31	4,771.71	6,022.73	6,747.42

Table B-29
Numbers and Income Distributions for Singles Aged 55 to 61: Option 3
(percentage in real 1980 income classes)

	Men			Women		
	1980	*1990*	*2005*	*1980*	*1990*	*2005*
Income Distribution						
$0 to $2,500	9.15	7.04	5.13	10.68	7.01	3.57
$2,500 to $5,000	11.34	8.62	6.21	18.99	15.29	11.24
$5,000 to $7,500	13.22	10.65	8.12	18.74	16.96	14.60
$7,500 to $10,000	12.91	11.15	9.09	14.87	14.76	14.06
$10,000 to $20,000	34.31	34.82	33.22	27.61	31.67	35.14
$20,000 and over	19.07	27.73	38.23	9.12	14.31	21.39
Difference from Baseline						
$0 to $2,500	0	−0.04	−0.06	0	−0.07	−0.08
$2,500 to $5,000	0	−0.07	−0.13	0	−0.13	−0.29
$5,000 to $7,500	0	−0.08	−0.16	0	−0.09	−0.26
$7,500 to $10,000	0	−0.06	−0.16	0	−0.03	−0.14
$10,000 to $20,000	0	−0.05	−0.26	0	0.11	0.15
$20,000 and over	0	0.29	0.77	0	0.21	0.63
Number (thousands)	812.65	884.72	1,377.59	1,401.43	1,345.43	1,767.86

Table B-30
Numbers and Income Distributions for Singles Aged 62 to 64: Option 3
(percentage in real 1980 income classes)

	Men			Women		
	1980	*1990*	*2005*	*1980*	*1990*	*2005*
Income Distribution						
$0 to $2,500	9.79	6.17	3.10	10.83	5.77	1.02
$2,500 to $5,000	18.84	15.01	10.79	28.38	25.78	20.38
$5,000 to $7,500	17.54	15.89	13.52	21.04	21.60	21.99
$7,500 to $10,000	13.67	13.53	12.80	13.35	14.49	15.86
$10,000 to $20,000	26.87	30.29	33.06	20.39	23.48	27.64
$20,000 and over	13.28	19.11	26.73	5.99	8.88	13.11
Difference from Baseline						
$0 to $2,500	0	−0.11	−0.11	0	−0.21	−0.13
$2,500 to $5,000	0	−0.16	−0.29	0	−0.29	−0.73
$5,000 to $7,500	0	−0.10	−0.24	0	−0.02	−0.18
$7,500 to $10,000	0	0.10	0.06	0	0.20	0.49
$10,000 to $20,000	0	0.10	0.06	0	0.20	0.49
$20,000 and over	0	0.31	0.71	0	0.26	0.48
Number (thousands)	333.33	321.63	449.27	807.83	772.48	1,081.18

Table B-31
Numbers and Income Distributions for Singles Aged 65 to 71: Option 3
(percentage in real 1980 income classes)

	Men			Women		
	1980	1990	2005	1980	1990	2005
Income Distribution						
$0 to $2,500	6.30	2.53	0	6.68	1.98	0
$2,500 to $5,000	36.38	35.87	29.50	41.42	41.01	32.25
$5,000 to $7,500	21.01	22.03	24.23	21.79	23.21	26.70
$7,500 to $10,000	11.80	12.48	14.06	11.21	12.09	14.24
$10,000 to $20,000	17.65	18.74	21.26	14.55	16.27	19.50
$20,000 and over	6.86	8.34	10.95	4.35	5.43	7.31
Difference from Baseline						
$0 to $2,500	0	0.09	0	0	0.10	0
$2,500 to $5,000	0	−0.05	−0.99	0	−0.09	−1.10
$5,000 to $7,500	0	−0.02	0.13	0	0	0.22
$7,500 to $10,000	0	0	0.17	0	0.01	0.22
$10,000 to $20,000	0	0.01	0.38	0	0	0.33
$20,000 and over	0	−0.03	0.31	0	−0.02	0.33
Number (thousands)	729.17	855.52	908.48	2,411.49	3,023.65	3,361

Table B-32
Numbers and Income Distributions for Singles Aged 72 and over: Option 3
(percentage in real 1980 income classes)

	Men			Women		
	1980	1990	2005	1980	1990	2005
Income Distribution						
$0 to $2,500	7.08	4.20	0.72	8.37	2.17	0
$2,500 to $5,000	40.41	38.90	32.29	47.51	48.16	30.50
$5,000 to $7,500	23.09	23.96	26.22	21.73	23.64	31.18
$7,500 to $10,000	11.84	12.68	14.95	9.84	10.89	15.15
$10,000 to $20,000	13.01	14.91	19.13	9.75	11.61	17.71
$20,000 and over	4.57	5.35	6.68	2.80	3.53	5.46
Difference from Baseline						
$0 to $2,500	0	0.09	−0.16	0	−0.03	0
$2,500 to $5,000	0	0.01	−0.72	0	−0.31	−0.96
$5,000 to $7,500	0	0	0.10	0	0.14	0.24
$7,500 to $10,000	0	−0.01	0.18	0	0.09	0.22
$10,000 to $20,000	0	−0.04	0.40	0	0.12	0.31
$20,000 and over	0	−0.06	0.21	0	−0.01	0.20
Number (thousands)	954.69	1,061.07	1,101.66	3,817.02	4,961.66	5,645.77

Table B-33
Numbers and Income Distributions for Families and Singles Aged 55 to 64: Option 3
(percentage in real 1980 income classes)

	Families of Two or More			*Singles*		
	1980	*1990*	*2005*	*1980*	*1990*	*2005*
Income Distribution						
$0 to $2,500	2.50	1.46	0.84	10.26	6.65	3.39
$2,500 to $5,000	2.93	1.85	1.13	19.38	15.92	11.83
$5,000 to $7,500	4.33	2.87	1.82	17.84	16.26	14.29
$7,500 to $10,000	5.56	3.87	2.56	13.91	13.62	12.89
$10,000 to $20,000	27.93	22.06	16.30	27.42	30.47	32.64
$20,000 and over	56.74	67.90	77.34	11.19	17.08	24.95
Difference from Baseline						
$0 to $2,500	0	0.03	−0.03	0	−0.10	−0.09
$2,500 to $5,000	0	−0.01	−0.04	0	−0.16	−0.34
$5,000 to $7,500	0	−0.03	−0.06	0	−0.07	−0.21
$7,500 to $10,000	0	−0.05	−0.08	0	−0.02	−0.10
$10,000 to $20,000	0	−0.28	−0.40	0	0.09	0.10
$20,000 and over	0	0.34	0.61	0	0.25	0.64
Number (thousands)	9,594.28	9,229.89	12,721.13	3,355.24	3,324.26	4,675.90

Table B-34
Total Income of Elderly Families and Singles, by Age Group: Option 4
(billions of real 1980 dollars)

Age Group	*1980*	*1985*	*1990*	*1995*	*2000*	*2005*
Men						
65 to 71	6.10	6.91	7.75	8.25	8.68	9.28
72 and over	7.12	7.83	8.57	9.02	9.46	10.06
All elderly	13.22	14.74	16.32	17.28	18.14	19.33
Women						
65 to 71	17.60	20.82	24.12	26.41	28.39	30.51
72 and over	23.87	28.42	34.14	39.28	43.87	46.32
All elderly	41.47	49.24	58.26	65.70	72.27	78.82
Families						
65 to 71	83.22	96.36	109.78	121.23	126.64	132.94
72 and over	60.15	67.92	75.83	82.70	86.88	91.09
All elderly	143.27	164.28	185.62	203.93	213.52	224.04
		Difference from Baseline				
Men						
65 to 71	0	0	−0.01	0	0.03	0.11
72 and over	0	−0.01	−0.03	−0.01	0.03	0.10
All elderly	0	−0.01	−0.04	−0.01	0.06	0.20
Women						
65 to 71	0	0	−0.03	0.01	0.09	0.26
72 and over	0	−0.01	−0.02	0.02	0.10	0.17
All elderly	0	−0.01	−0.05	0.03	0.19	0.43
Families						
65 to 71	0	0.30	0.43	0.92	1.35	2.17
72 and over	0	0	−0.01	0.32	0.52	0.80
All elderly	0	0.30	0.43	1.24	1.87	2.96

Table B-35
Numbers and Income Distributions for Families and Singles under Age 55: Option 4
(percentage in real 1980 income classes)

	Families of Two or More			*Singles*		
	1980	*1990*	*2005*	*1980*	*1990*	*2005*
Income Distribution						
$0 to $2,500	3.51	2.69	2.06	11.17	8.06	5.95
$2,500 to $5,000	2.70	1.79	1.21	11.06	8.03	5.54
$5,000 to $7,500	3.85	2.54	1.67	13.03	10.20	7.51
$7,500 to $10,000	5.04	3.35	2.21	13.03	11.17	8.91
$10,000 to $20,000	28.23	20.74	14.34	36.31	38.04	36.01
$20,000 and over	56.68	68.89	78.52	15.41	24.51	36.08
Difference from Baseline						
$0 to $2,500	0	0.06	0.01	0	0.12	0.06
$2,500 to $5,000	0	−0.02	−0.04	0	−0.26	−0.27
$5,000 to $7,500	0	−0.06	−0.07	0	−0.32	−0.41
$7,500 to $10,000	0	−0.10	−0.11	0	−0.27	−0.44
$10,000 to $20,000	0	−0.64	−0.80	0	−0.16	−0.79
$20,000 and over	0	0.76	1	0	0.88	1.85
Number (thousands)	41,708.86	49,971.84	54,093.01	15,419.63	21,978.56	26,113.18

Table B-36
Numbers and Income Distributions for Families and Singles Aged 55 to 61: Option 4
(percentage in real 1980 income classes)

	Families of Two or More			*Singles*		
	1980	*1990*	*2005*	*1980*	*1990*	*2005*
Income Distribution						
$0 to $2,500	2.40	1.34	0.74	10.12	7.04	4.36
$2,500 to $5,000	2.47	1.47	0.83	16.18	12.36	8.80
$5,000 to $7,500	3.64	2.26	1.32	16.71	14.20	11.44
$7,500 to $10,000	4.79	3.12	1.90	14.15	13.19	11.65
$10,000 to $20,000	26.17	19.42	13.26	30.07	33.05	34.18
$20,000 and over	60.54	72.38	81.95	12.77	20.16	29.57
Difference from Baseline						
$0 to $2,500	0	0.07	0.05	0	−0.04	0.03
$2,500 to $5,000	0	−0.01	−0.01	0	−0.39	−0.45
$5,000 to $7,500	0	−0.06	−0.05	0	−0.34	−0.54
$7,500 to $10,000	0	−0.11	−0.10	0	−0.18	−0.39
$10,000 to $20,000	0	−0.70	−0.82	0	0.18	−0.15
$20,000 and over	0	0.81	0.94	0	0.77	1.50
Number (thousands)	7,000.34	6,775.09	8,933.18	2,214.08	2,230.15	3,145.45

Table B-37
Numbers and Income Distributions for Families and Singles Aged 62 to 64: Option 4
(percentage in real 1980 income classes)

	Families of Two or More			*Singles*		
	1980	*1990*	*2005*	*1980*	*1990*	*2005*
Income Distribution						
$0 to $2,500	2.77	1.87	1.28	10.53	5.96	1.78
$2,500 to $5,000	4.19	2.83	1.84	25.60	22.20	17.13
$5,000 to $7,500	6.19	4.36	2.91	20.02	19.76	19.14
$7,500 to $10,000	7.63	5.66	3.94	13.45	14.22	14.88
$10,000 to $20,000	32.70	27.79	21.91	22.28	25.71	29.51
$20,000 and over	46.50	57.50	68.12	8.12	12.16	17.57
Difference from Baseline						
$0 to $2,500	0	0.01	0	0	−0.10	0.03
$2,500 to $5,000	0	−0.08	−0.09	0	−0.67	−1.03
$5,000 to $7,500	0	−0.15	−0.17	0	−0.21	−0.56
$7,500 to $10,000	0	−0.63	−0.99	0	0.40	0.63
$10,000 to $20,000	0	−0.63	−0.99	0	0.40	0.63
$20,000 and over	0	1.03	1.47	0	0.55	1.01
Number (thousands)	2,593.94	2,454.80	3,787.94	1,141.16	1,094.11	1,530.45

Table B-38
Numbers and Income Distributions for Families and Singles Aged 65 to 71: Option 4
(percentage in real 1980 income classes)

	Families of Two or More			*Singles*		
	1980	*1990*	*2005*	*1980*	*1990*	*2005*
Income Distribution						
$0 to $2,500	0.24	0	0	6.59	2.33	0
$2,500 to $5,000	5.92	2.76	0.38	40.25	39.63	32.61
$5,000 to $7,500	12.27	10.01	6.10	21.61	22.90	25.71
$7,500 to $10,000	13.59	12.87	11.23	11.35	12.20	13.99
$10,000 to $20,000	38.10	39.59	40.97	15.27	16.89	19.71
$20,000 and over	29.88	34.77	41.32	4.93	6.07	7.98
Difference from Baseline						
$0 to $2,500	0	0	0	0	0.32	0
$2,500 to $5,000	0	0.24	0.09	0	−0.33	−0.13
$5,000 to $7,500	0	0.07	0.13	0	−0.06	−0.27
$7,500 to $10,000	0	−0.11	−0.23	0	0.03	−0.01
$10,000 to $20,000	0	−0.34	−0.71	0	0.07	0.18
$20,000 and over	0	0.14	0.72	0	−0.02	0.22
Number (thousands)	4,618.36	5,487.92	5,872.10	3,140.66	3,879.17	4,269.47

Table B-39
Numbers and Income Distributions for Families and Singles Aged 72 and over: Option 4
(percentage in real 1980 income classes)

	Families of Two or More			*Singles*		
	1980	*1990*	*2005*	*1980*	*1990*	*2005*
Income Distribution						
$0 to $2,500	0	0	0	8.11	2.88	0.14
$2,500 to $5,000	8.79	3.74	0.28	46.09	46.24	32.27
$5,000 to $7,500	19.70	17.50	11.83	22	23.63	29.57
$7,500 to $10,000	17.29	17.72	17.41	10.24	11.21	14.78
$10,000 to $20,000	34.83	38.11	42.43	10.40	12.20	17.64
$20,000 and over	19.39	22.92	28.05	3.15	3.84	5.60
Difference from Baseline						
$0 to $2,500	0	0	0	0	0.35	0
$2,500 to $5,000	0	0.32	0.06	0	−0.54	0.55
$5,000 to $7,500	0	0.12	0.23	0	0.04	−0.59
$7,500 to $10,000	0	−0.16	−0.24	0	0.08	−0.12
$10,000 to $20,000	0	0	0	0	0	0
$20,000 and over	0	0.11	0	0	−0.03	0.14
Number (thousands)	4,014.17	4,548.31	4,784.31	4,771.71	6,022.73	6,747.42

Table B-40
Numbers and Income Distributions for Singles Aged 55 to 61: Option 4
(percentage in real 1980 income classes)

	Men			*Women*		
	1980	*1990*	*2005*	*1980*	*1990*	*2005*
Income Distribution						
$0 to $2,500	9.15	7.04	5.18	10.68	7.05	3.71
$2,500 to $5,000	11.34	8.44	6.07	18.99	14.94	10.93
$5,000 to $7,500	13.22	10.44	7.92	18.74	16.68	14.19
$7,500 to $10,000	12.91	10.98	8.88	14.87	14.65	13.80
$10,000 to $20,000	34.31	34.73	32.84	27.61	31.94	35.22
$20,000 and over	19.07	28.38	39.11	9.12	14.75	22.15
Difference from Baseline						
$0 to $2,500	0	−0.04	−0.01	0	−0.04	0.07
$2,500 to $5,000	0	−0.25	−0.27	0	−0.48	−0.60
$5,000 to $7,500	0	−0.28	−0.37	0	−0.37	−0.67
$7,500 to $10,000	0	−0.23	−0.37	0	−0.14	−0.40
$10,000 to $20,000	0	−0.14	−0.64	0	0.39	0.23
$20,000 and over	0	0.95	1.65	0	0.65	1.38
Number (thousands)	812.65	884.72	1,377.59	1,401.43	1,345.43	1,767.86

Table B-41
Numbers and Income Distributions for Singles Aged 62 to 64: Option 4
(percentage in real 1980 income classes)

	Men			Women		
	1980	*1990*	*2005*	*1980*	*1990*	*2005*
Income Distribution						
$0 to $2,500	9.79	6.18	3.19	10.83	5.87	1.19
$2,500 to $5,000	18.84	14.74	10.58	28.38	25.31	19.85
$5,000 to $7,500	17.54	15.69	13.25	21.04	21.45	21.58
$7,500 to $10,000	13.67	13.46	12.62	13.35	14.53	15.81
$10,000 to $20,000	26.87	30.45	33.02	20.39	23.74	28.05
$20,000 and over	13.28	19.47	27.33	5.99	9.11	13.52
Difference from Baseline						
$0 to $2,500	0	−0.09	−0.02	0	−0.11	0.05
$2,500 to $5,000	0	−0.43	−0.50	0	−0.77	−1.26
$5,000 to $7,500	0	−0.30	−0.51	0	−0.18	−0.59
$7,500 to $10,000	0	0.26	0.02	0	0.46	0.89
$10,000 to $20,000	0	0.26	0.02	0	0.46	0.89
$20,000 and over	0	0.67	1.31	0	0.49	0.89
Number (thousands)	333.33	321.63	449.27	807.83	772.48	1,081.18

Table B-42
Numbers and Income Distributions for Singles Aged 65 to 71: Option 4
(percentage in real 1980 income classes)

	Men			Women		
	1980	*1990*	*2005*	*1980*	*1990*	*2005*
Income Distribution						
$0 to $2,500	6.30	2.73	0	6.68	2.21	0
$2,500 to $5,000	36.38	35.67	30.23	41.42	40.74	33.25
$5,000 to $7,500	21.01	21.97	23.92	21.79	23.16	26.19
$7,500 to $10,000	11.80	12.49	13.91	11.21	12.11	14.02
$10,000 to $20,000	17.65	18.79	21.09	14.55	16.35	19.33
$20,000 and over	6.86	8.35	10.85	4.35	5.42	7.21
Difference from Baseline						
$0 to $2,500	0	0.29	0	0	0.33	0
$2,500 to $5,000	0	−0.25	−0.25	0	−0.36	−0.09
$5,000 to $7,500	0	−0.08	−0.19	0	−0.05	−0.29
$7,500 to $10,000	0	0.01	0.02	0	0.04	−0.01
$10,000 to $20,000	0	0.06	0.21	0	0.07	0.17
$20,000 and over	0	−0.02	0.22	0	−0.03	0.23
Number (thousands)	729.17	855.52	908.48	2,411.49	3,023.65	3,361

Table B-43
Numbers and Income Distributions for Singles Aged 72 and over: Option 4
(percentage in real 1980 income classes)

	Men			Women		
	1980	1990	2005	1980	1990	2005
Income Distribution						
$0 to $2,500	7.08	4.21	0.87	8.37	2.59	0
$2,500 to $5,000	40.41	38.78	32.95	47.51	47.84	32.13
$5,000 to $7,500	23.09	23.97	25.95	21.73	23.56	30.27
$7,500 to $10,000	11.84	12.71	14.72	9.84	10.89	14.80
$10,000 to $20,000	13.01	14.97	18.86	9.75	11.60	17.40
$20,000 and over	4.57	5.37	6.65	2.80	3.51	5.40
Difference from Baseline						
$0 to $2,500	0	0.11	−0.01	0	0.40	0
$2,500 to $5,000	0	−0.11	−0.07	0	−0.63	0.68
$5,000 to $7,500	0	0.01	−0.17	0	0.05	−0.68
$7,500 to $10,000	0	0.02	−0.06	0	0.10	−0.14
$10,000 to $20,000	0	0.02	0.14	0	0.12	0
$20,000 and over	0	−0.04	0.17	0	−0.03	0.13
Number (thousands)	954.69	1,061.07	1,101.66	3,817.02	4,961.66	5,645.77

Table B-44
Numbers and Income Distributions for Families and Singles Aged 55 to 64: Option 4
(percentage)

	Families of Two or More			Singles		
	1980	1990	2005	1980	1990	2005
Income Distribution						
$0 to $2,500	2.50	1.48	0.90	10.26	6.69	3.51
$2,500 to $5,000	2.93	1.83	1.13	19.38	15.60	11.53
$5,000 to $7,500	4.33	2.82	1.80	17.84	16.03	13.96
$7,500 to $10,000	5.56	3.79	2.50	13.91	13.53	12.70
$10,000 to $20,000	27.93	21.65	15.83	27.42	30.63	32.65
$20,000 and over	56.74	68.42	77.83	11.19	17.52	25.64
Difference from Baseline						
$0 to $2,500	0	0.05	0.04	0	−0.06	0.03
$2,500 to $5,000	0	−0.03	−0.03	0	−0.48	−0.64
$5,000 to $7,500	0	−0.08	−0.09	0	−0.30	−0.55
$7,500 to $10,000	0	−0.13	−0.14	0	−0.11	−0.28
$10,000 to $20,000	0	−0.68	−0.87	0	0.25	0.11
$20,000 and over	0	0.87	1.10	0	0.69	1.34
Number (thousands)	9,594.28	9,229.89	12,721.13	3,355.24	3,324.26	4,675.90

References

Anderson, Joseph. "An Economic-Demographic Model of the United States Labor Market." Washington, D.C.: ICF Incorporated, 1980.

Anderson, Joseph. "Population Change and the American Labor Market: 1950-2000." Statement to the House Select Subcommittee on Population, Washington, D.C., 2 June 1978.

Ando, Albert, and Franco Modigliani. "The 'Life-Cycle' Hypothesis of Saving: Aggregate Implications and Tests." *American Economic Review* March 1963.

Barrington, Evan. "The Effect of Mandatory Retirement on the Labor Supply of Older Workers." Ph.D. dissertation, Massachusetts Institute of Technology, 1980.

Barro, Robert J. "The Impact of Social Security on Private Saving: Evidence from the U.S. Time Series." Washington, D.C.: American Enterprise Institute for Public Policy Research, 1978.

Bayo, Francisco R., William D. Richie, and Joseph F. Faber. "Long-Range Cost Estimates of Old-Age, Survivors, and Disability Insurance System, 1978." *Social Security Administration Actuarial Study No. 78* 1978.

Borzilleri, Thomas C. "The Need for a Separate Consumer Price Index for Older Persons: A Review and New Evidence." *The Gerontologist,* 18, no. 3 (1978).

Borzilleri, Thomas C. "In-Kind Benefit Programs and Retirement Income." Report to the President's Commission on Pension Policy, Washington, D.C., March 1980.

Burkhauser, Richard V. "The Early Pension System, and Its Effect on Exit from the Labor Market." Ph.D. dissertation, University of Chicago, 1976.

Burkhauser, Richard V., and Jennifer Warlich. "Disentangling the Annuity from the Redistributive Aspects of Social Security." Presented at the Annual Meeting of the American Economic Association, Chicago, Ill., 1978.

Caton, Christopher. "Forecast Summary: Twenty-Five Years of Change." *Data Resources U.S. Long-Term Review* Fall 1980.

Caton, Christopher, and Christopher Probyn. "The Inflationary Impact of the Productivity Slowdown." *Data Resources Review of the U.S. Economy* June 1979.

Chen, Yung-Ping. "Elderly Homeowner May Need HELP." *Philadelphia Inquirer,* 25 August 1980.

Clark, Robert L., David T. Barker, and R. Steven Cantrell. "Outlawing Age Discrimination: Economic and Institutional Responses to the Elimination of Mandatory Retirement." Report to Administration on Aging, Washington, D.C., September 1979.

Clark, Robert, Juanita Kreps, and Joseph Spengler. "The Economics of Aging." *Journal of Economic Literature* September 1978.

Clark, Robert, and John Menefee. "Increasing Federal Expenditures for the Elderly." Presented to the 31st Annual Meeting of the Gerontological Society, Dallas, November 1978 (revised version forthcoming in *The Gerontologist*).

Congressional Budget Office. "Poverty Status of Families under Alternative Definitions of Income." Background Paper no. 17, Washington, D.C., February 1977.

Data Resources, Inc., "Note of TRENDLONG0980 and TRENDLONG2005." *Data Resources U.S. Long-Term Review Fall 1980.*

Duffy, Martin, Evan Barrington, J. Michael Flanagan, and Lawrence Olson. "Inflation and the Elderly." Report to National Retired Teacher's Association and American Association of Retired Persons, Lexington, Mass., Data Resources, Inc., 1980.

Duffy, Martin, and Lawrence Olson. "Pensions in an Inflationary Environment." Lexington, Mass., Data Resources, Inc. 1980.

Eckstein, Otto. *Core Inflation.* Englewood Cliff, N.J.: Prentice-Hall, 1981.

Esposito, Louis. "Effect of Social Security on Saving: Review of Studies Using U.S. Time-Series Data." *Social Security Bulletin* June 1978.

Feldstein, Martin S., and Anthony Pellechio. "Social Security Wealth: The Impact of Alternative Inflation Adjustments." In *Financing Social Security,* edited by Colin D. Campbell. Washington, D.C.: American Enterprise Institute for Public Policy Research, 1979.

Fox, Alan. "Work, Retirement Patterns, and Replacement Rates of Married Couples: Findings from the Retirement History Survey." *Social Security Bulletin* January 1979.

Freeland, Mark, George Olat, and Carol Ellen Schendlen. "Projections of National Health Expenditures, 1980, 1985, 1990." *Health Care Financing Review* Winter 1980.

Freeman, Richard B. "The Effect of Demographic Factors on Age-Earnings Profiles." *Journal of Human Resources* Summer 1979.

Gordon, Josephine G., and Robert N. Schoeplein. "Tax Impact from Elimination of the Retirement Test." *Social Security Bulletin* September 1979.

Grad, Susan, and Karen Foster. "Income of the Population Aged 55 and Older, 1976." *Social Security Bulletin* July 1979.

Joe, Thomas, and Alan Bogatay, eds. *"The Social Security Disability Insurance Program and Supplemental Security Income Programs: A Series of Papers."* Chicago: University of Chicago Press, 1980.

Kurz, Mordecai. "The Effects of Pensions on Capital Formation: A Framework for Sample Analysis." Preliminary report to the President's Commission on Pension Policy, Menlo Park, Calif., SRI International, January 1980.

Kurz, Mordecai, and Mary Avrin. "Current Issues of the U.S. Pension System." Report to the President's Commission on Pension Policy, Stanford, Calif.: Stanford University, 1979.

Leonard, Jonathan S. "The Social Security Disability Program and Labor Force Participation." National Bureau of Economic Research Working Paper no. 392, August 1979.

Moon, Marilyn. *The Measurement of Economic Welfare.* New York: Academic Press, 1977.

Moon, Marilyn, and Eugene Smolensky. *Improving Measures of Economic Well-Being.* New York: Academic Press, 1977.

Parsons, Donald O. "The Decline in Male Labor Force Participation." *Journal of Political Economy* February 1980.

Pellechio, Anthony. "The Effect of the Social Security Retirement Test on the Earnings of Retirement Aged Workers." Testimony before the Senate Subcommittee on Social Security, Washington, D.C., April 1980.

Sander, Kenneth G. "The Retirement Test: Its Effect on Older Workers' Earnings." *Social Security Bulletin,* June 1968.

Scholen, Ken, and Yung-Ping Chen. *Unlocking Home Equity for the Elderly.* Cambridge, Mass.: Ballinger, 1980.

Schulz, James, Allan Borowski, Barry L. Friedman, Leslie C. Kelly, Thomas D. Leavitt, and William Spector. "The Economic Impact of Private Pensions on Retirement Income." Program in the Economics and Politics of Aging, Florence Heller Graduate School, Brandeis University, 1979.

U.S. Senate, Special Committee on Aging. "Encouraging Options for Work and Retirement Policy." Washington, D.C.: U.S. Government Printing Office, 1980.

Vroman, Wayne. "Older Worker Earnings and 1965 Social Security Act Amendments." Social Security Administration Research Report no. 38, 1971.

Wertheimer, Richard F., and Sheila R. Zedlewski. "The Direct Effects of Mandatory Retirement Age Limits on Older Workers," Washington, D.C., Urban Institute Working Paper 1348-01, August 1980.

Index

Index

About the Authors

Lawrence Olson is manager of the DRI Public Economics Service. He received the Ph.D. in economics from the University of Chicago. He has worked for DRI since 1978, directing a number of research projects, including studies of wage and salary distributions for whites and nonwhites, the wage effects of vocational schooling, the impact of private colleges on Massachusetts, and changing patterns of marriage and divorce. He directed projects to forecast future labor force availability for a multibillion-dollar national gas pipeline in Alaska, state and local expenditures on elementary and secondary education, the job outlook for college graduates, and the implications of the changing age patterns for the U.S. economy. He has worked on a number of projects dealing with the elderly, including a study of how they are affected by inflation and an analysis of options for pension indexing. Prior to coming to DRI, he was assistant professor of economics and education at the University of Rochester (1974-1978).

Christopher Caton is director of long-term studies, DRI National Forecasting Group. He received the Ph.D. in econometrics and mathematical economics from the University of Pennsylvania and the B.A. in economics from the University of Adelaide. He directs long-term macroeconomic forecasting at DRI, including forecasts to 1990 that are updated every quarter and twenty-five-year forecasts that are revised once a year. He also directs the *DRI Long-Term Review of the U.S. Economy,* in which he has published numerous articles. Other periodicals to which he has contributed include *Economic Record, Review of Economic Studies, Econometrics,* and *International Economica Review.* Before coming to DRI, he was senior finance officer in the Short-Term Forecasting Section of the Australian Treasury and senior finance officer in the Econometric Applications Section of the Australian Bureau of Statistics.

Martin Duffy is a vice-president of DRI with responsibility for the Consumer and Insurance Division. He received the B.A. in history and the B.S. in electrical engineering from Tufts University, the M.B.A. from The Wharton School of the University of Pennsylvania, and has pursued additional graduate studies in economics at the University of Pennsylvania. In 1979 and 1980, he directed a large DRI special study on inflation and the elderly, and he has been widely quoted on pensions, retirement, and the economics of the elderly in numerous periodicals (including the *Wall Street Journal,*

Fortune, and the *Christian Science Monitor*). He testified on the economy, inflation, and the elderly before the House Budget Committee on Human Resources in April 1980 and the Senate Special Committee on Aging in December 1980. Before his work at DRI, he was assistant to the financial vice-president for long-range financial and economic planning at Harvard University. Prior to his Harvard employment, he was assistant director of the Fels Center for Government and assistant dean of men at the University of Pennsylvania.

About the Contributors

Michael Shannon is an economist with the DRI Consumer Economic Services. He received the B.A. in economics from Dartmouth College. At DRI, he does forecasting and model development for the DECO Models.

Robert Tannenwald was a senior economist with the DRI National Forecasting Group, with responsibility for the business fixed investment and state and local sectors, at the time this book was written. He is currently a Ph.D. candidate in political economy and government at Harvard University. Prior to his work at DRI, he served as analyst in taxation and fiscal policy for the Congressional Research Service of the Library of Congress.